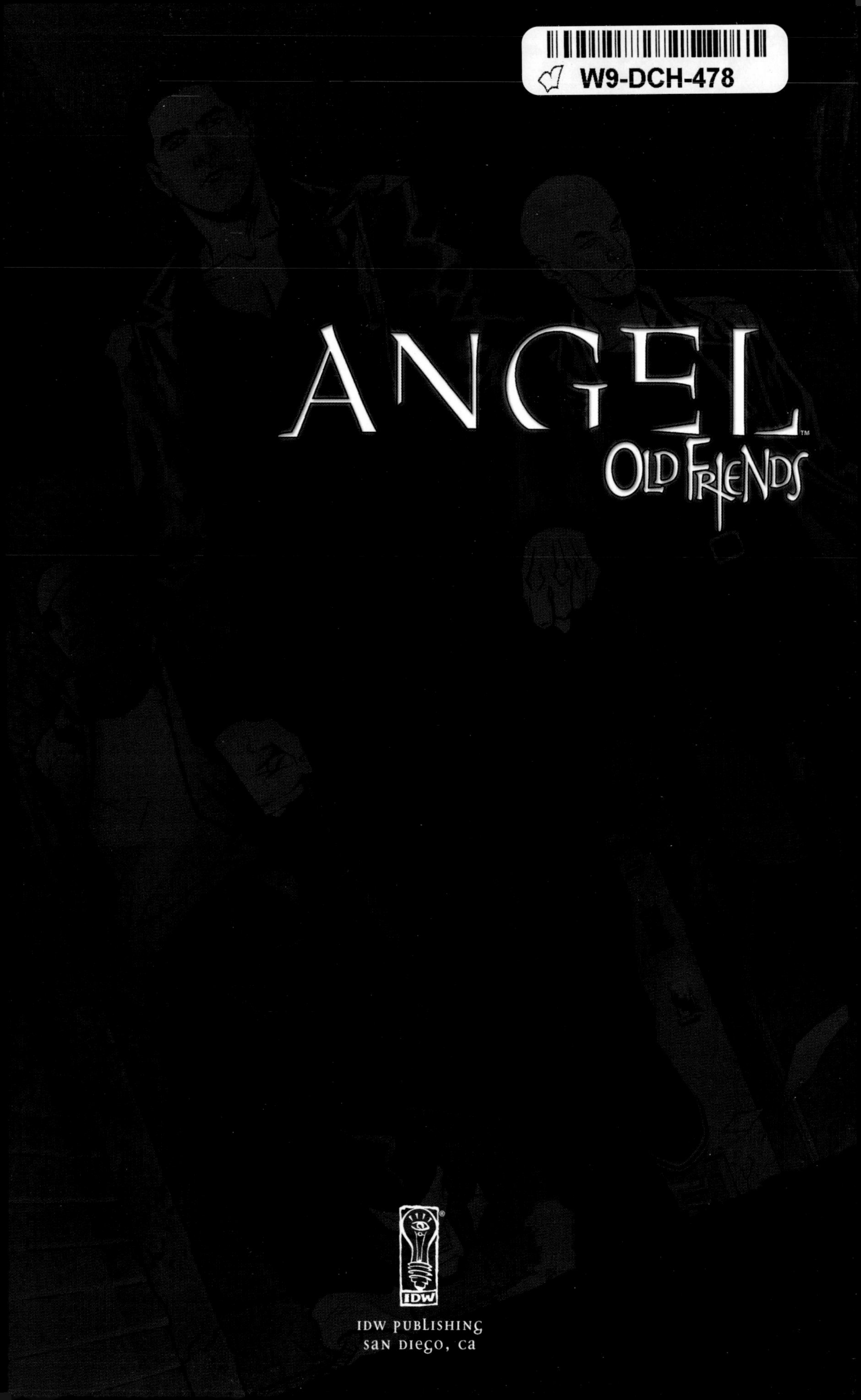

ANGEL™
OLD FRIENDS

IDW PUBLISHING
SAN DIEGO, CA

IDW Publishing is:
Robbie Robbins, President
Chris Ryall, Publisher/Editor-in-Chief
Ted Adams, Vice President
Kris Oprisko, Vice President
Neil Uyetake, Art Director
Dan Taylor, Editor
Aaron Myers, Assistant Editor
Tom B. Long, Designer
Chance Boren, Editorial Assistant
Matthew Ruzicka, CPA, Controller
Alex Garner, Creative Director
Yumiko Miyano, Business Development
Rick Privman, Business Development

ISBN: 1-933239-76-X
09 08 07 06 1 2 3 4 5

www.IDWPUBLISHING.com

ANGEL created by Joss Whedon and David Greenwalt • Thanks to Debbie Olshan at Fox Worldwide Publishing for her invaluable assistance.

ANGEL
OLD FRIENDS

written by
Jeff Mariotte

art by
David Messina

art assistant
Elena Casagrande

color assistants
**Davide Amici and
Matteo Gherardi**

designed by
Neil Uyetake

lettered by
Tom B. Long

edited by
**Chris Ryall and
Aaron Myers**

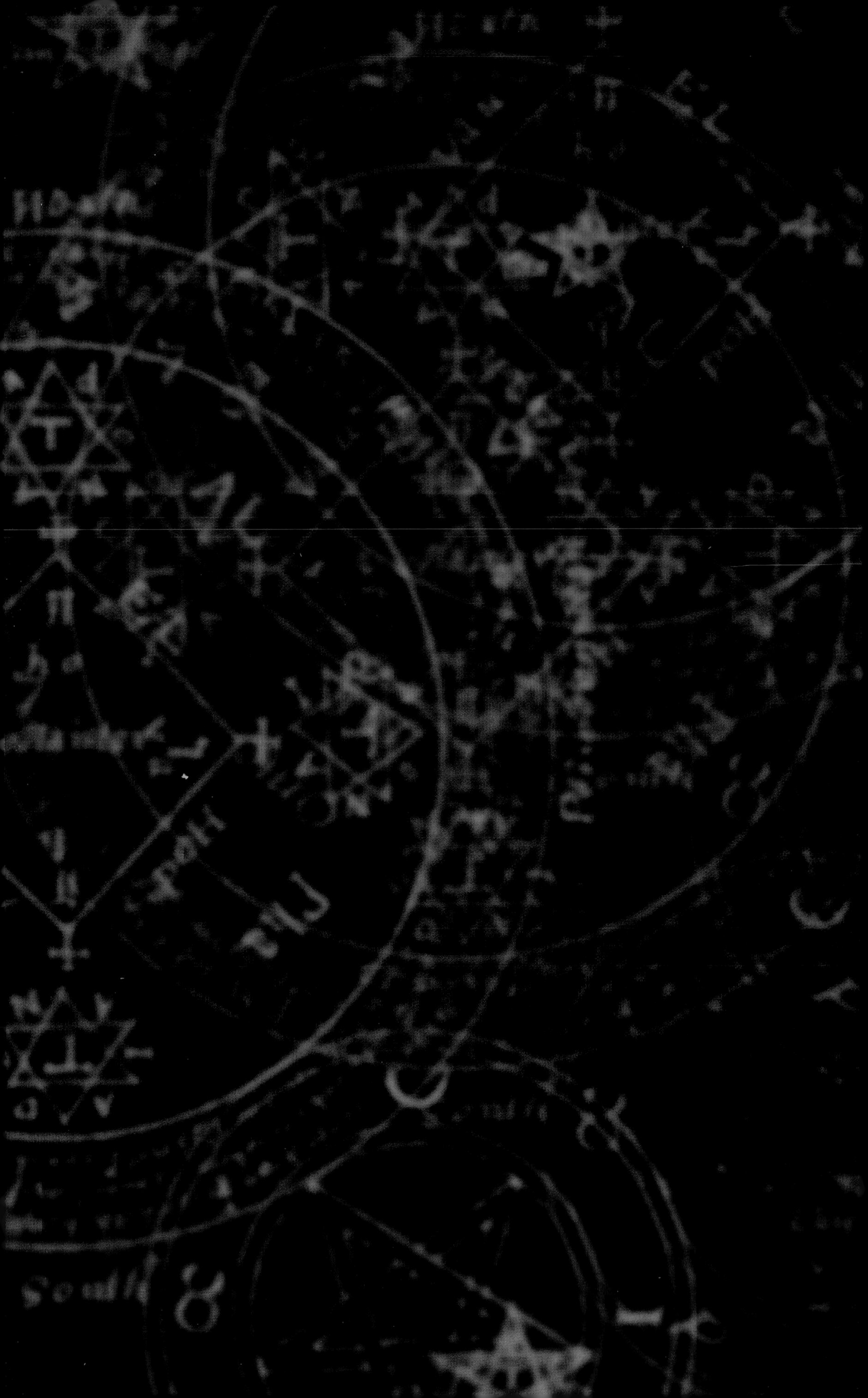

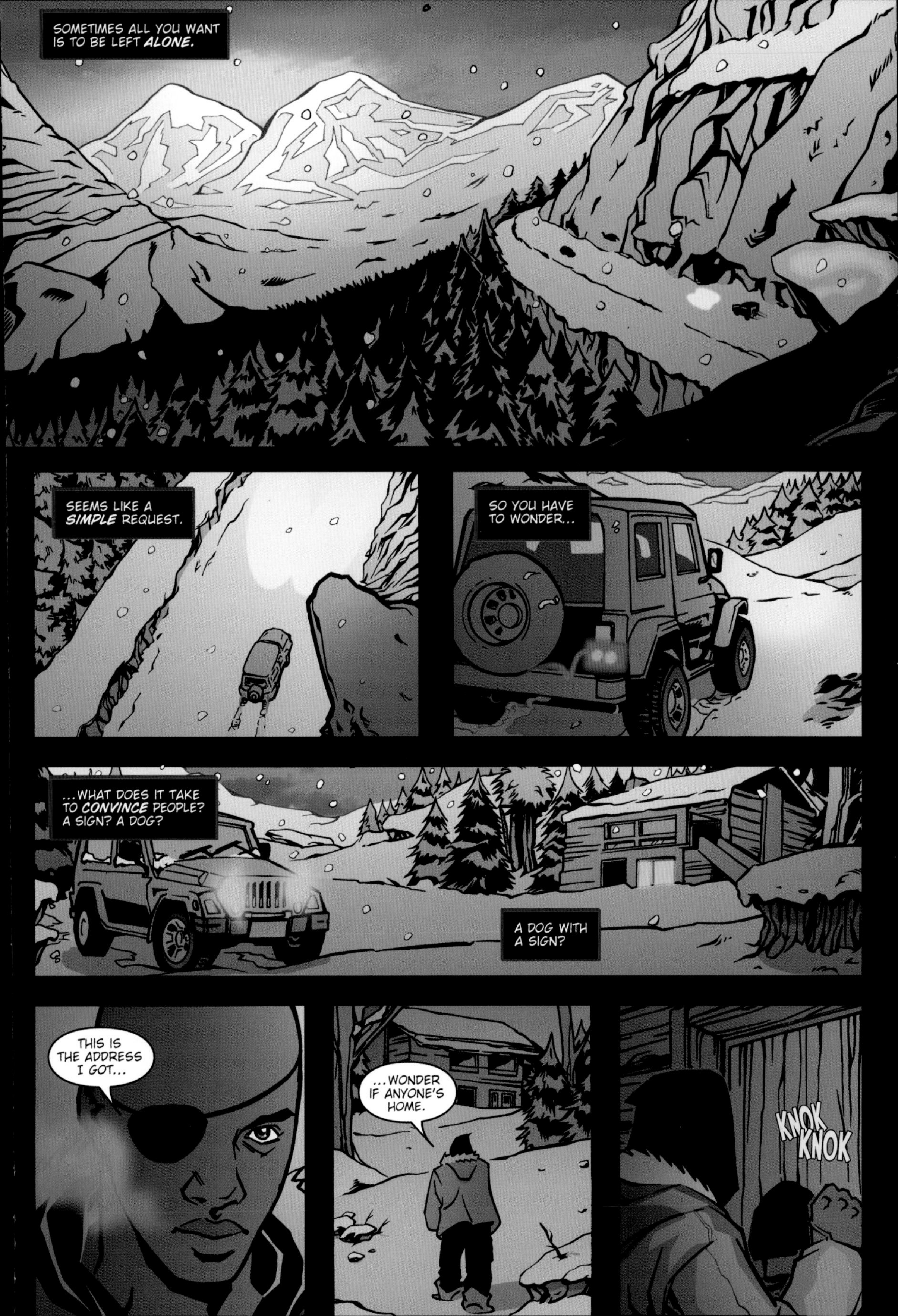
SOMETIMES ALL YOU WANT IS TO BE LEFT ALONE.
SEEMS LIKE A SIMPLE REQUEST.
SO YOU HAVE TO WONDER...
...WHAT DOES IT TAKE TO CONVINCE PEOPLE? A SIGN? A DOG?
A DOG WITH A SIGN?
THIS IS THE ADDRESS I GOT...
...WONDER IF ANYONE'S HOME.
KNOK KNOK

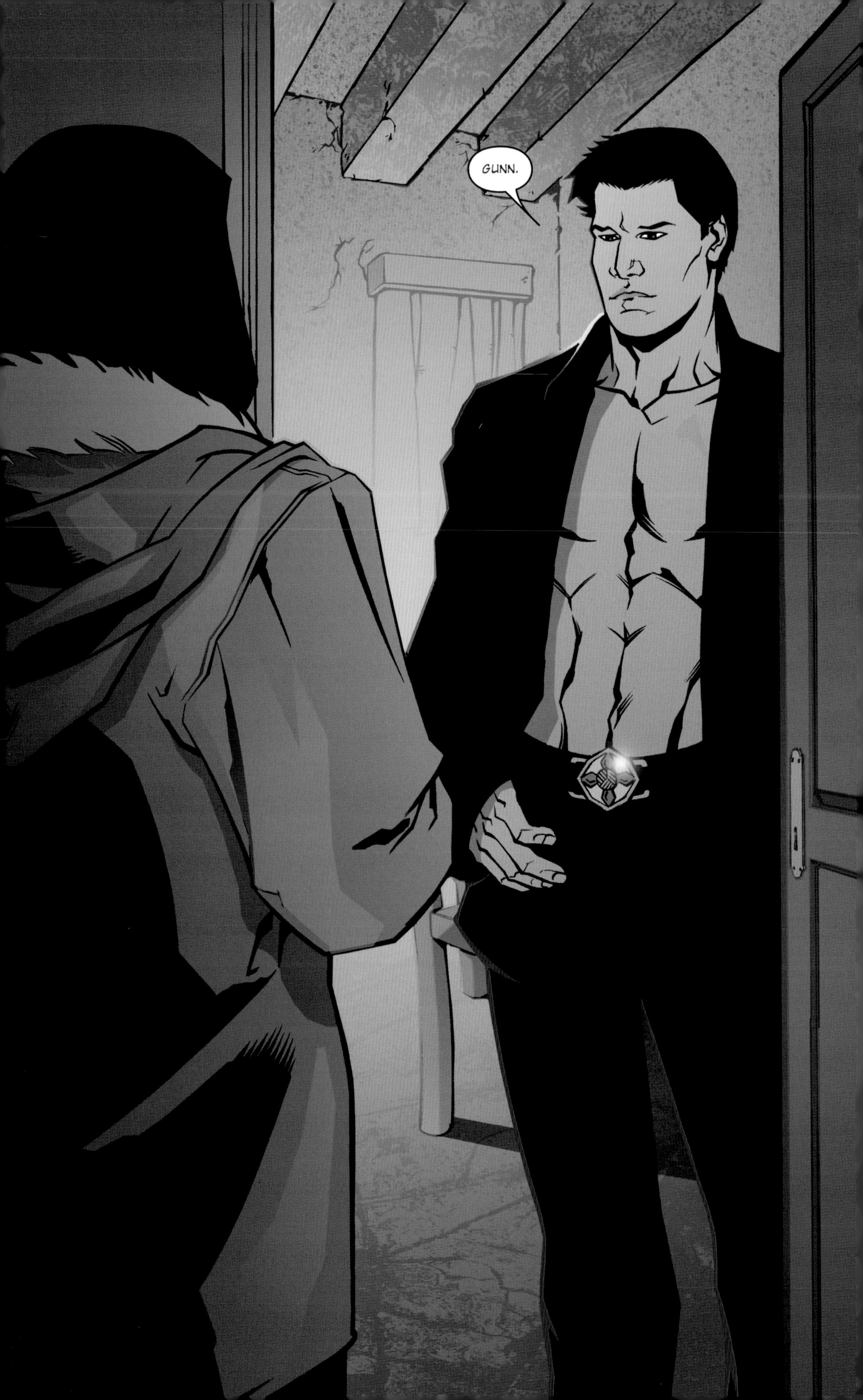
GUNN.

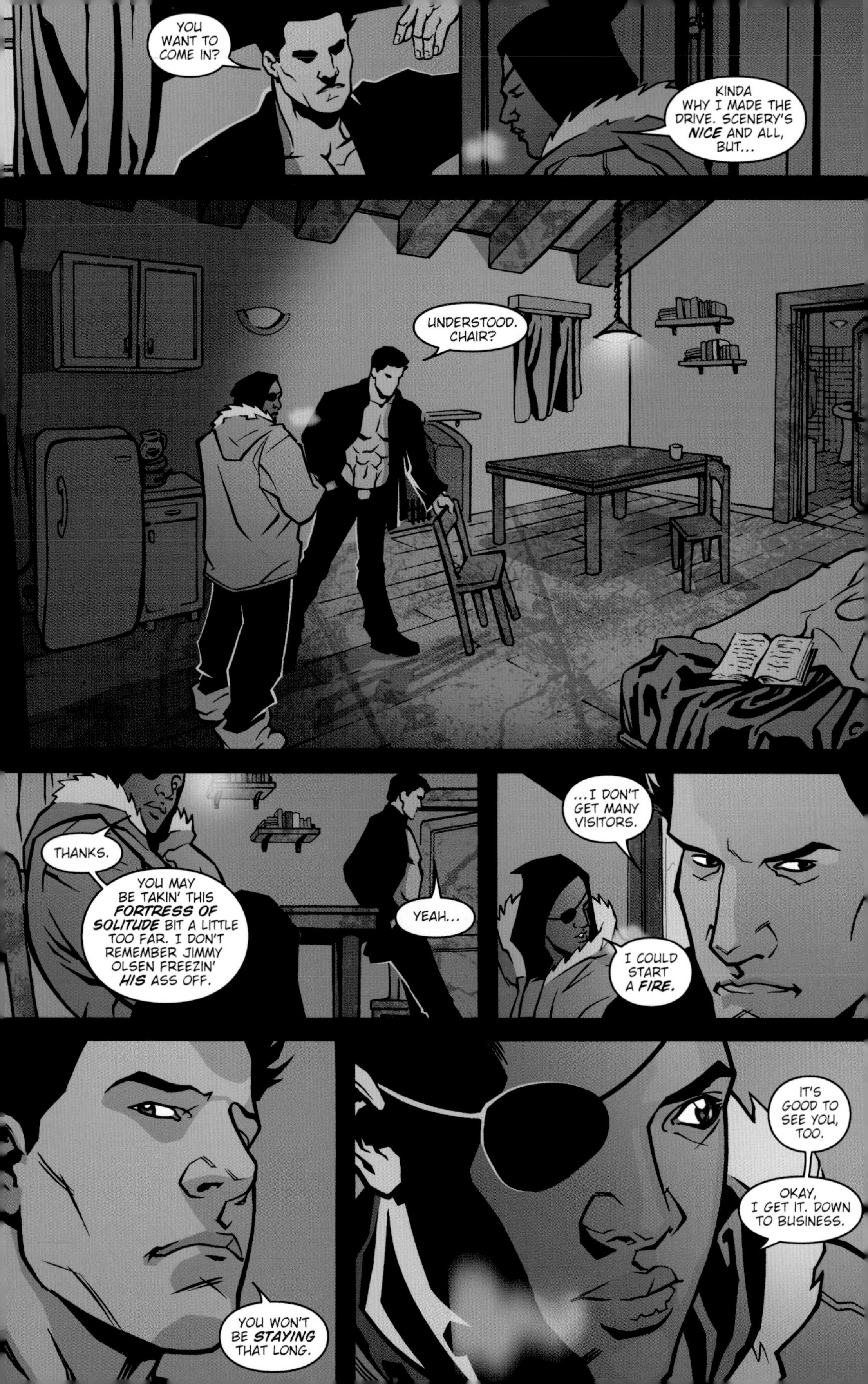
YOU WANT TO COME IN?
KINDA WHY I MADE THE DRIVE. SCENERY'S NICE AND ALL, BUT...
UNDERSTOOD. CHAIR?
THANKS.
YOU MAY BE TAKIN' THIS FORTRESS OF SOLITUDE BIT A LITTLE TOO FAR. I DON'T REMEMBER JIMMY OLSEN FREEZIN' HIS ASS OFF.
YEAH...
...I DON'T GET MANY VISITORS.
I COULD START A FIRE.
YOU WON'T BE STAYING THAT LONG.
IT'S GOOD TO SEE YOU, TOO.
OKAY, I GET IT. DOWN TO BUSINESS.

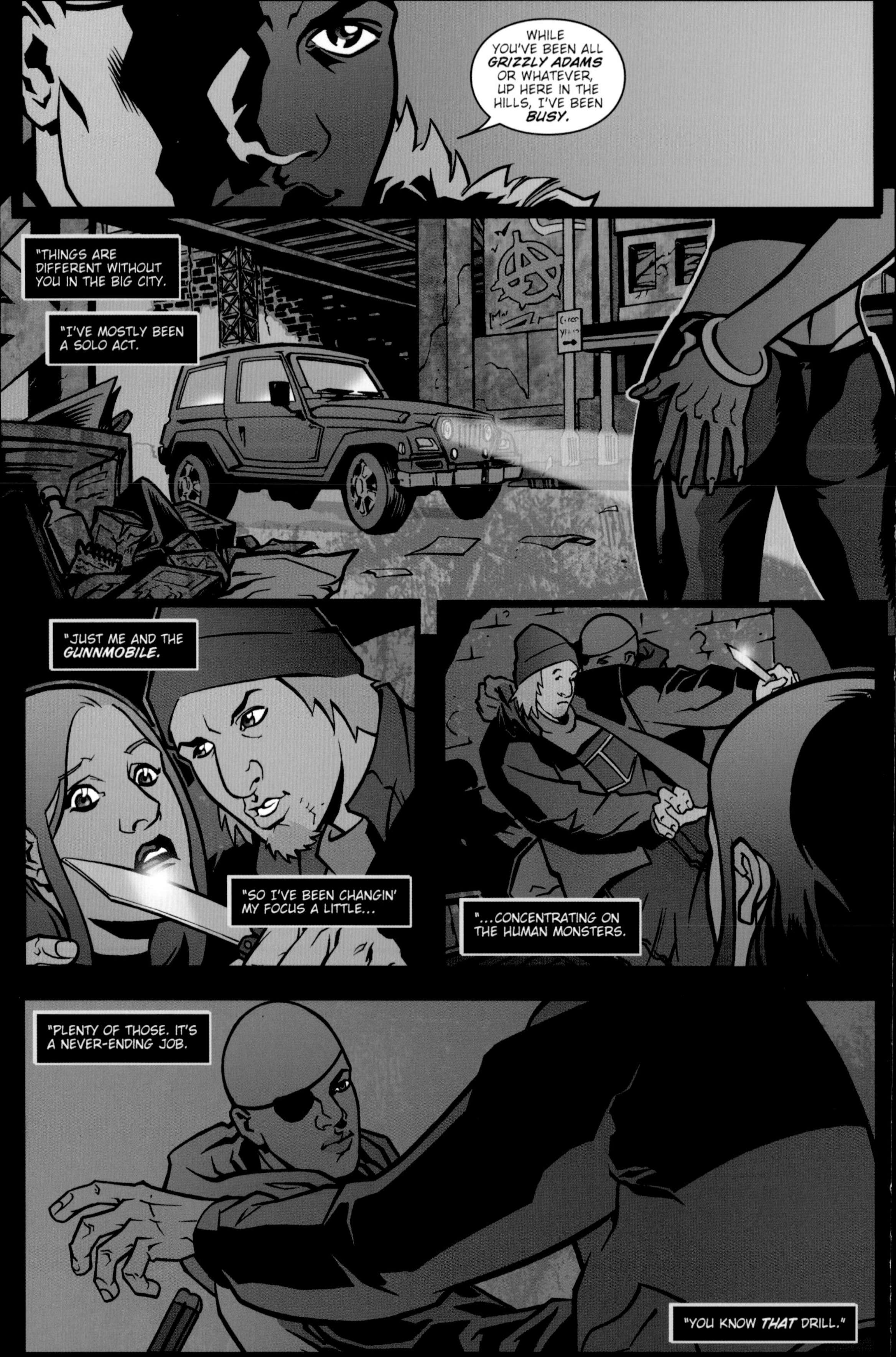
WHILE YOU'VE BEEN ALL GRIZZLY ADAMS OR WHATEVER, UP HERE IN THE HILLS, I'VE BEEN BUSY.
"THINGS ARE DIFFERENT WITHOUT YOU IN THE BIG CITY.
"I'VE MOSTLY BEEN A SOLO ACT.
"JUST ME AND THE GUNNMOBILE.
"SO I'VE BEEN CHANGIN' MY FOCUS A LITTLE...
"...CONCENTRATING ON THE HUMAN MONSTERS.
"PLENTY OF THOSE. IT'S A NEVER-ENDING JOB.
"YOU KNOW THAT DRILL."

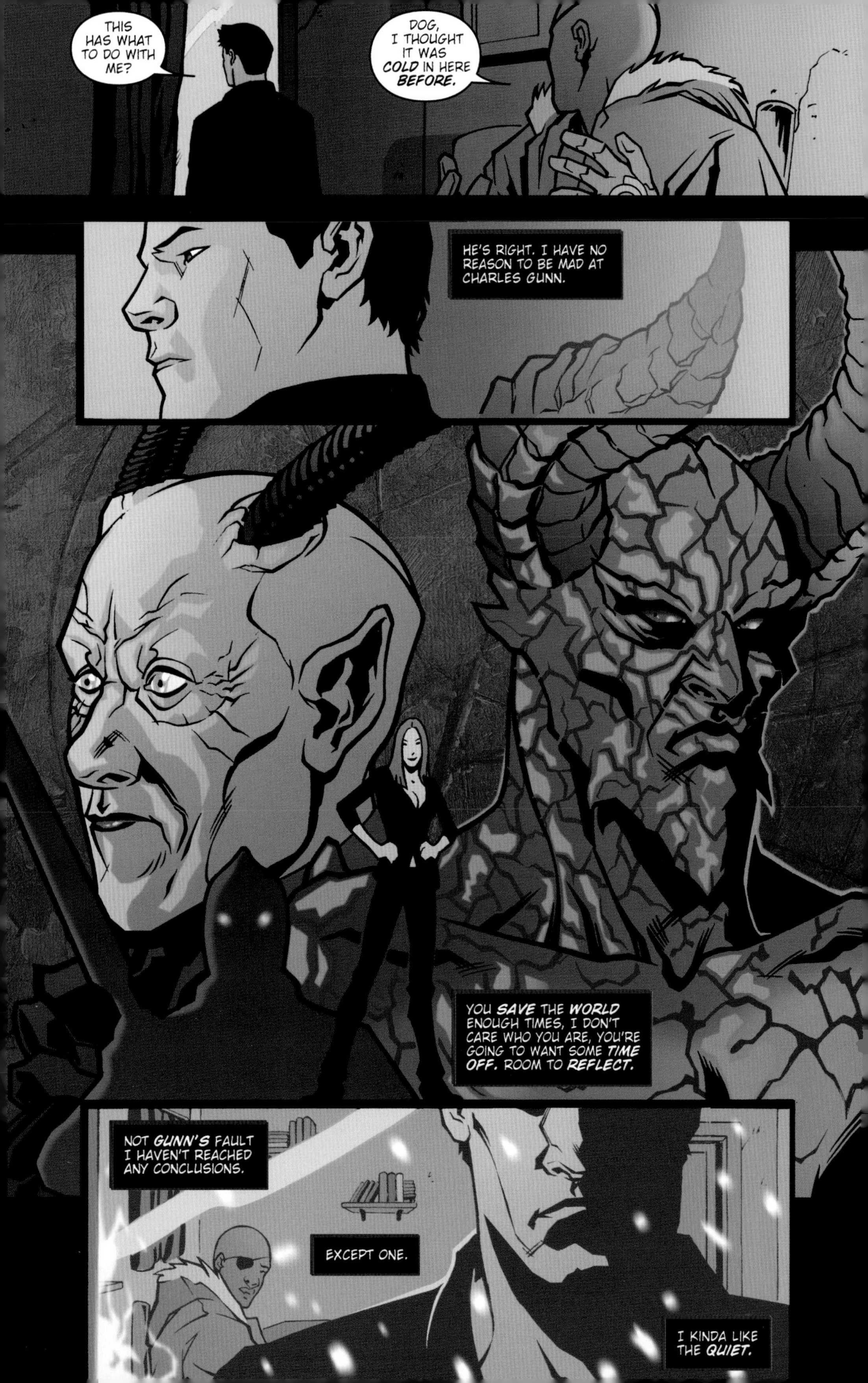
THIS HAS WHAT TO DO WITH ME?
DOG, I THOUGHT IT WAS COLD IN HERE BEFORE.
HE'S RIGHT. I HAVE NO REASON TO BE MAD AT CHARLES GUNN.
YOU SAVE THE WORLD ENOUGH TIMES, I DON'T CARE WHO YOU ARE, YOU'RE GOING TO WANT SOME TIME OFF. ROOM TO REFLECT.
NOT GUNN'S FAULT I HAVEN'T REACHED ANY CONCLUSIONS.
EXCEPT ONE.
I KINDA LIKE THE QUIET.

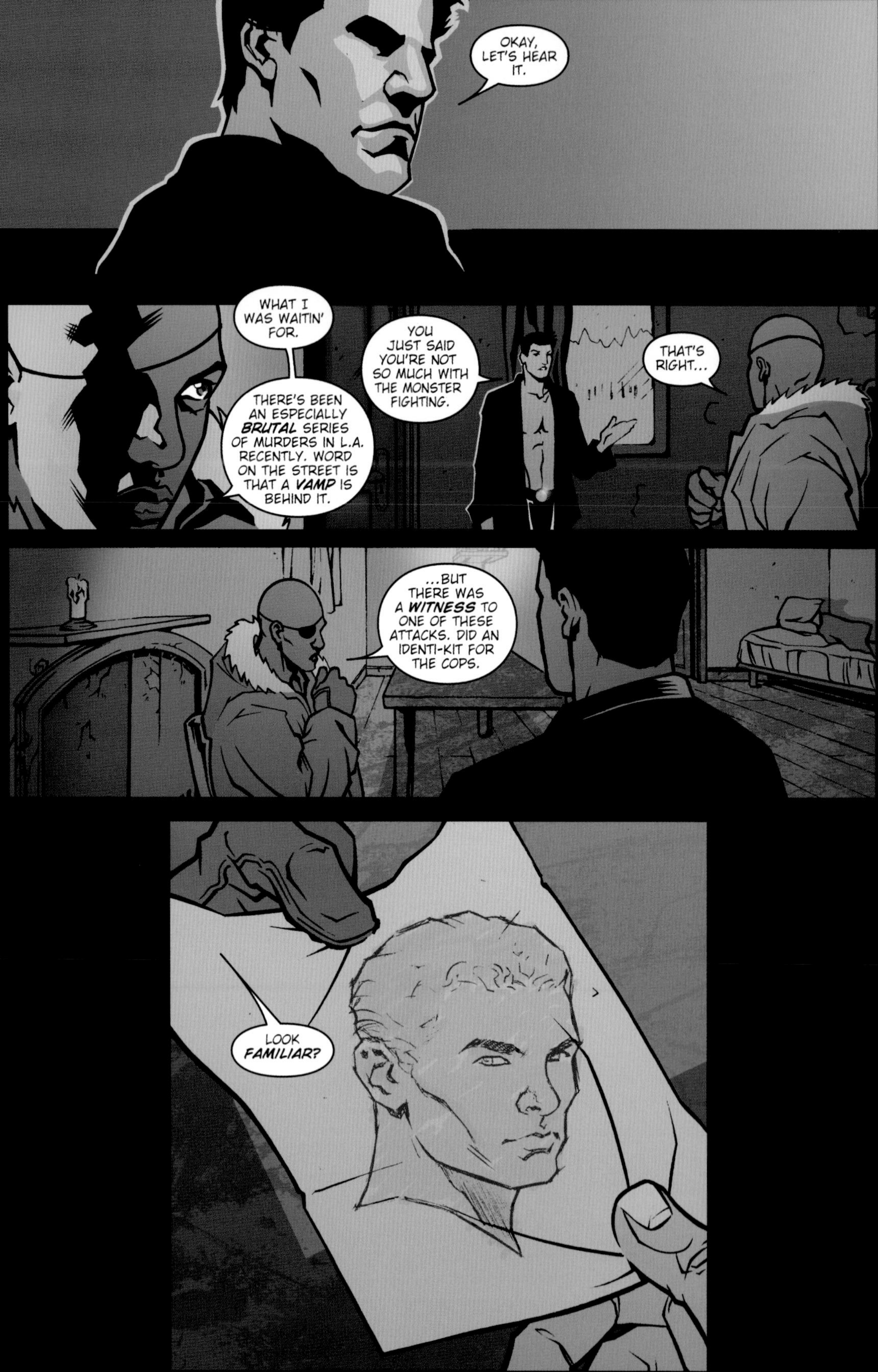
OKAY, LET'S HEAR IT.
WHAT I WAS WAITIN' FOR.
THERE'S BEEN AN ESPECIALLY BRUTAL SERIES OF MURDERS IN L.A. RECENTLY. WORD ON THE STREET IS THAT A VAMP IS BEHIND IT.
YOU JUST SAID YOU'RE NOT SO MUCH WITH THE MONSTER FIGHTING.
THAT'S RIGHT...
...BUT THERE WAS A WITNESS TO ONE OF THESE ATTACKS. DID AN IDENTI-KIT FOR THE COPS.
LOOK FAMILIAR?

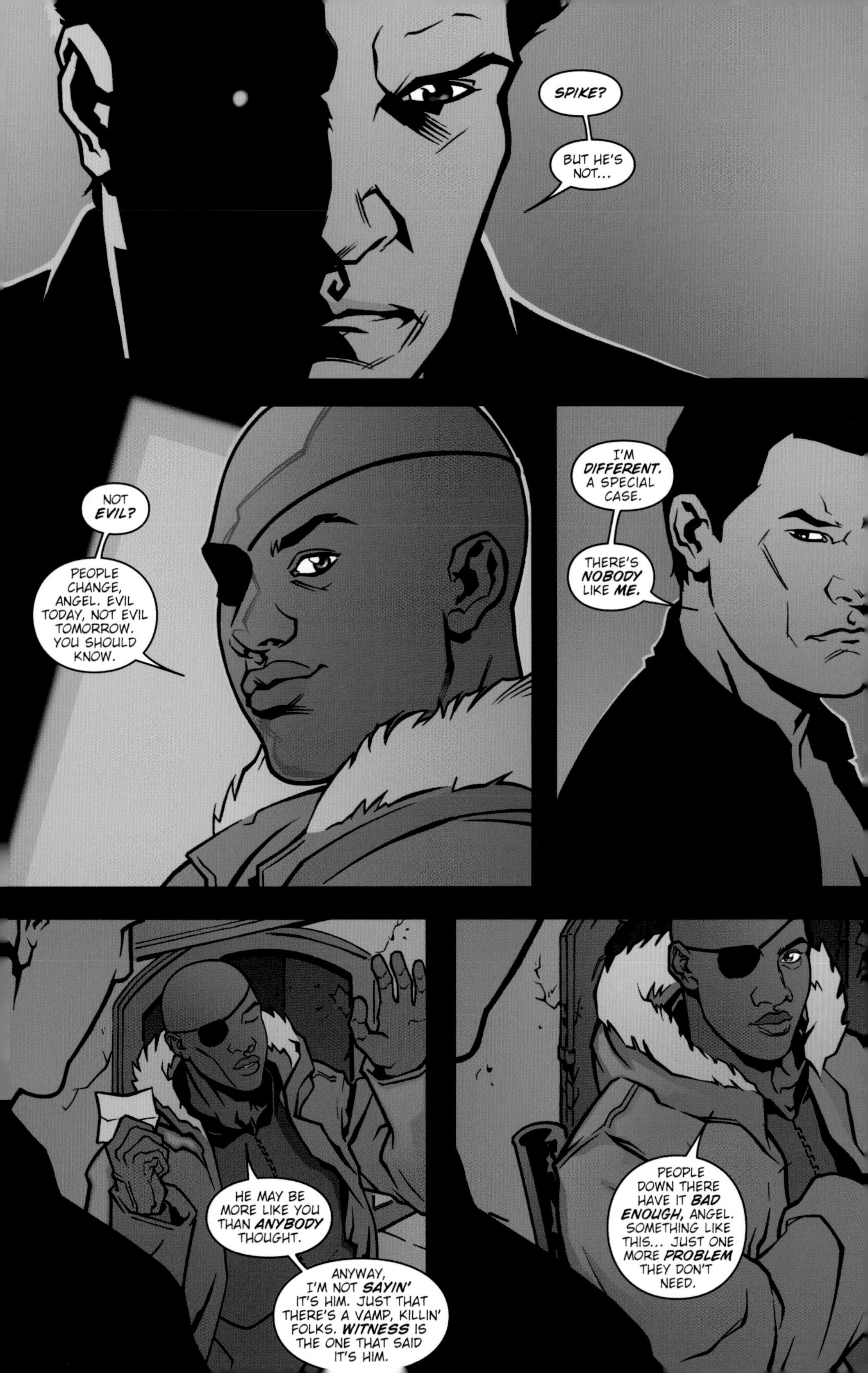
SPIKE?
BUT HE'S NOT...
NOT EVIL?
PEOPLE CHANGE, ANGEL. EVIL TODAY, NOT EVIL TOMORROW. YOU SHOULD KNOW.
I'M DIFFERENT. A SPECIAL CASE.
THERE'S NOBODY LIKE ME.
HE MAY BE MORE LIKE YOU THAN ANYBODY THOUGHT.
ANYWAY, I'M NOT SAYIN' IT'S HIM. JUST THAT THERE'S A VAMP, KILLIN' FOLKS. WITNESS IS THE ONE THAT SAID IT'S HIM.
PEOPLE DOWN THERE HAVE IT BAD ENOUGH, ANGEL. SOMETHING LIKE THIS... JUST ONE MORE PROBLEM THEY DON'T NEED.

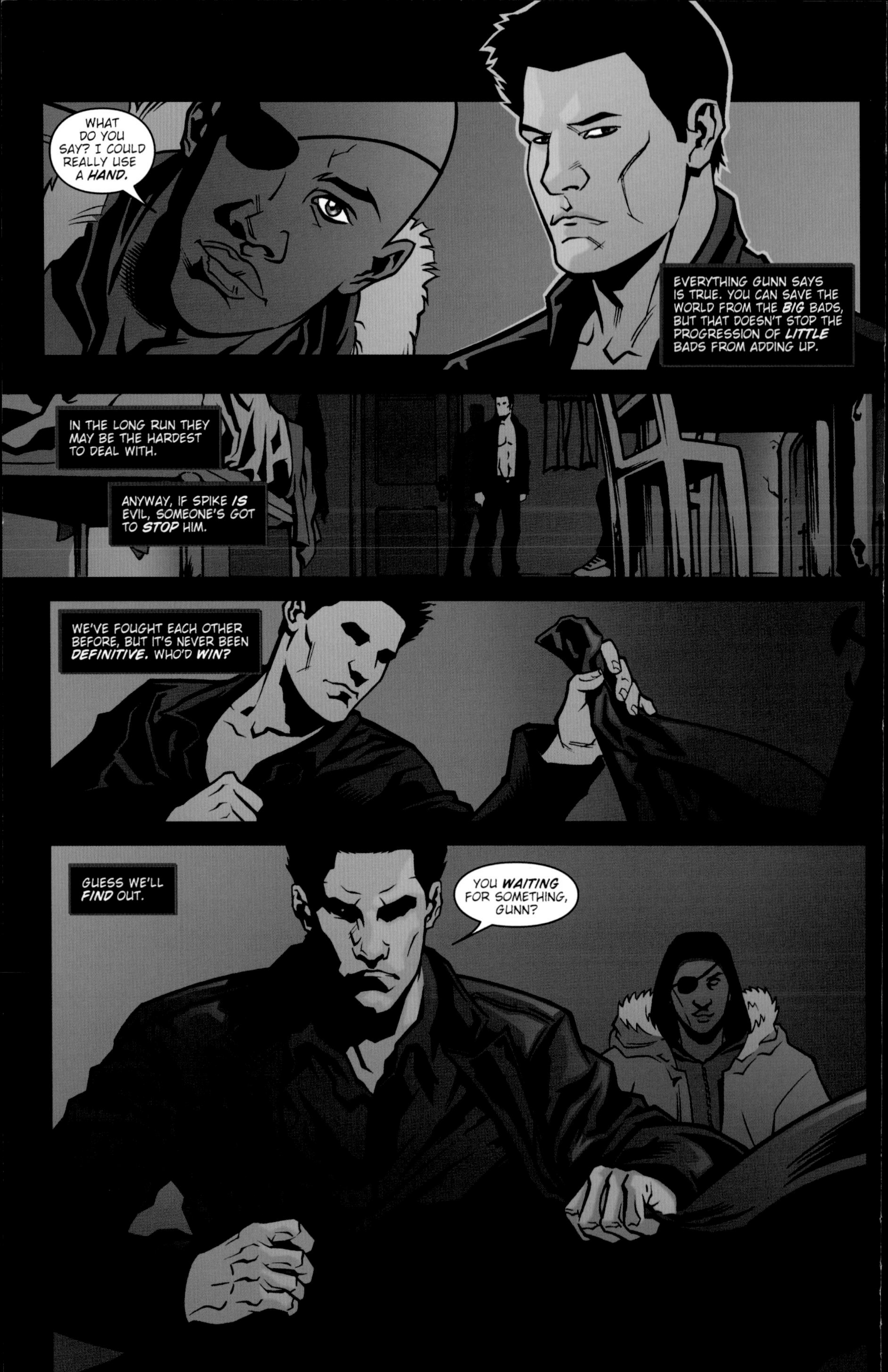
WHAT DO YOU SAY? I COULD REALLY USE A HAND.
EVERYTHING GUNN SAYS IS TRUE. YOU CAN SAVE THE WORLD FROM THE BIG BADS, BUT THAT DOESN'T STOP THE PROGRESSION OF LITTLE BADS FROM ADDING UP.
IN THE LONG RUN THEY MAY BE THE HARDEST TO DEAL WITH.
ANYWAY, IF SPIKE IS EVIL, SOMEONE'S GOT TO STOP HIM.
WE'VE FOUGHT EACH OTHER BEFORE, BUT IT'S NEVER BEEN DEFINITIVE. WHO'D WIN?
GUESS WE'LL FIND OUT.
YOU WAITING FOR SOMETHING, GUNN?

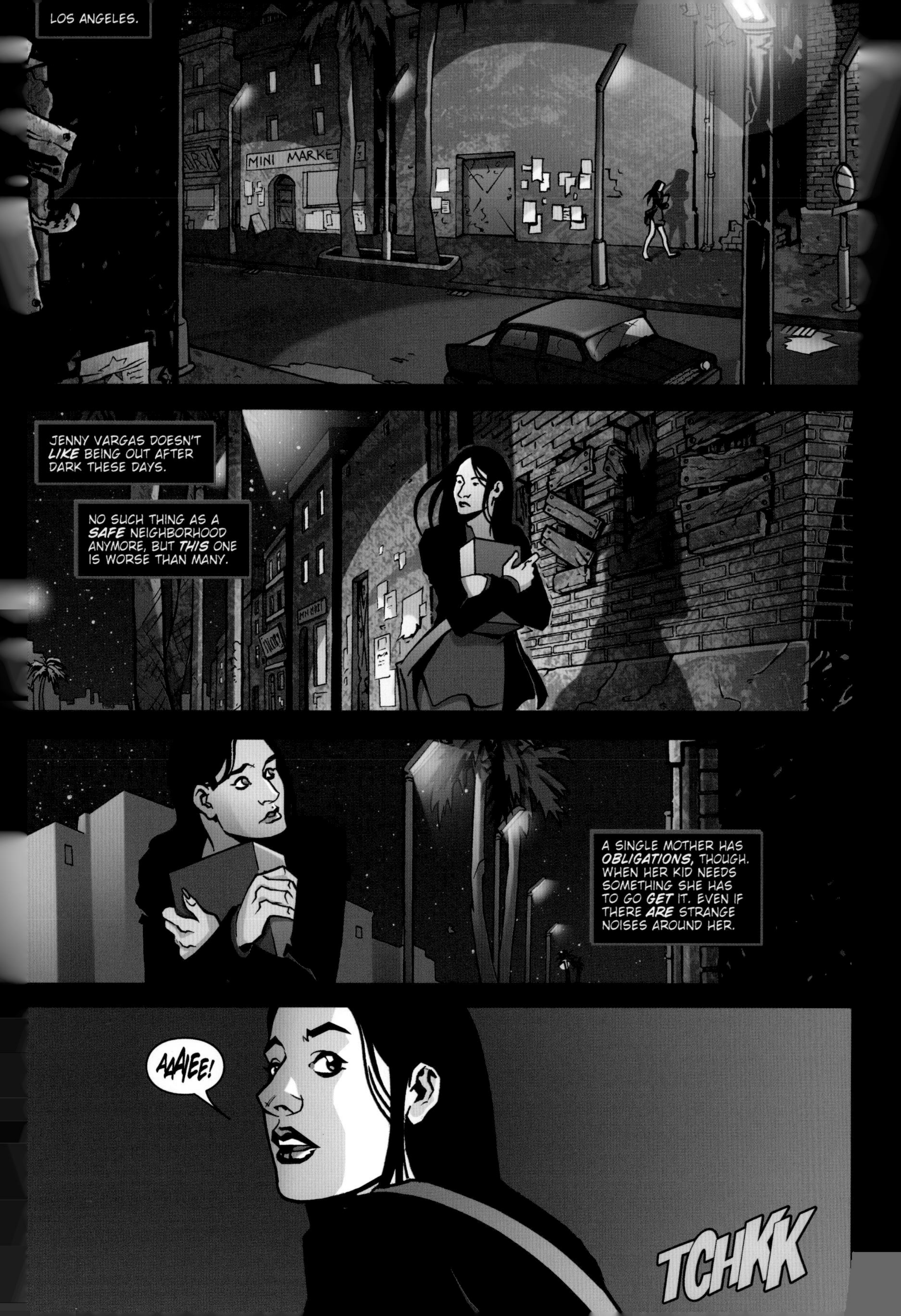
LOS ANGELES.
MINI MARKET
JENNY VARGAS DOESN'T LIKE BEING OUT AFTER DARK THESE DAYS.
NO SUCH THING AS A SAFE NEIGHBORHOOD ANYMORE, BUT THIS ONE IS WORSE THAN MANY.
A SINGLE MOTHER HAS OBLIGATIONS, THOUGH. WHEN HER KID NEEDS SOMETHING SHE HAS TO GO GET IT. EVEN IF THERE ARE STRANGE NOISES AROUND HER.
AAAIEE!
TCHKK

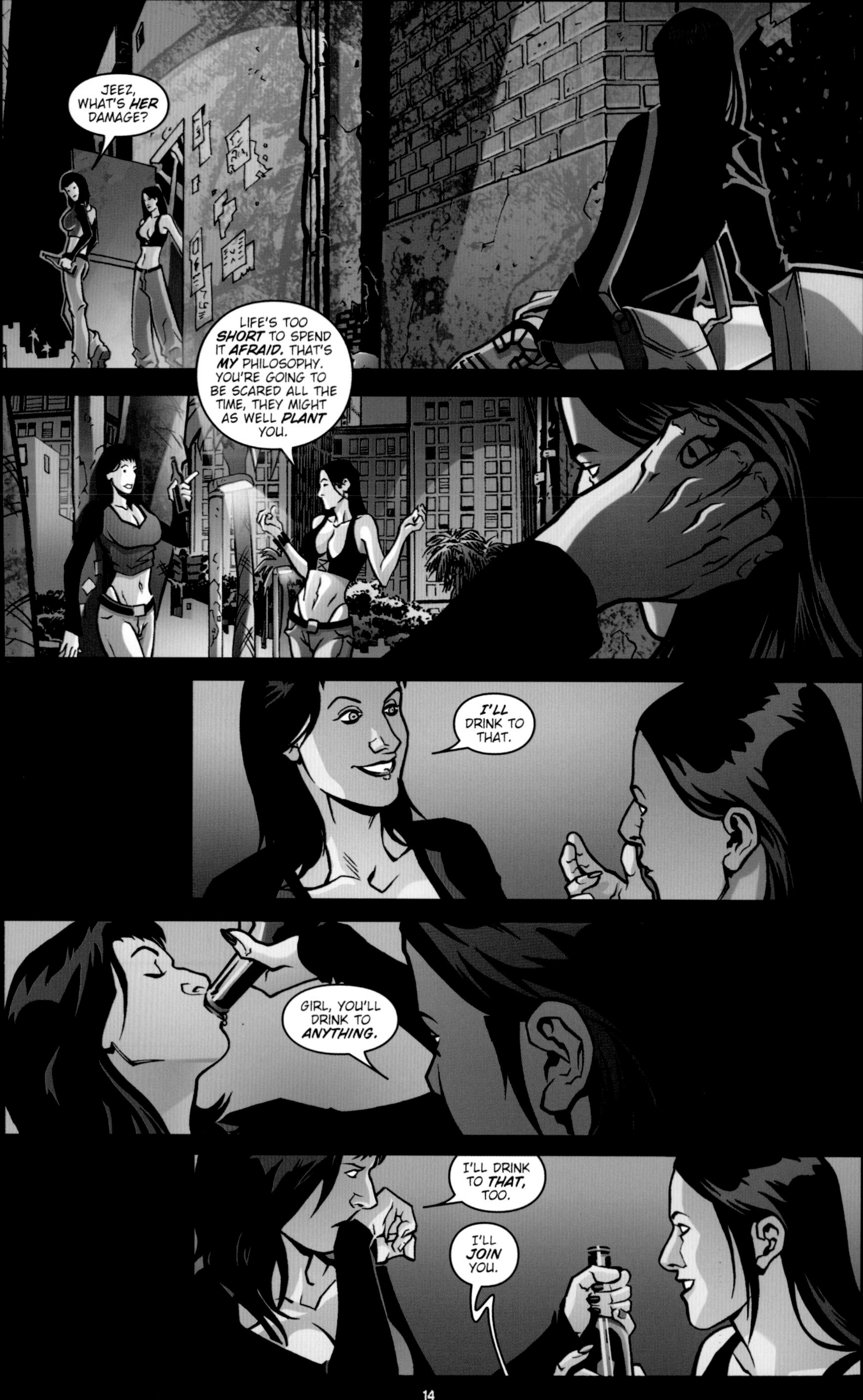
JEEZ, WHAT'S HER DAMAGE?
LIFE'S TOO SHORT TO SPEND IT AFRAID. THAT'S MY PHILOSOPHY. YOU'RE GOING TO BE SCARED ALL THE TIME, THEY MIGHT AS WELL PLANT YOU.
I'LL DRINK TO THAT.
GIRL, YOU'LL DRINK TO ANYTHING.
I'LL DRINK TO THAT, TOO.
I'LL JOIN YOU.

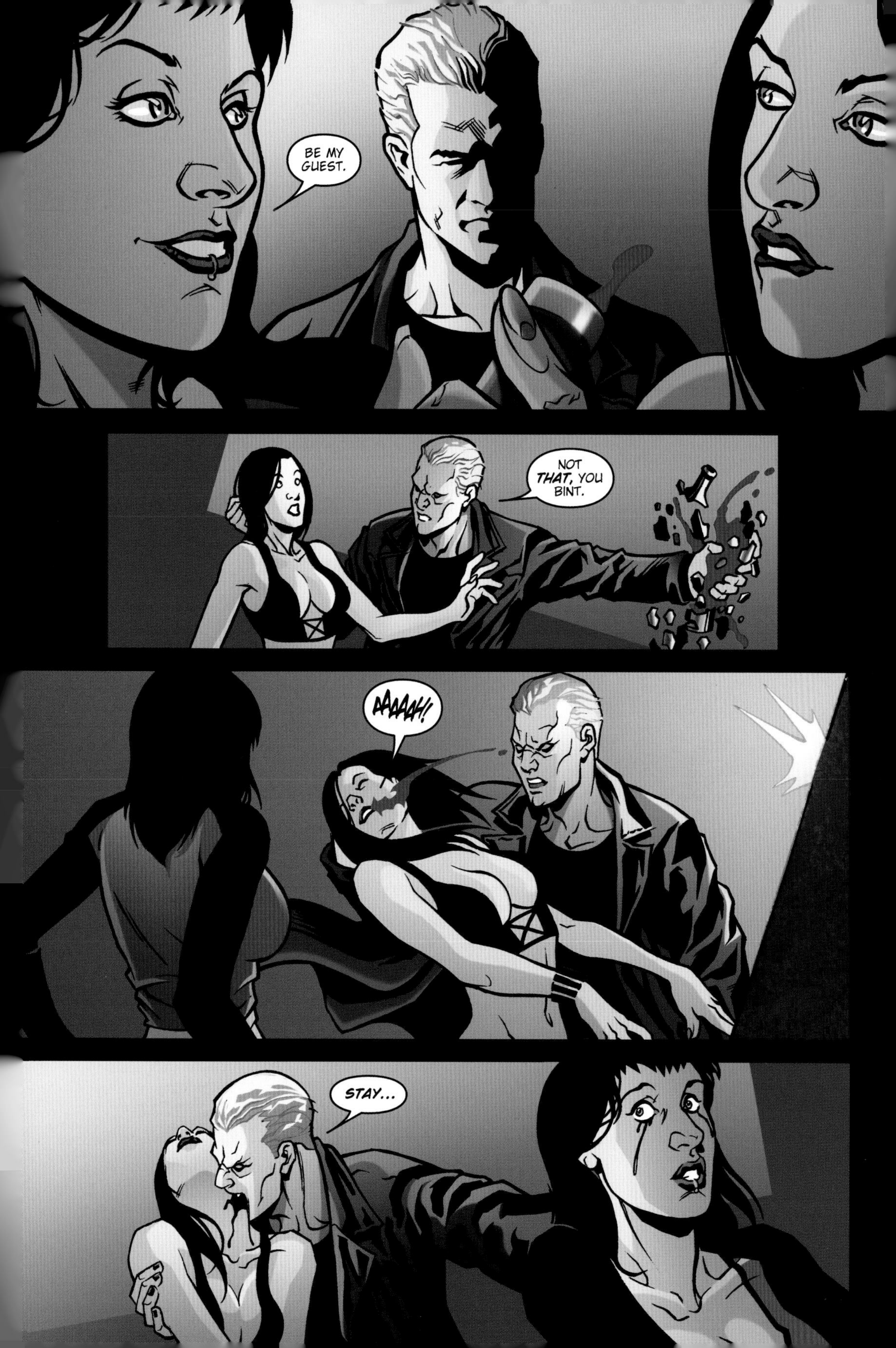
BE MY GUEST.
NOT THAT, YOU BINT.
AAAAAH!
STAY...

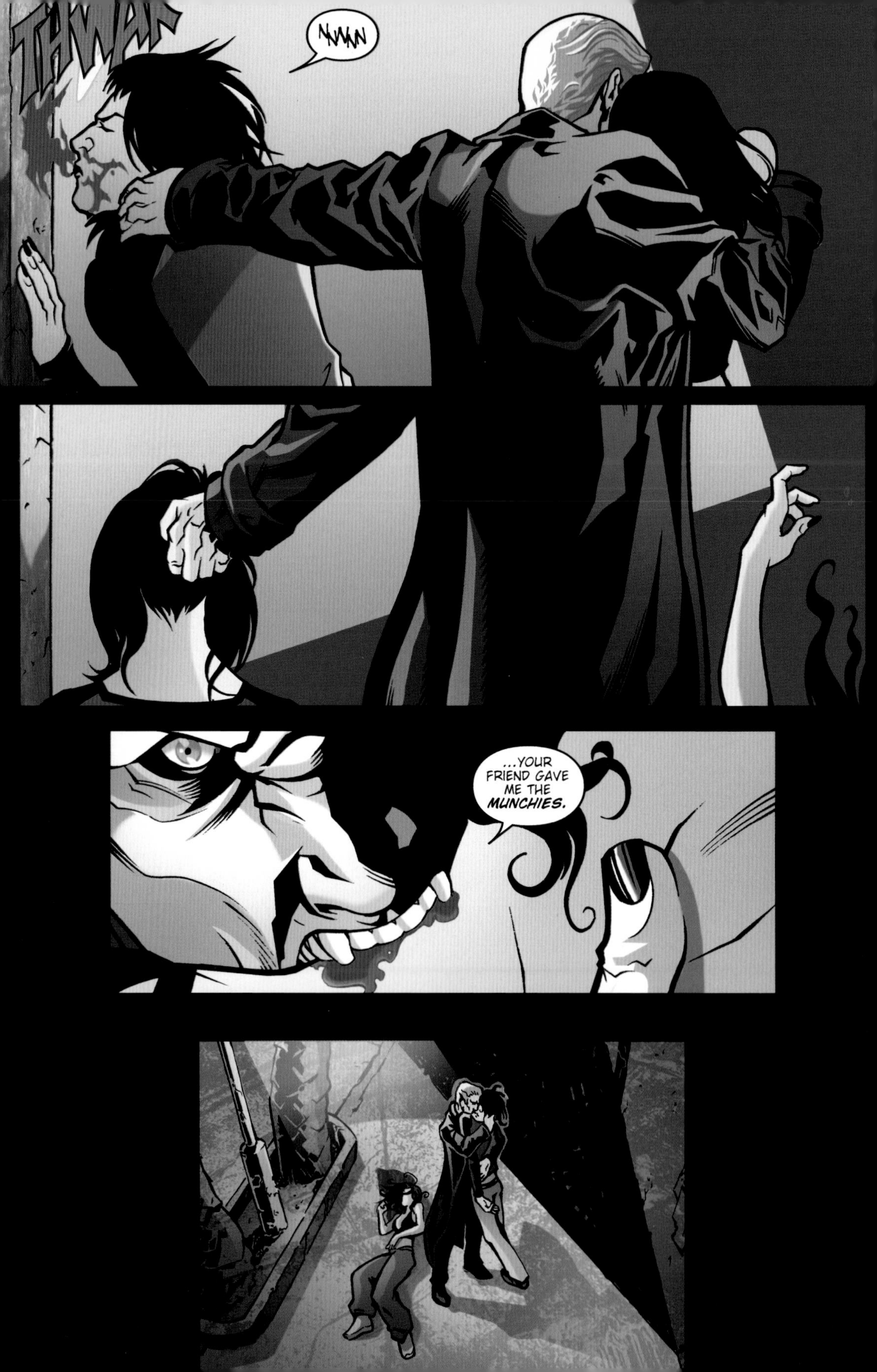
THWAP
...YOUR FRIEND GAVE ME THE MUNCHIES.

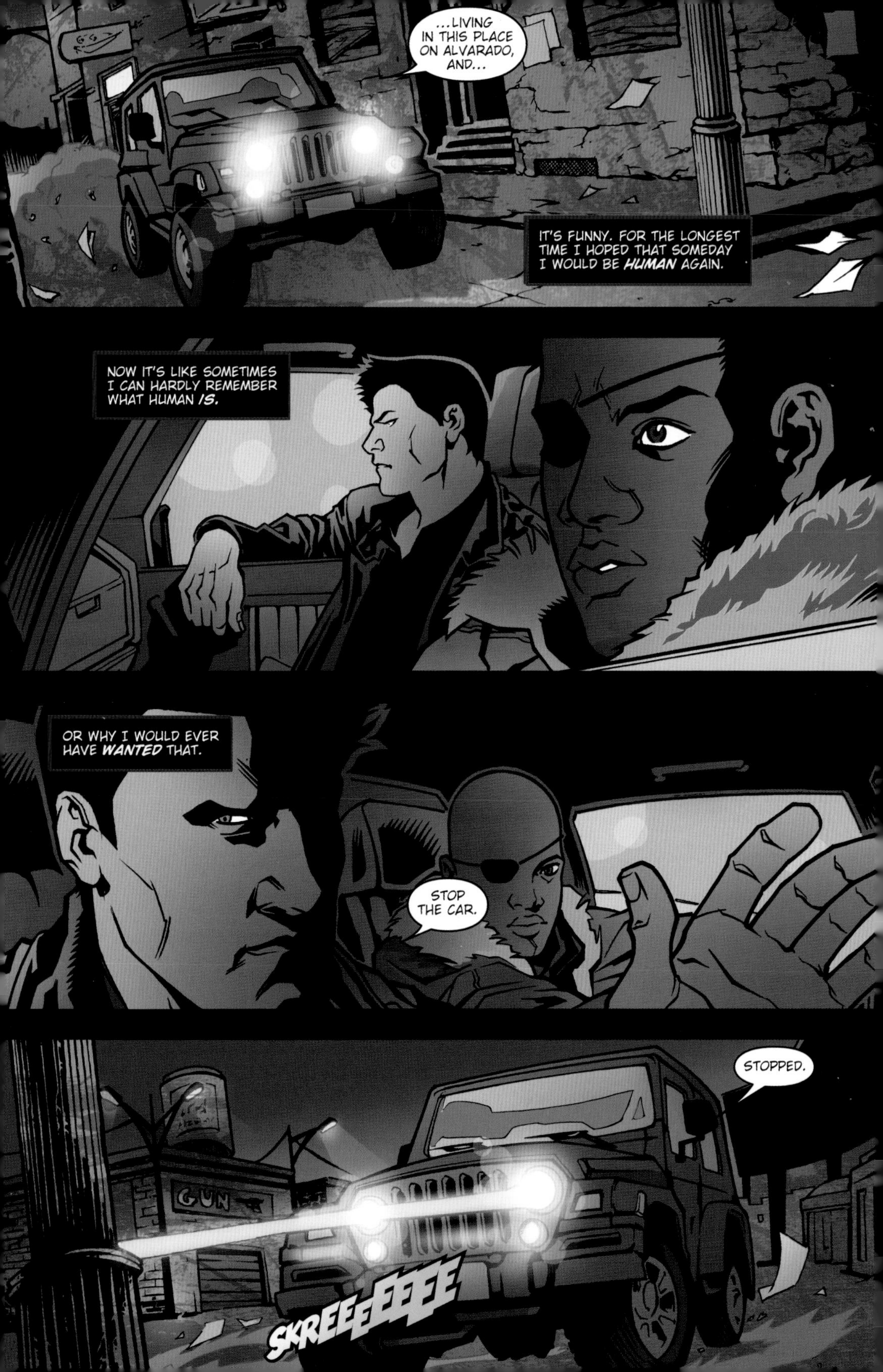
...LIVING IN THIS PLACE ON ALVARADO, AND...
IT'S FUNNY. FOR THE LONGEST TIME I HOPED THAT SOMEDAY I WOULD BE HUMAN AGAIN.
NOW IT'S LIKE SOMETIMES I CAN HARDLY REMEMBER WHAT HUMAN IS.
OR WHY I WOULD EVER HAVE WANTED THAT.
STOP THE CAR.
STOPPED.
GUN
SKREEEEEEE

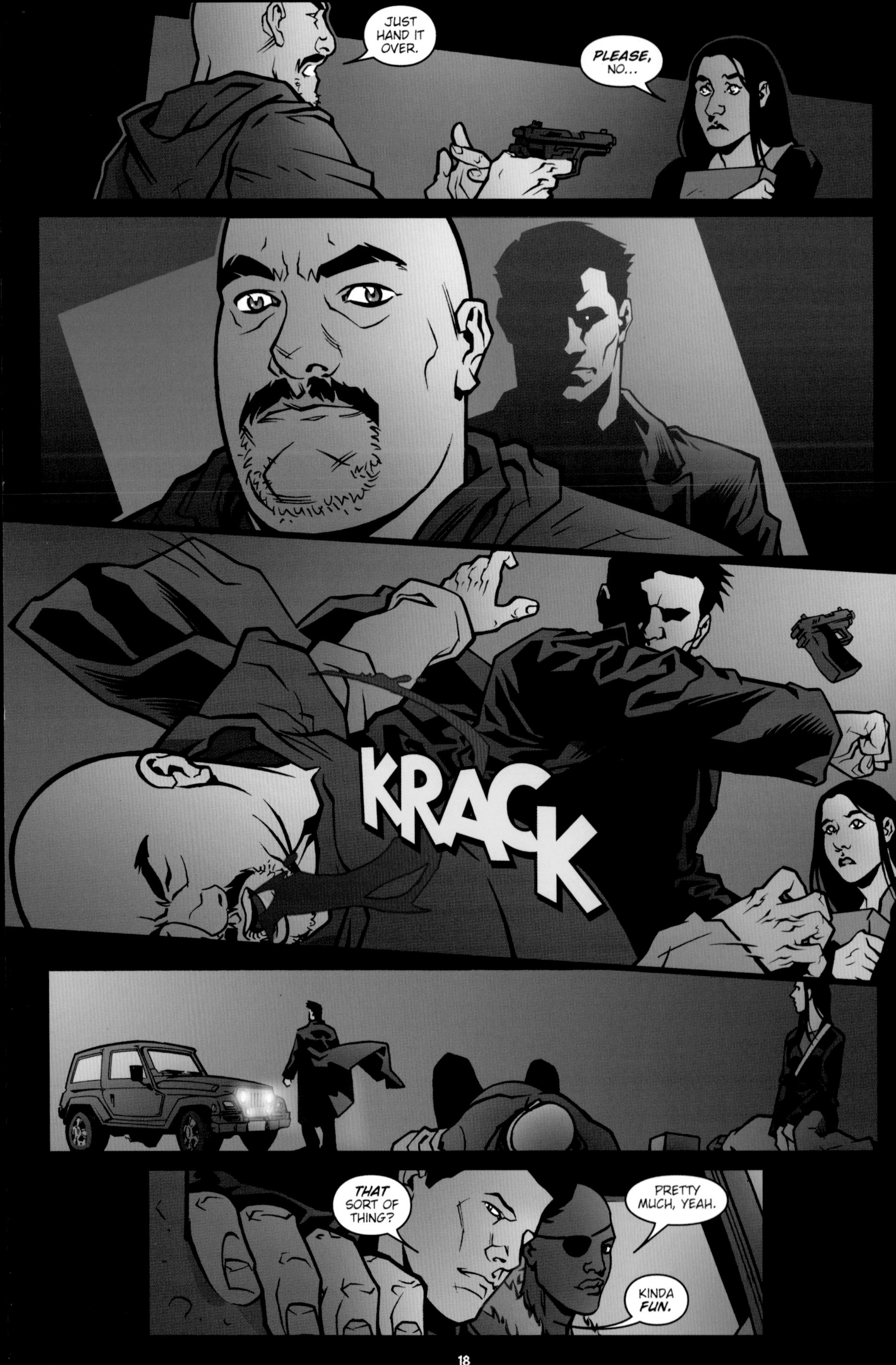
JUST HAND IT OVER.
PLEASE, NO...
KRACK
THAT SORT OF THING?
PRETTY MUCH, YEAH.
KINDA *FUN.*

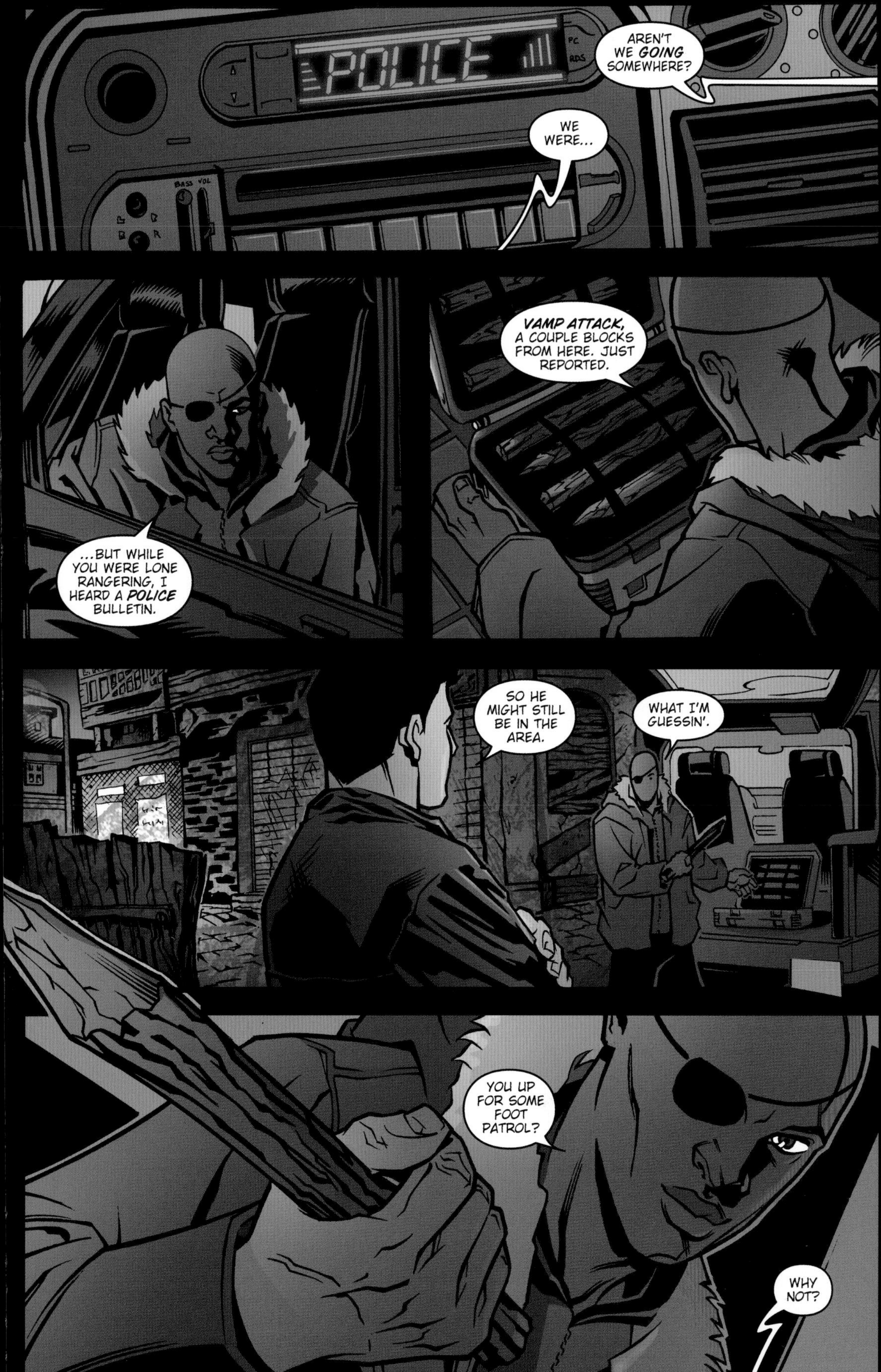
POLICE
AREN'T WE GOING SOMEWHERE?
WE WERE...
...BUT WHILE YOU WERE LONE RANGERING, I HEARD A POLICE BULLETIN.
VAMP ATTACK, A COUPLE BLOCKS FROM HERE. JUST REPORTED.
SO HE MIGHT STILL BE IN THE AREA.
WHAT I'M GUESSIN'.
YOU UP FOR SOME FOOT PATROL?
WHY NOT?

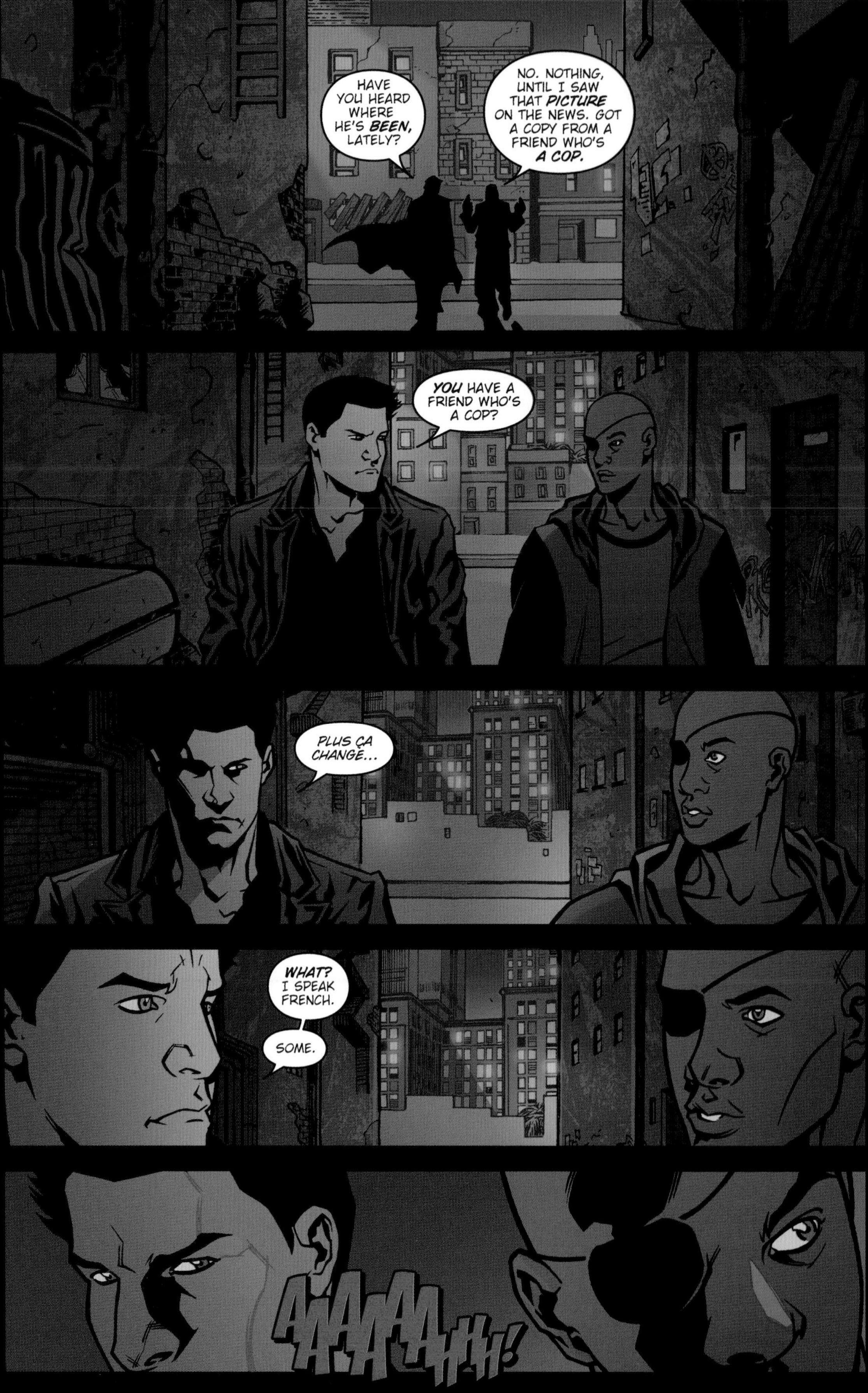
HAVE YOU HEARD WHERE HE'S BEEN, LATELY?
NO. NOTHING, UNTIL I SAW THAT PICTURE ON THE NEWS. GOT A COPY FROM A FRIEND WHO'S A COP.
YOU HAVE A FRIEND WHO'S A COP?
PLUS ÇA CHANGE...
WHAT? I SPEAK FRENCH.
SOME.
AAAAAAAHHH!

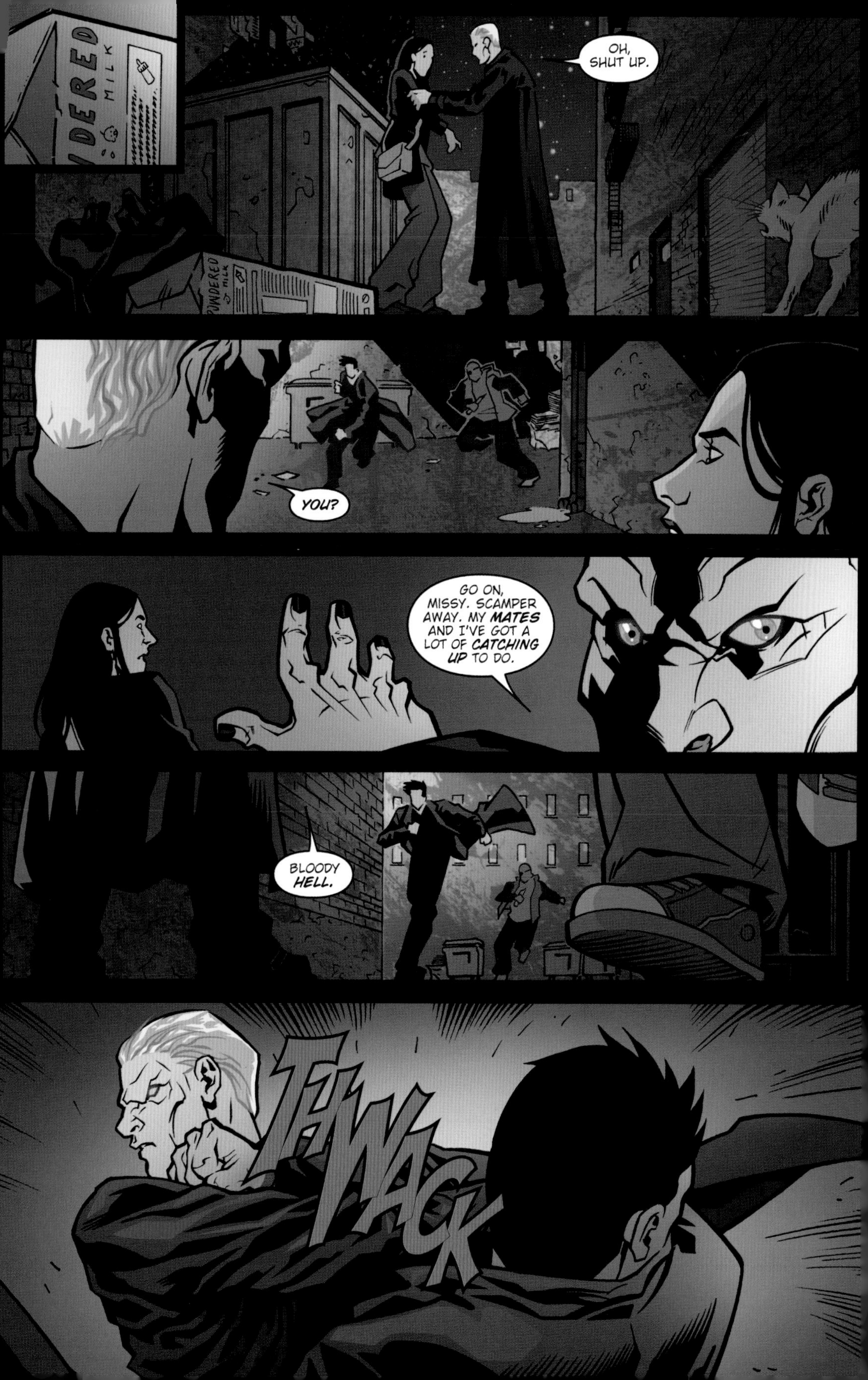
POWDERED MILK
OH, SHUT UP.
POWDERED MILK
YOU?
GO ON, MISSY. SCAMPER AWAY. MY MATES AND I'VE GOT A LOT OF CATCHING UP TO DO.
BLOODY HELL.
THWACK

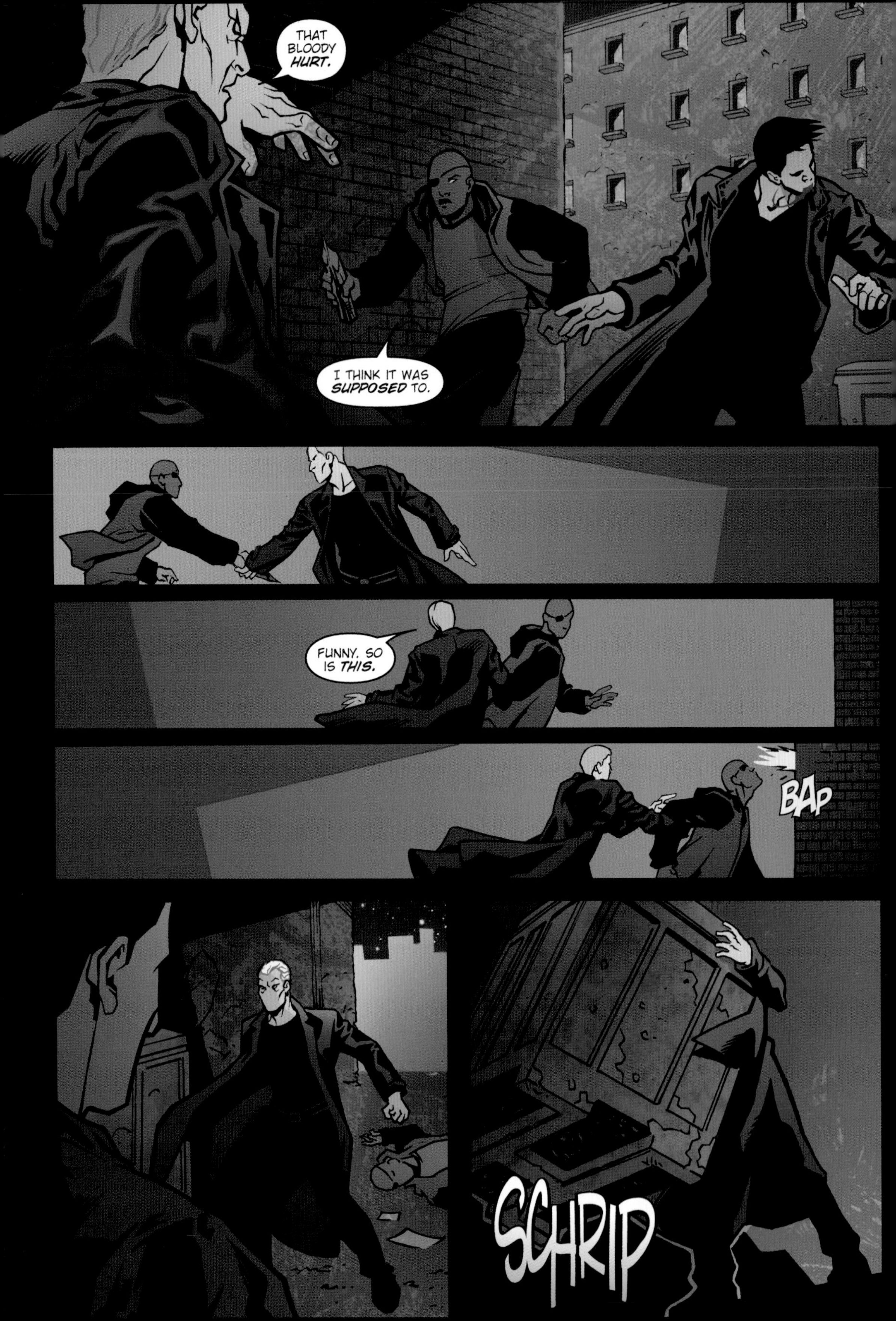
THAT BLOODY HURT.
I THINK IT WAS SUPPOSED TO.
FUNNY. SO IS THIS.
BAP
SCHRIP

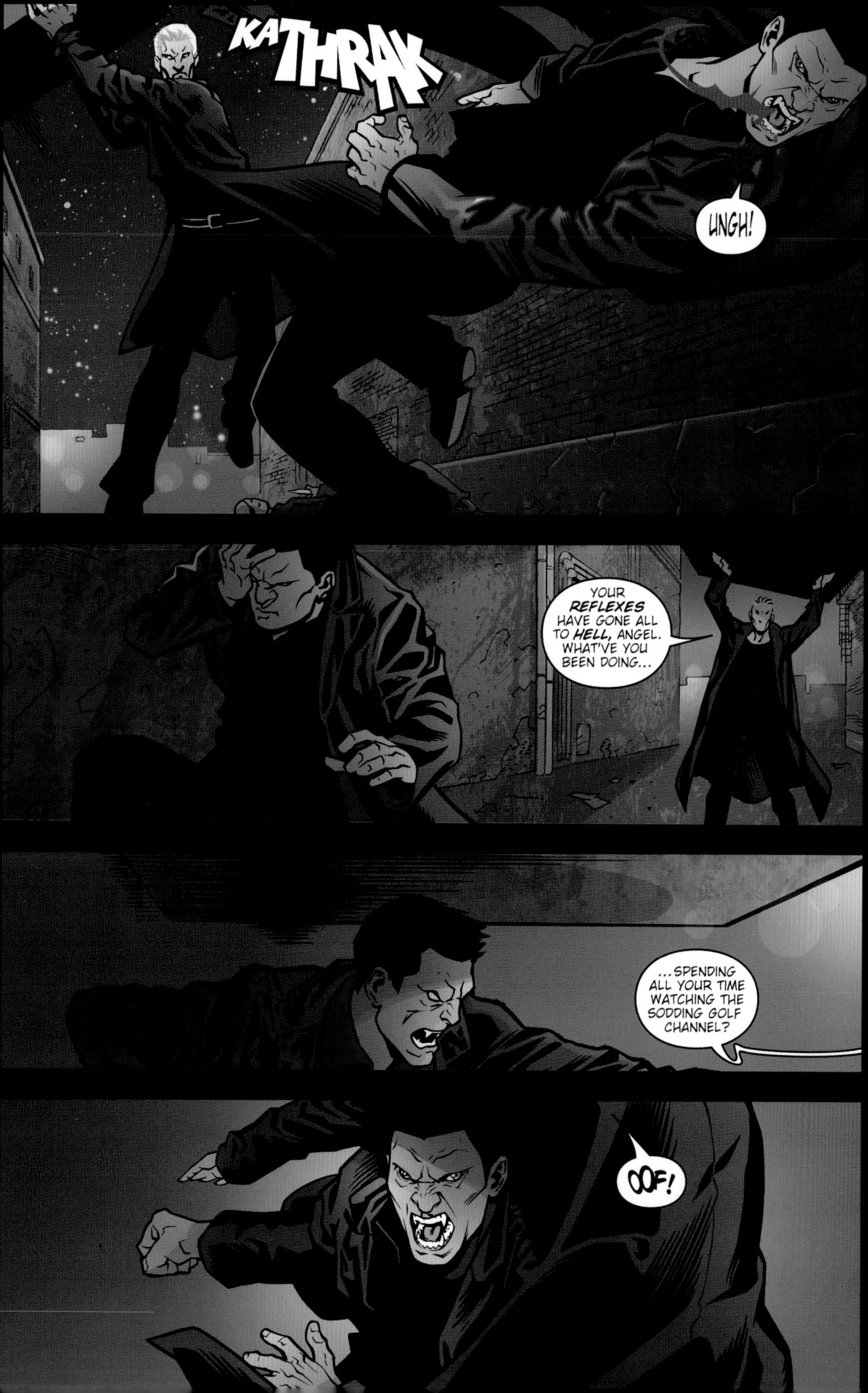
KATHRAK
UNGH!
YOUR REFLEXES HAVE GONE ALL TO HELL, ANGEL. WHAT'VE YOU BEEN DOING...
...SPENDING ALL YOUR TIME WATCHING THE SODDING GOLF CHANNEL?
OOF!

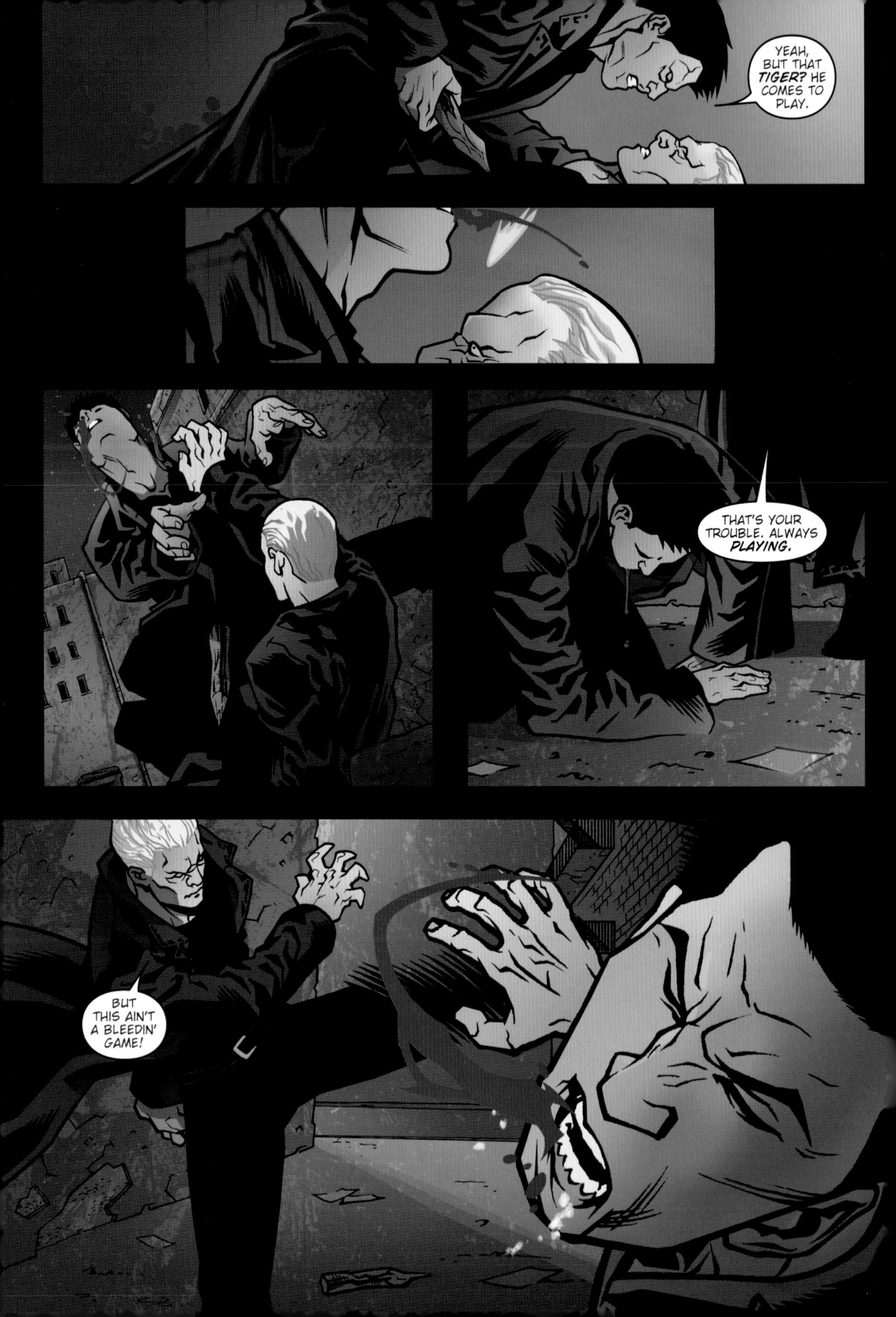
YEAH, BUT THAT TIGER? HE COMES TO PLAY.
THAT'S YOUR TROUBLE. ALWAYS PLAYING.
BUT THIS AIN'T A BLEEDIN' GAME!

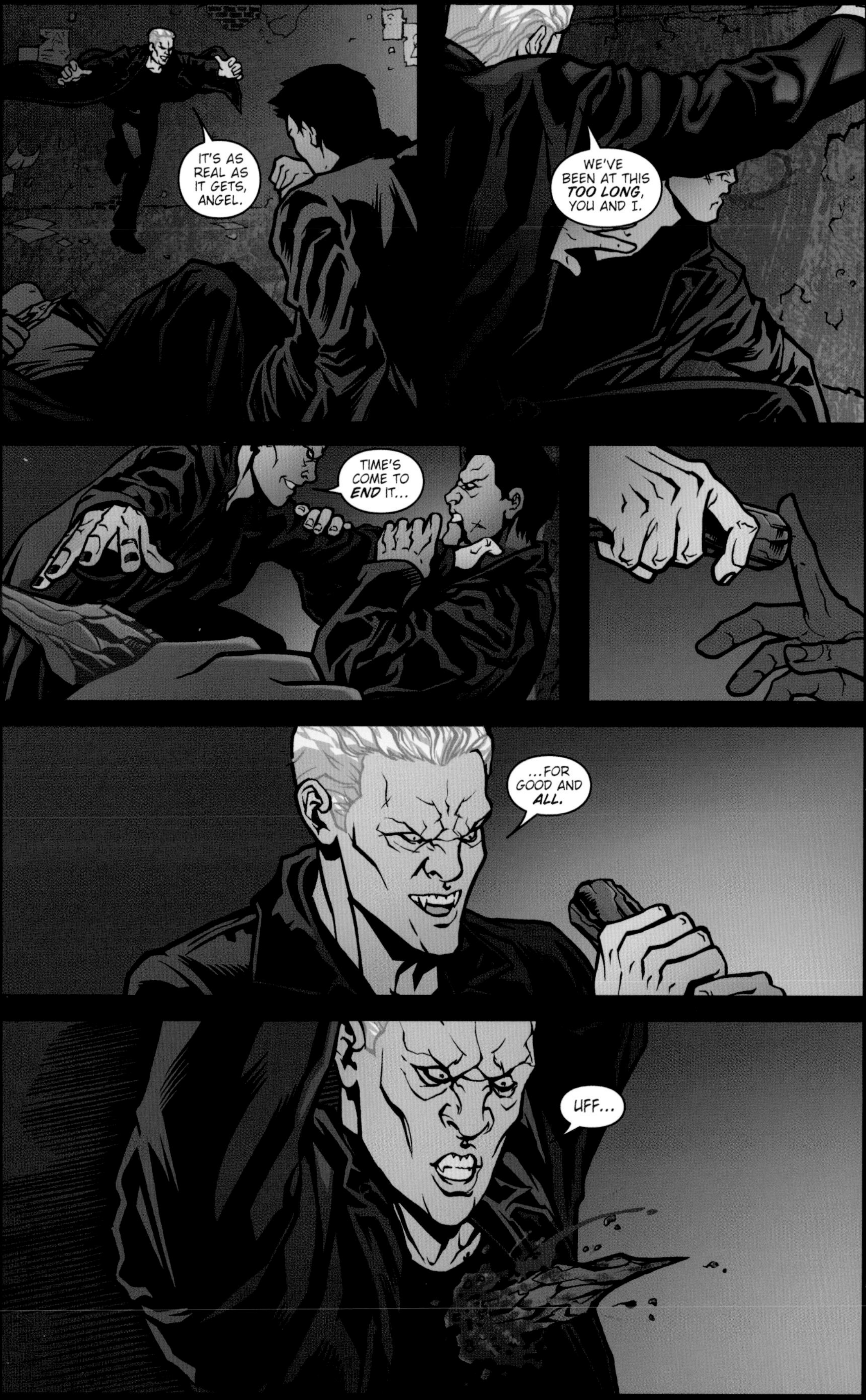
IT'S AS REAL AS IT GETS, ANGEL.
WE'VE BEEN AT THIS *TOO LONG*, YOU AND I.
TIME'S COME TO *END* IT...
...FOR GOOD AND *ALL.*
UFF...

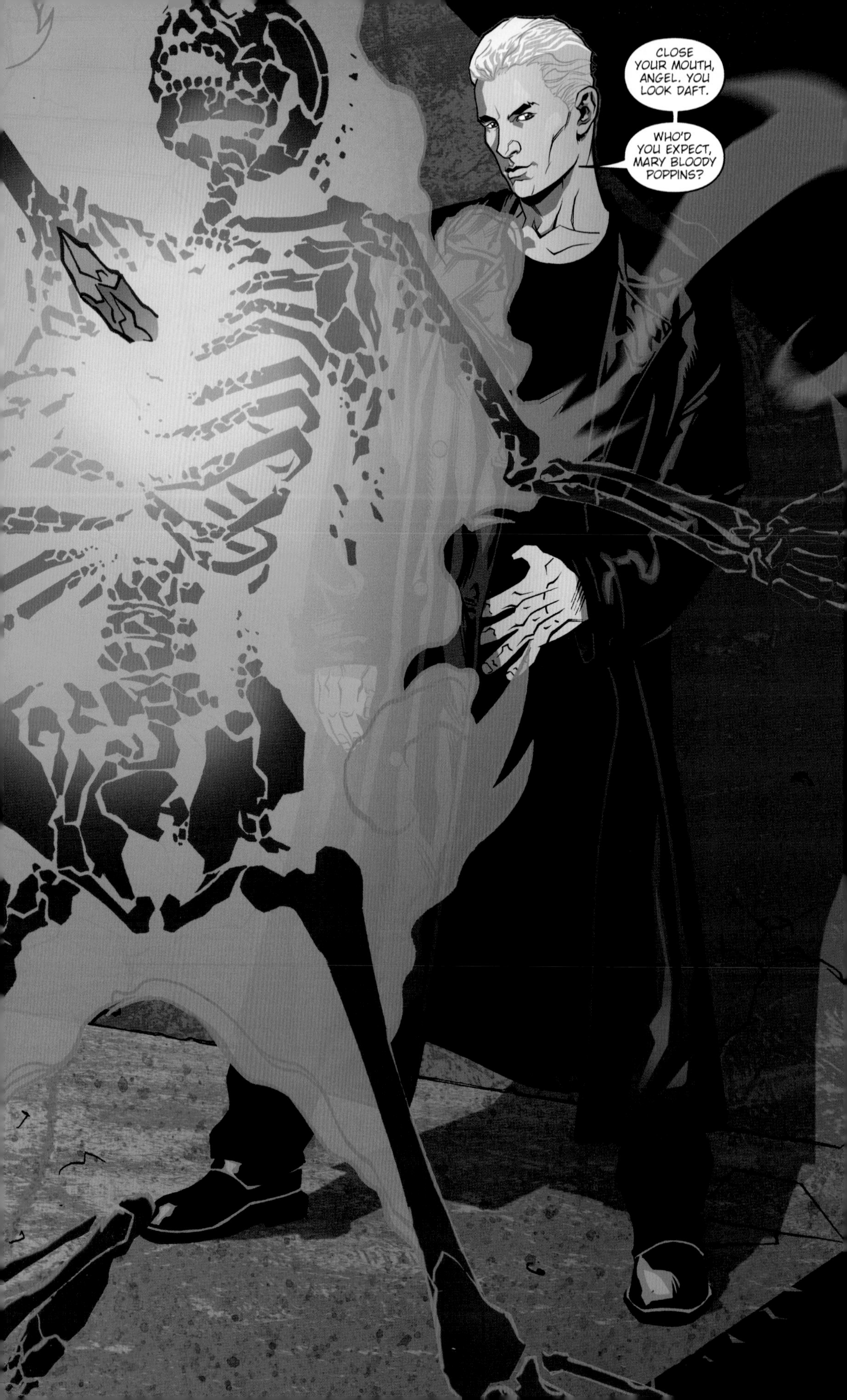
CLOSE YOUR MOUTH, ANGEL. YOU LOOK DAFT.
WHO'D YOU EXPECT, MARY BLOODY POPPINS?

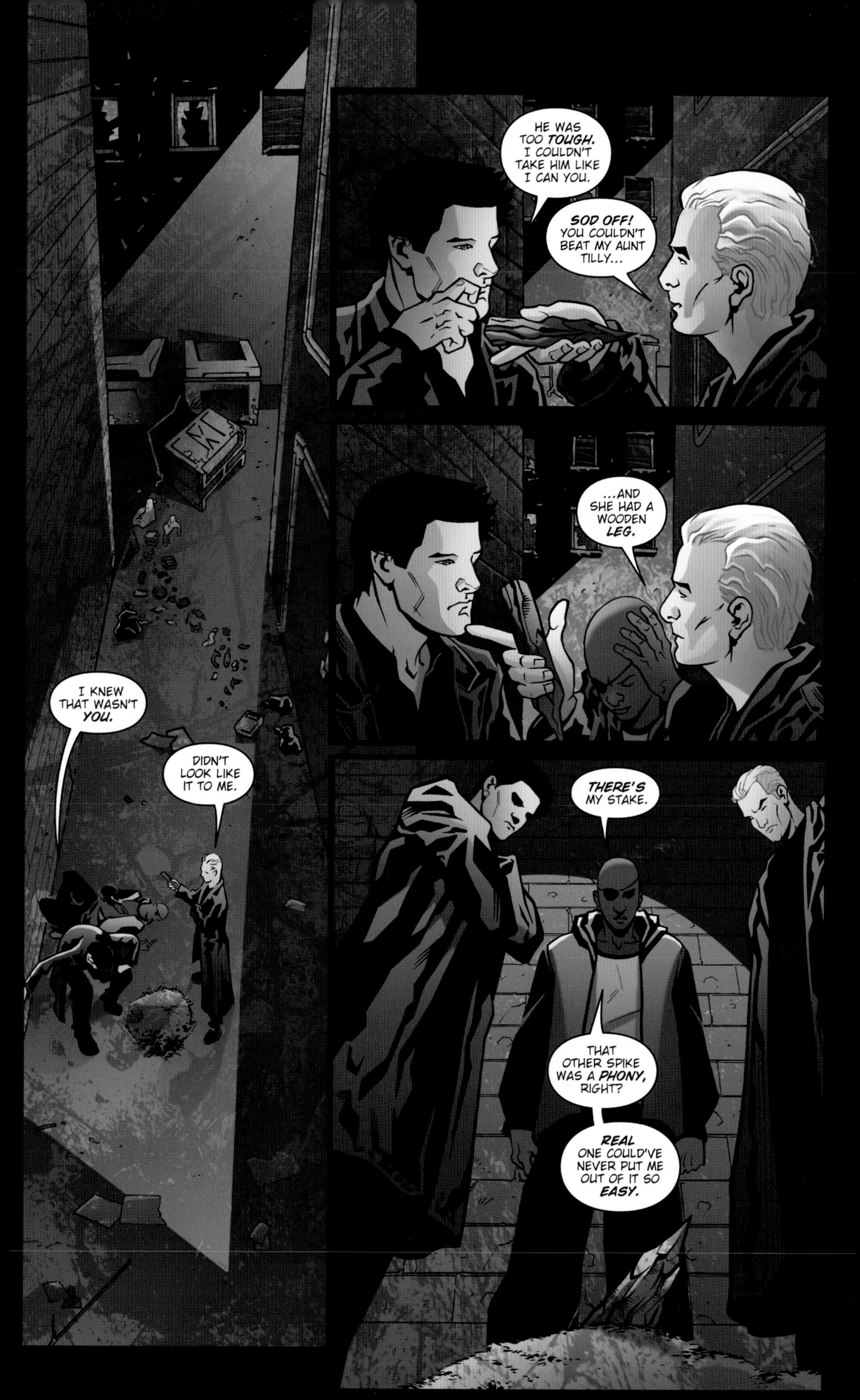
HE WAS TOO TOUGH. I COULDN'T TAKE HIM LIKE I CAN YOU.
SOD OFF! YOU COULDN'T BEAT MY AUNT TILLY...
...AND SHE HAD A WOODEN LEG.
I KNEW THAT WASN'T YOU.
DIDN'T LOOK LIKE IT TO ME.
THERE'S MY STAKE.
THAT OTHER SPIKE WAS A PHONY, RIGHT?
REAL ONE COULD'VE NEVER PUT ME OUT OF IT SO EASY.

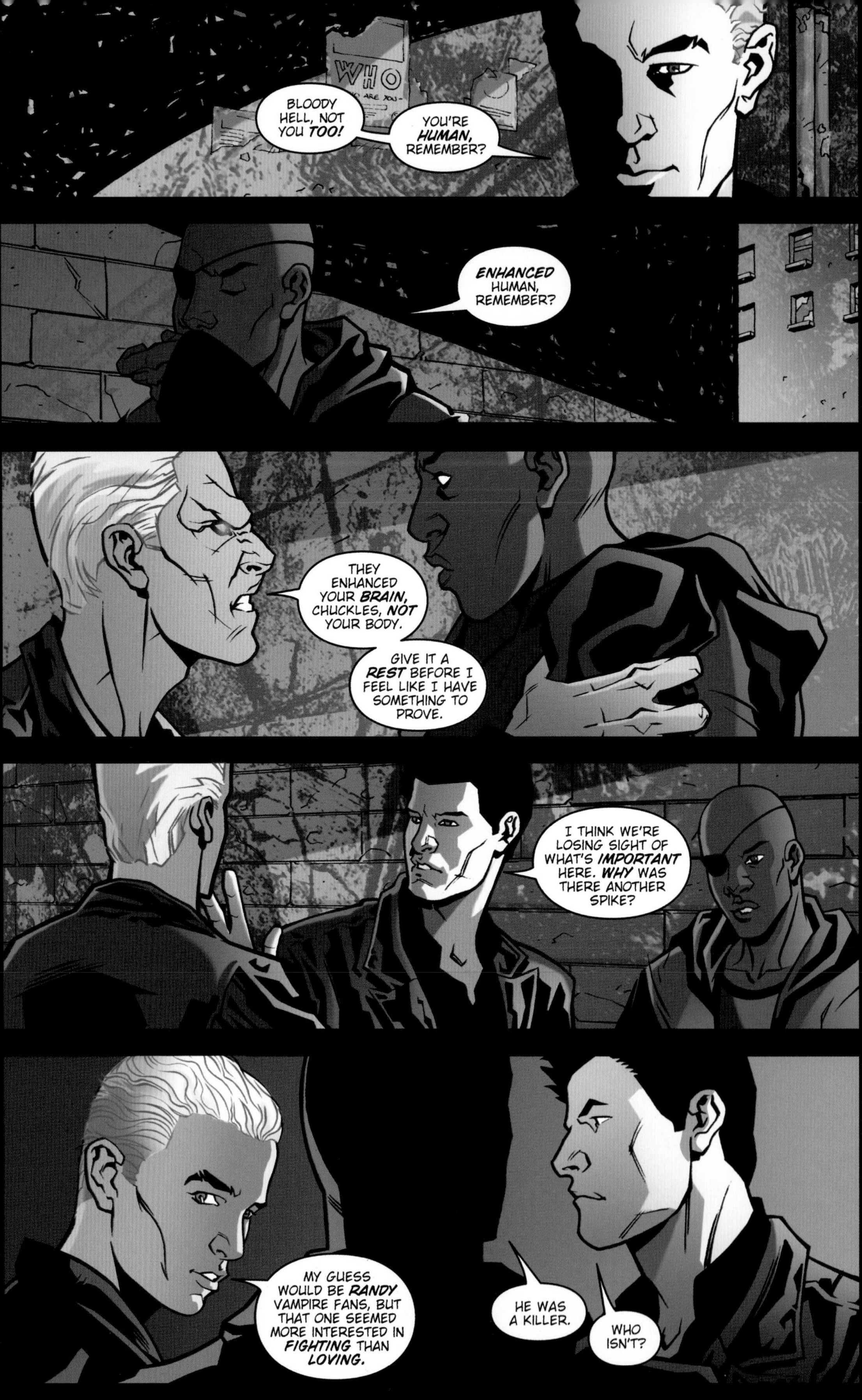
WHO
BLOODY HELL, NOT YOU **TOO!**
YOU'RE ***HUMAN,*** REMEMBER?
ENHANCED HUMAN, REMEMBER?
THEY ENHANCED YOUR ***BRAIN,*** CHUCKLES, ***NOT*** YOUR BODY.
GIVE IT A ***REST*** BEFORE I FEEL LIKE I HAVE SOMETHING TO PROVE.
I THINK WE'RE LOSING SIGHT OF WHAT'S ***IMPORTANT*** HERE. ***WHY*** WAS THERE ANOTHER SPIKE?
MY GUESS WOULD BE ***RANDY*** VAMPIRE FANS, BUT THAT ONE SEEMED MORE INTERESTED IN ***FIGHTING*** THAN ***LOVING.***
HE WAS A KILLER.
WHO ISN'T?

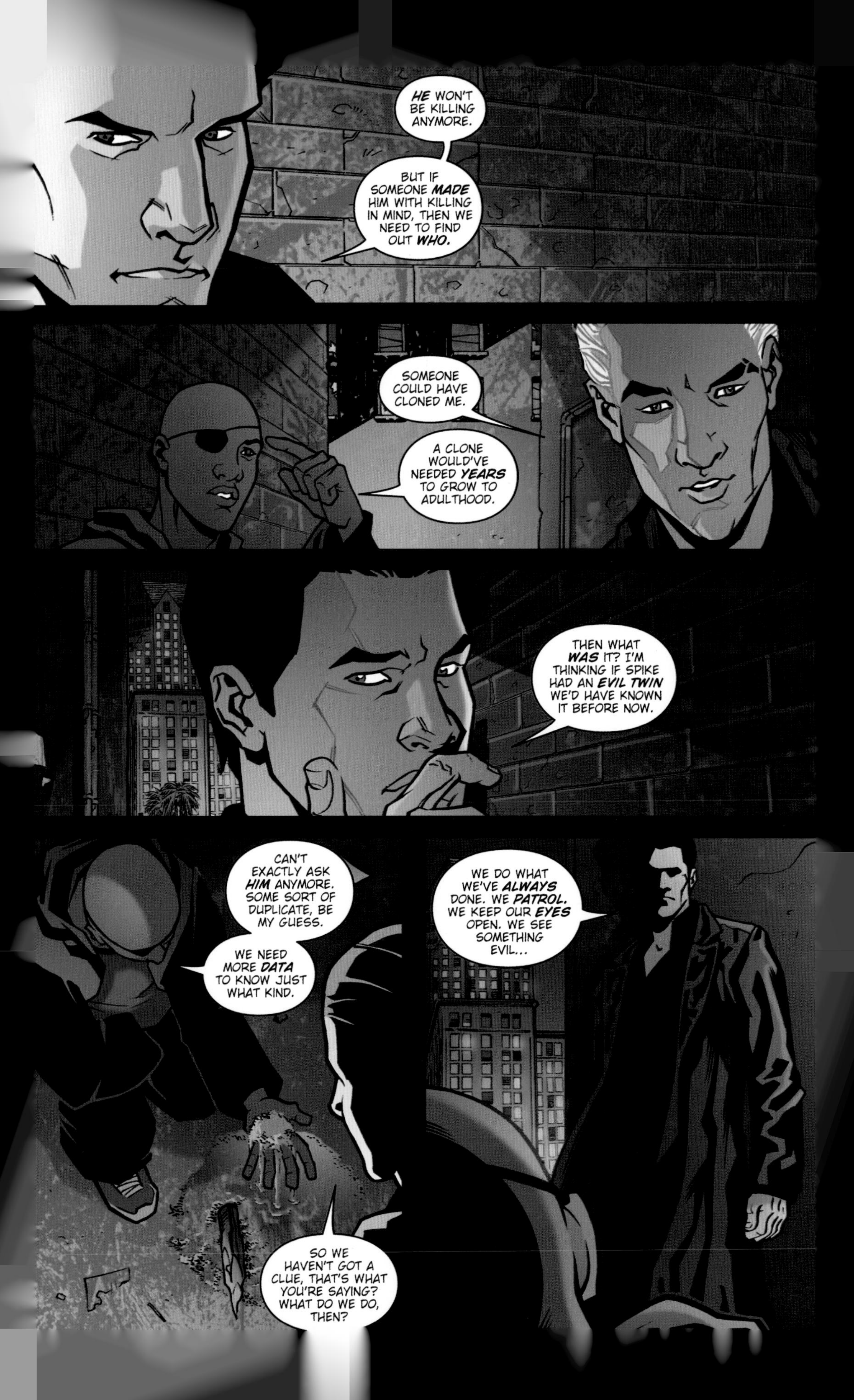
HE WON'T BE KILLING ANYMORE.
BUT IF SOMEONE MADE HIM WITH KILLING IN MIND, THEN WE NEED TO FIND OUT WHO.
SOMEONE COULD HAVE CLONED ME.
A CLONE WOULD'VE NEEDED YEARS TO GROW TO ADULTHOOD.
THEN WHAT WAS IT? I'M THINKING IF SPIKE HAD AN EVIL TWIN WE'D HAVE KNOWN IT BEFORE NOW.
CAN'T EXACTLY ASK HIM ANYMORE. SOME SORT OF DUPLICATE, BE MY GUESS.
WE NEED MORE DATA TO KNOW JUST WHAT KIND.
SO WE HAVEN'T GOT A CLUE, THAT'S WHAT YOU'RE SAYING? WHAT DO WE DO, THEN?
WE DO WHAT WE'VE ALWAYS DONE. WE PATROL. WE KEEP OUR EYES OPEN. WE SEE SOMETHING EVIL...

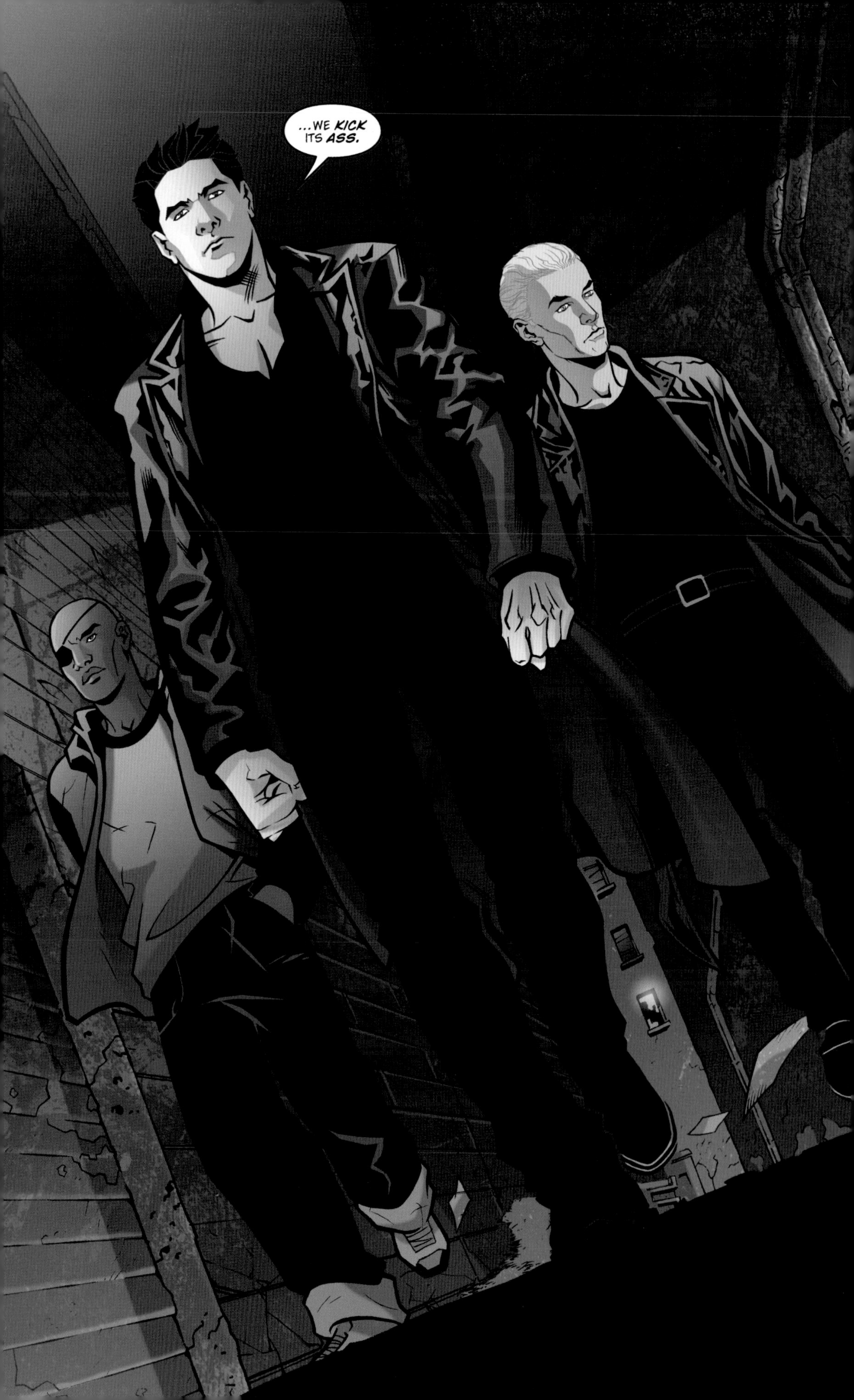
...WE KICK ITS ASS.

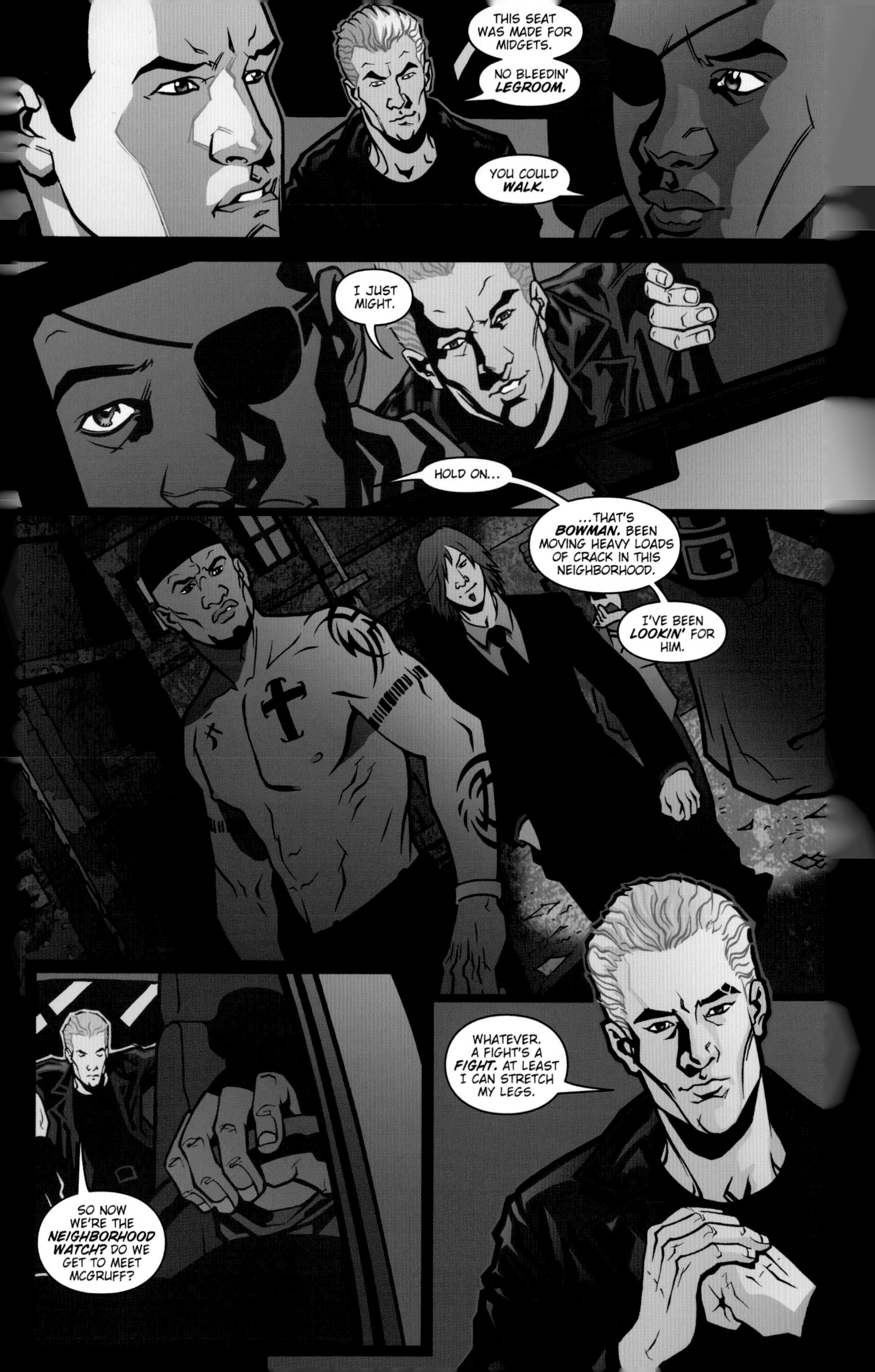
THIS SEAT WAS MADE FOR MIDGETS.
NO BLEEDIN' LEGROOM.
YOU COULD WALK.
I JUST MIGHT.
HOLD ON...
...THAT'S BOWMAN. BEEN MOVING HEAVY LOADS OF CRACK IN THIS NEIGHBORHOOD.
I'VE BEEN LOOKIN' FOR HIM.
SO NOW WE'RE THE NEIGHBORHOOD WATCH? DO WE GET TO MEET MCGRUFF?
WHATEVER. A FIGHT'S A FIGHT. AT LEAST I CAN STRETCH MY LEGS.

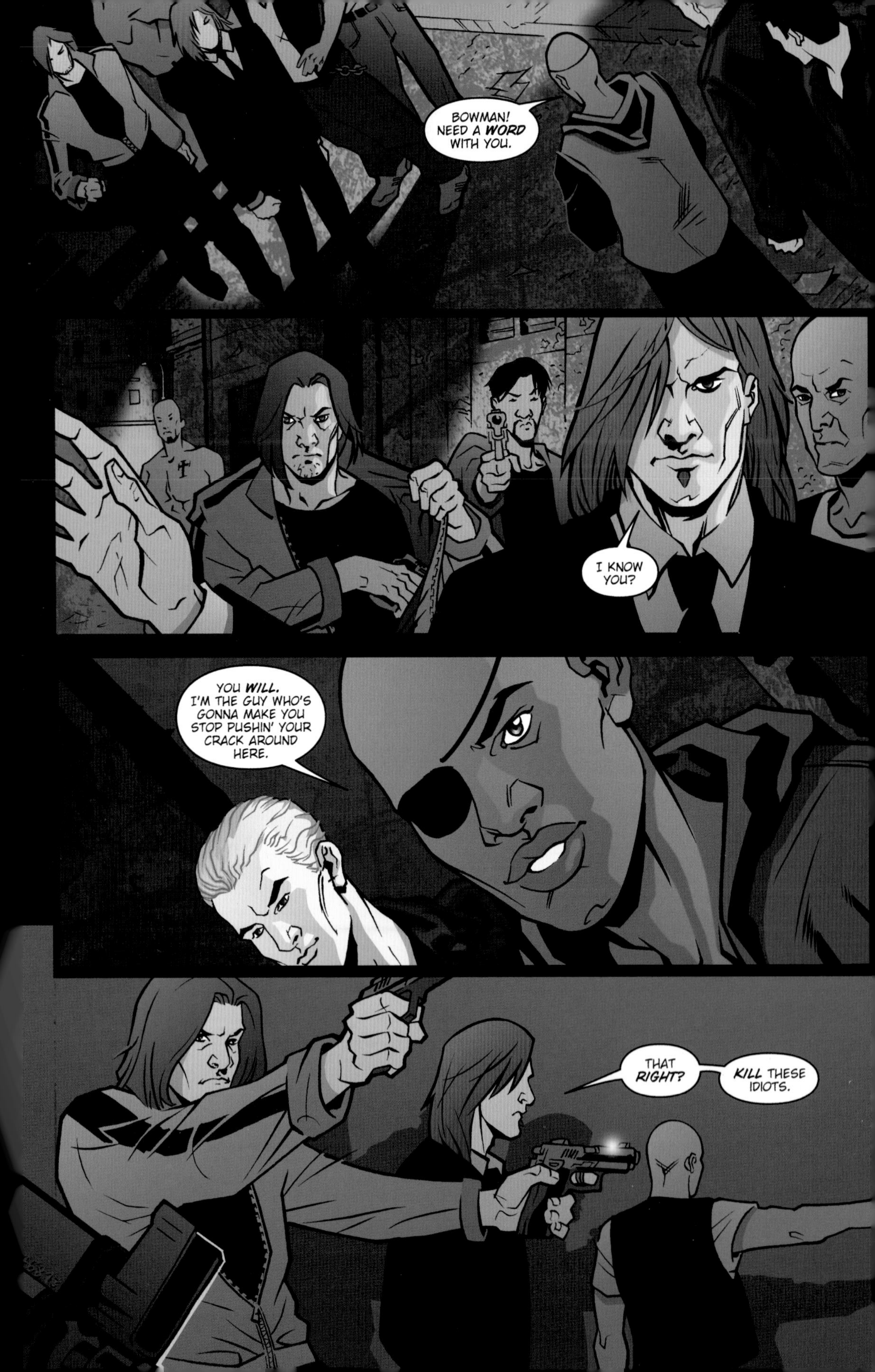
BOWMAN! NEED A WORD WITH YOU.
I KNOW YOU?
YOU WILL. I'M THE GUY WHO'S GONNA MAKE YOU STOP PUSHIN' YOUR CRACK AROUND HERE.
THAT RIGHT?
KILL THESE IDIOTS.

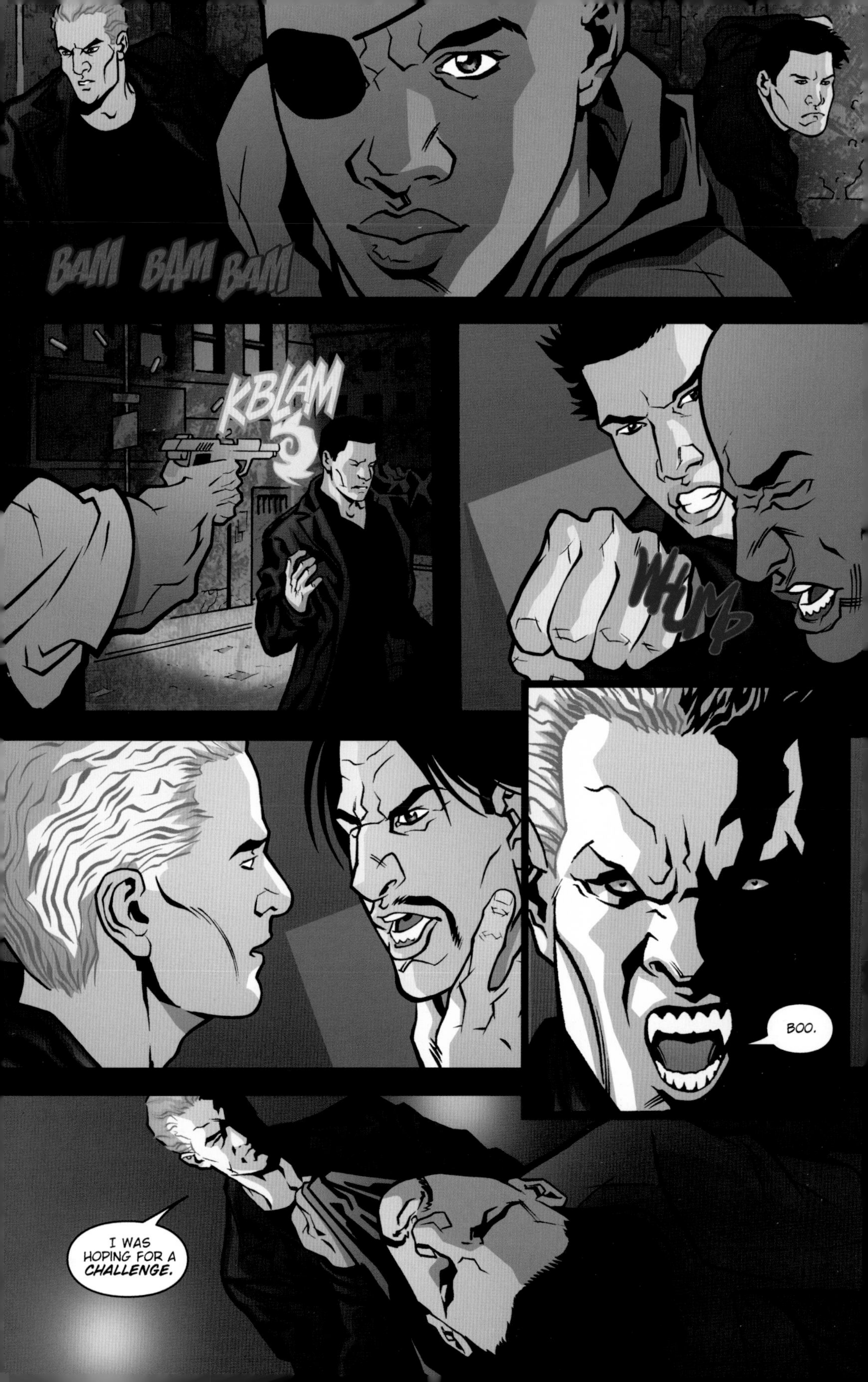
BAM BAM BAM
KBLAM
WHUMP
BOO.
I WAS HOPING FOR A CHALLENGE.

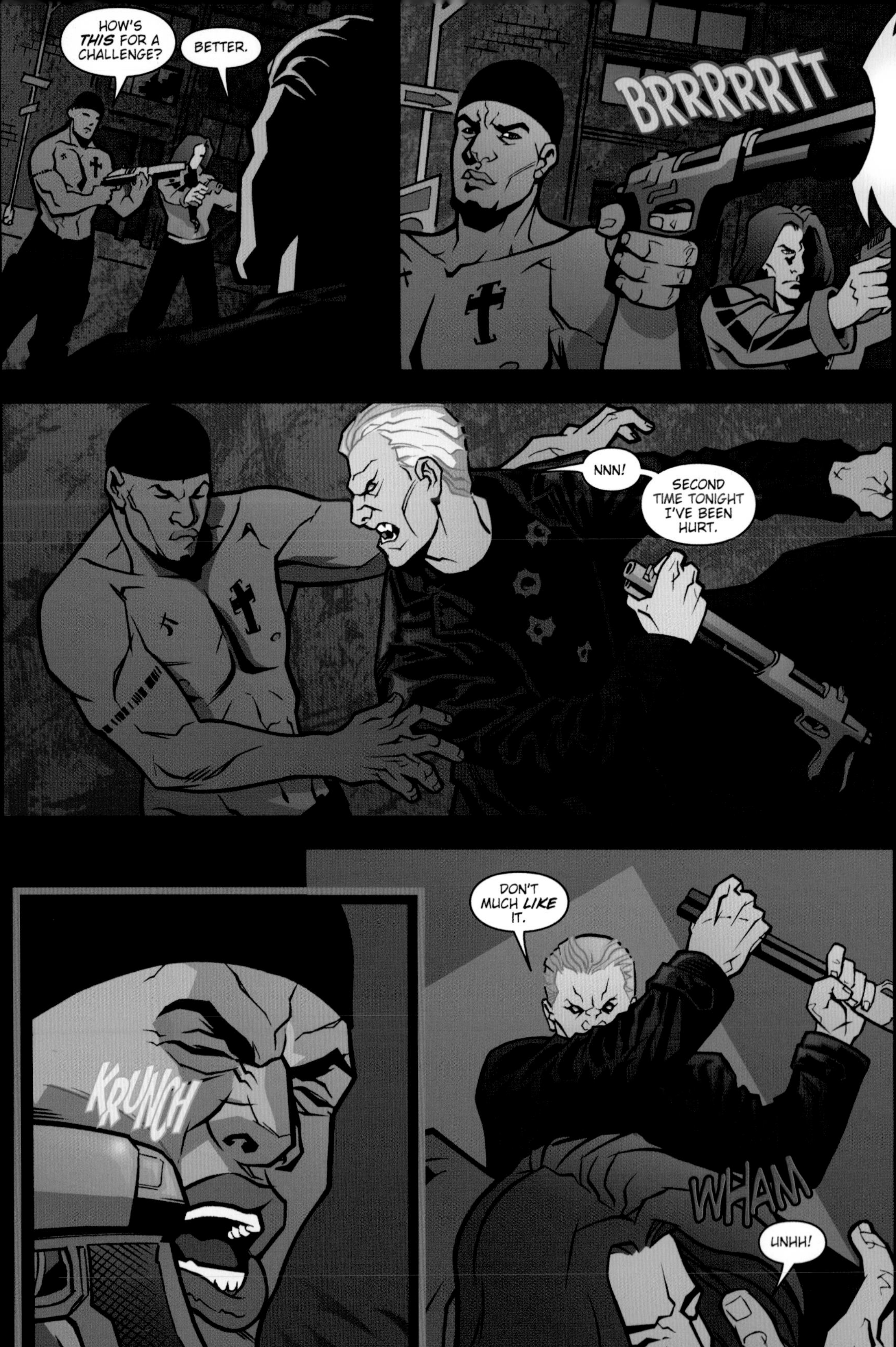
HOW'S THIS FOR A CHALLENGE?
BETTER.
BRRRRRTT
NNN!
SECOND TIME TONIGHT I'VE BEEN HURT.
KRUNCH
DON'T MUCH LIKE IT.
WHAM
UNHH!

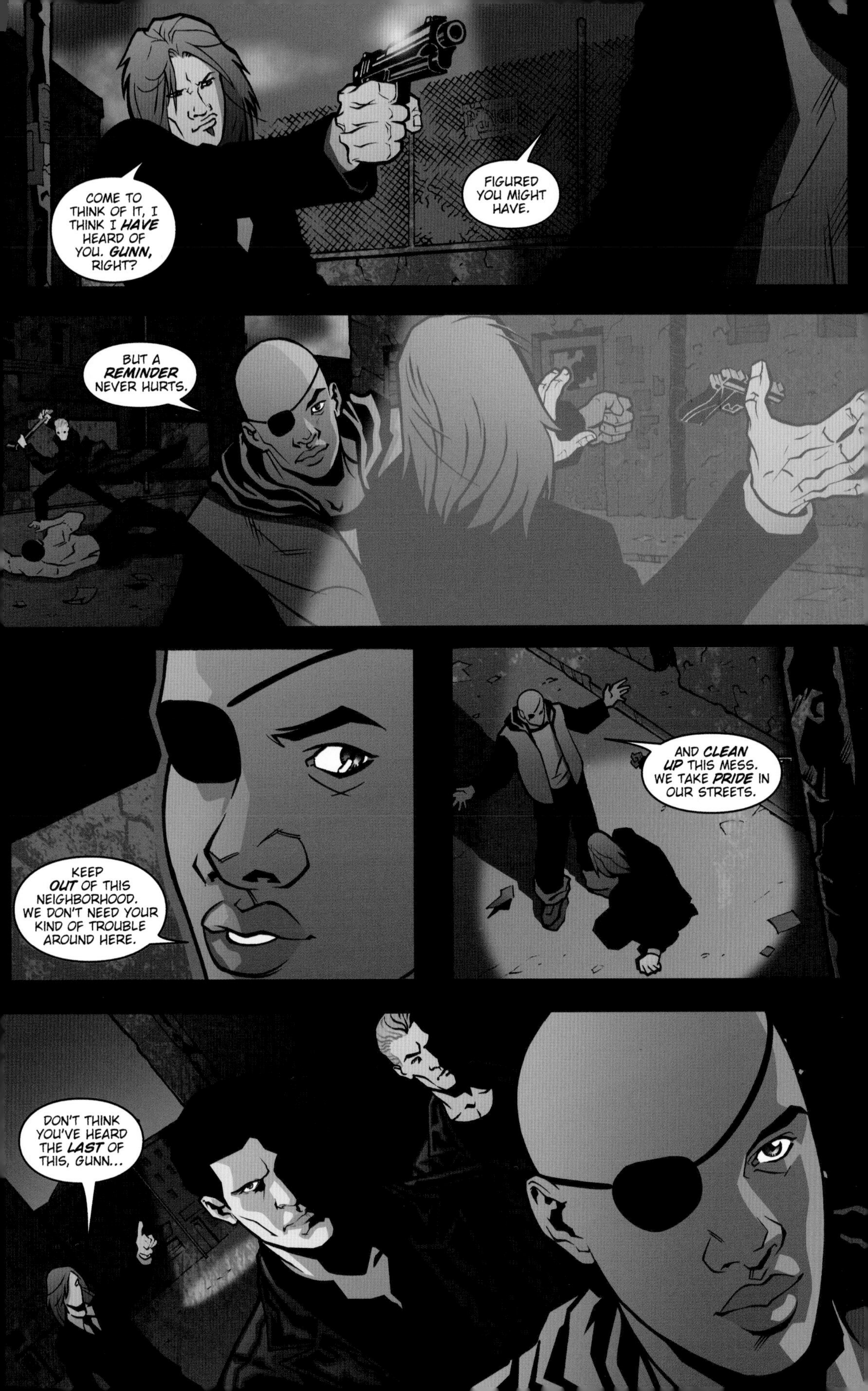
COME TO THINK OF IT, I THINK I HAVE HEARD OF YOU. GUNN, RIGHT?
FIGURED YOU MIGHT HAVE.
BUT A REMINDER NEVER HURTS.
KEEP OUT OF THIS NEIGHBORHOOD. WE DON'T NEED YOUR KIND OF TROUBLE AROUND HERE.
AND CLEAN UP THIS MESS. WE TAKE PRIDE IN OUR STREETS.
DON'T THINK YOU'VE HEARD THE LAST OF THIS, GUNN...

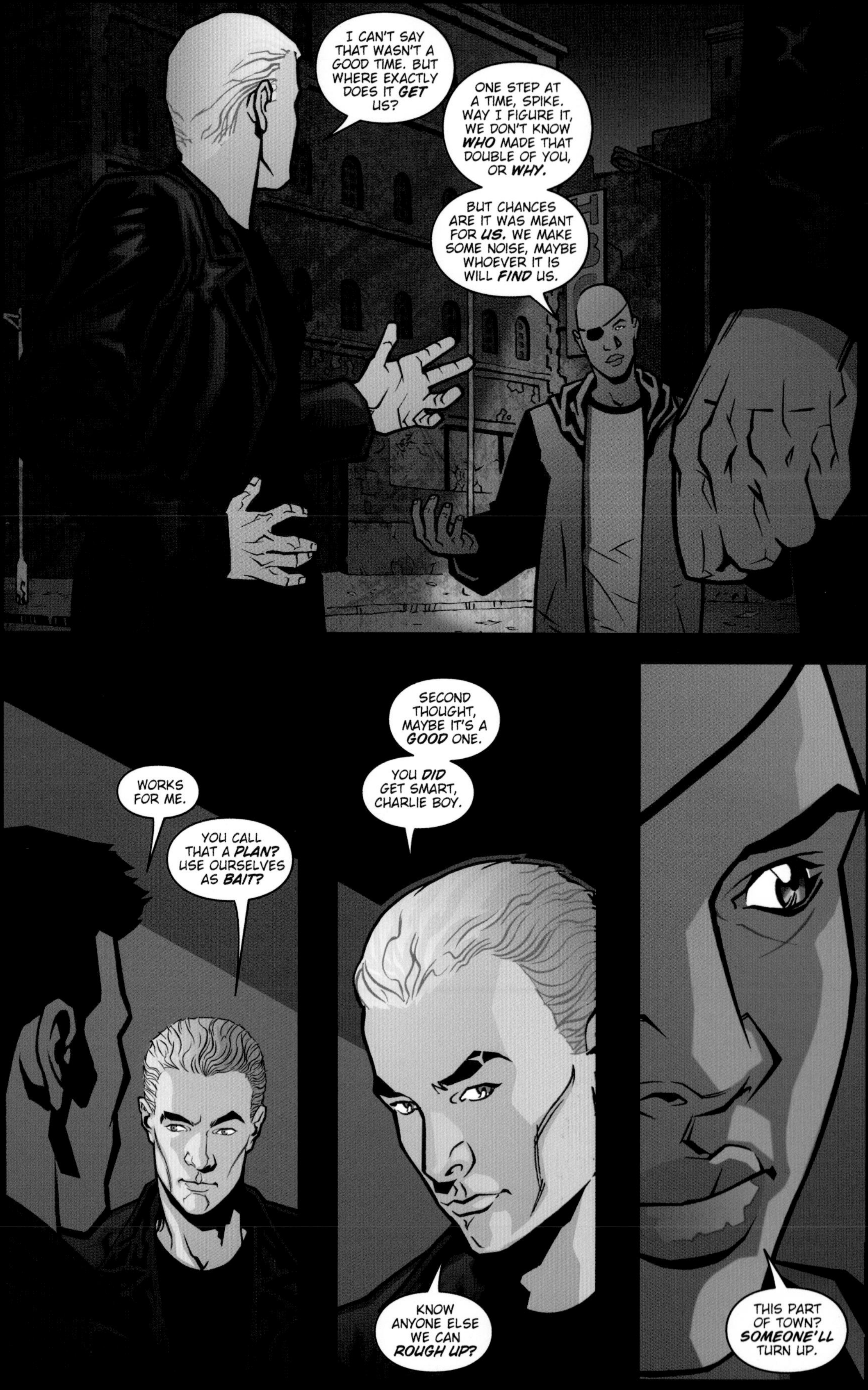
I CAN'T SAY THAT WASN'T A GOOD TIME. BUT WHERE EXACTLY DOES IT GET US?
ONE STEP AT A TIME, SPIKE. WAY I FIGURE IT, WE DON'T KNOW WHO MADE THAT DOUBLE OF YOU, OR WHY.
BUT CHANCES ARE IT WAS MEANT FOR US. WE MAKE SOME NOISE, MAYBE WHOEVER IT IS WILL FIND US.
WORKS FOR ME.
YOU CALL THAT A PLAN? USE OURSELVES AS BAIT?
SECOND THOUGHT, MAYBE IT'S A GOOD ONE.
YOU DID GET SMART, CHARLIE BOY.
KNOW ANYONE ELSE WE CAN ROUGH UP?
THIS PART OF TOWN? SOMEONE'LL TURN UP.

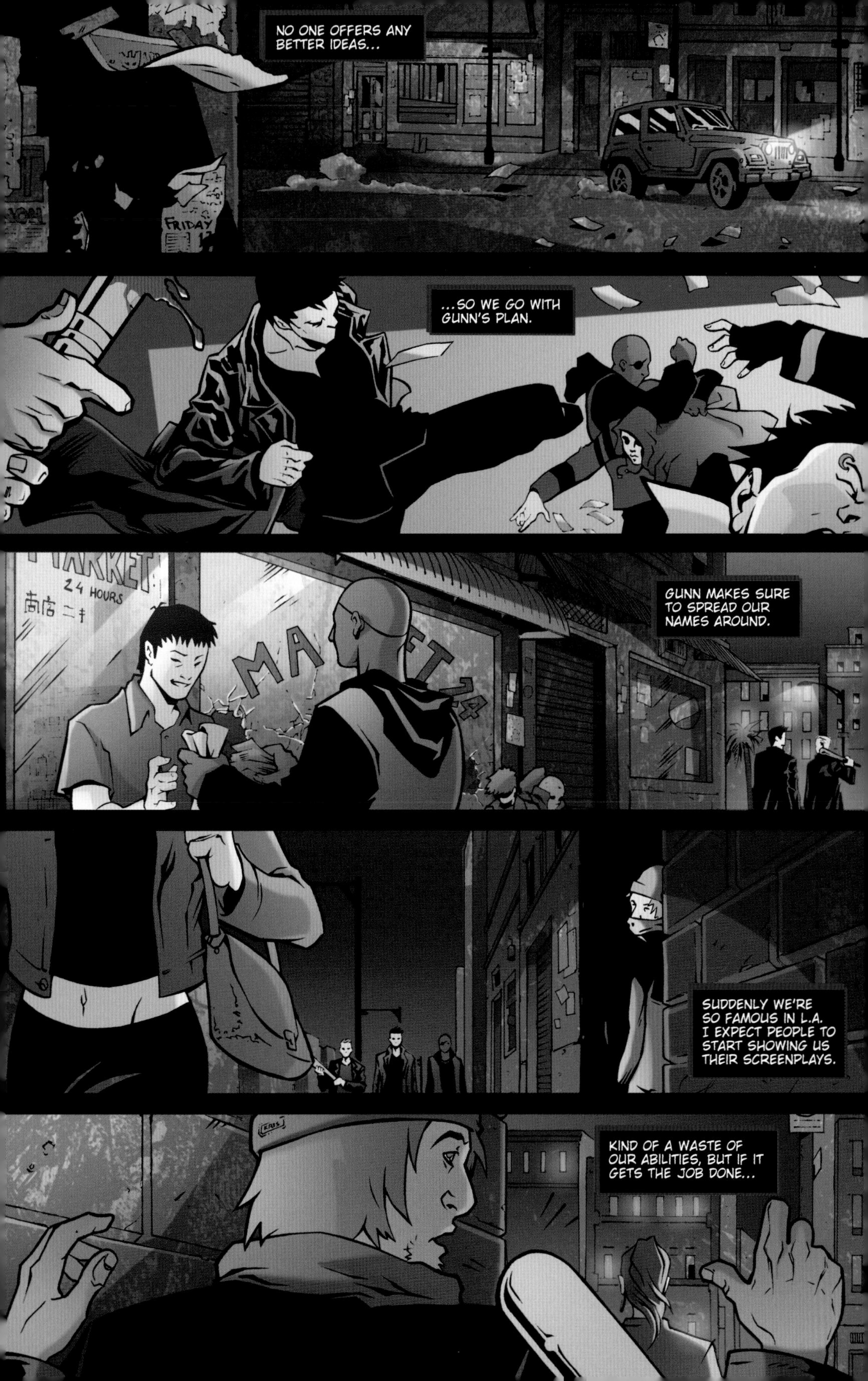
NO ONE OFFERS ANY BETTER IDEAS...
FRIDAY
...SO WE GO WITH GUNN'S PLAN.
MARKET
24 HOURS
GUNN MAKES SURE TO SPREAD OUR NAMES AROUND.
SUDDENLY WE'RE SO FAMOUS IN L.A. I EXPECT PEOPLE TO START SHOWING US THEIR SCREENPLAYS.
KIND OF A WASTE OF OUR ABILITIES, BUT IF IT GETS THE JOB DONE...

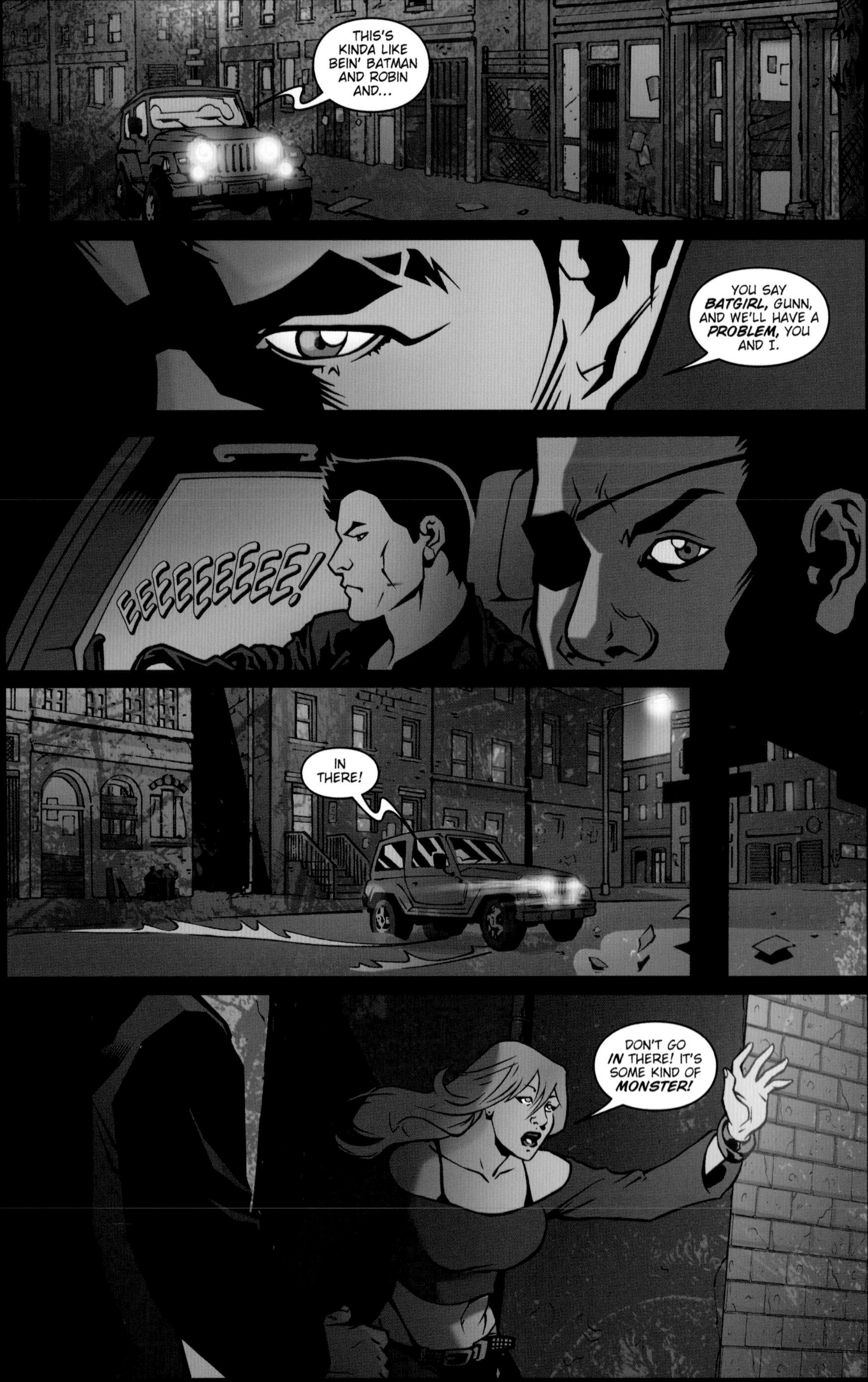
THIS'S KINDA LIKE BEIN' BATMAN AND ROBIN AND...
YOU SAY BATGIRL, GUNN, AND WE'LL HAVE A PROBLEM, YOU AND I.
EEEEEEEEEE!
IN THERE!
DON'T GO IN THERE! IT'S SOME KIND OF MONSTER!

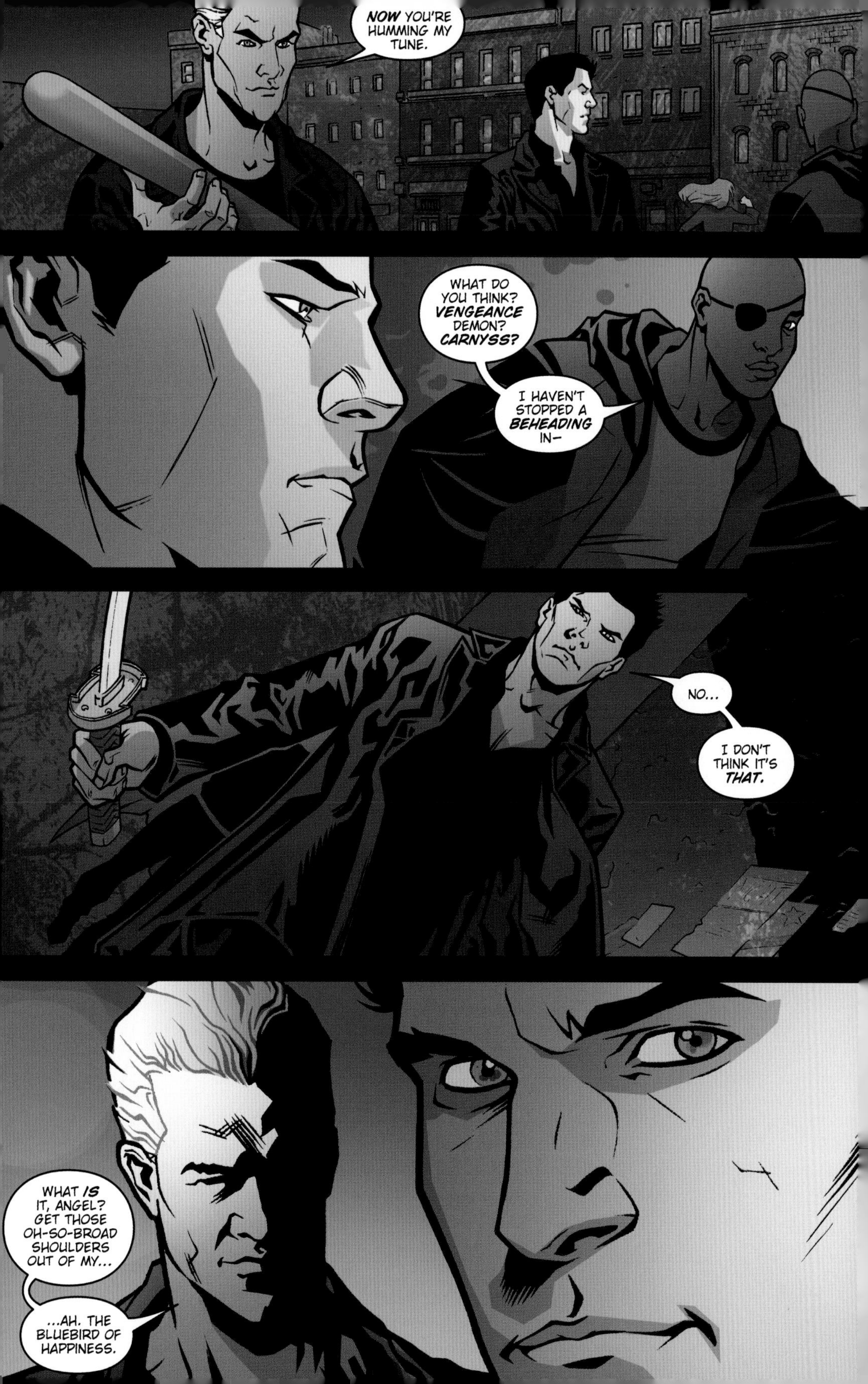
NOW YOU'RE HUMMING MY TUNE.
WHAT DO YOU THINK? VENGEANCE DEMON? CARNYSS?
I HAVEN'T STOPPED A BEHEADING IN—
NO...
I DON'T THINK IT'S THAT.
WHAT IS IT, ANGEL? GET THOSE OH-SO-BROAD SHOULDERS OUT OF MY...
...AH. THE BLUEBIRD OF HAPPINESS.

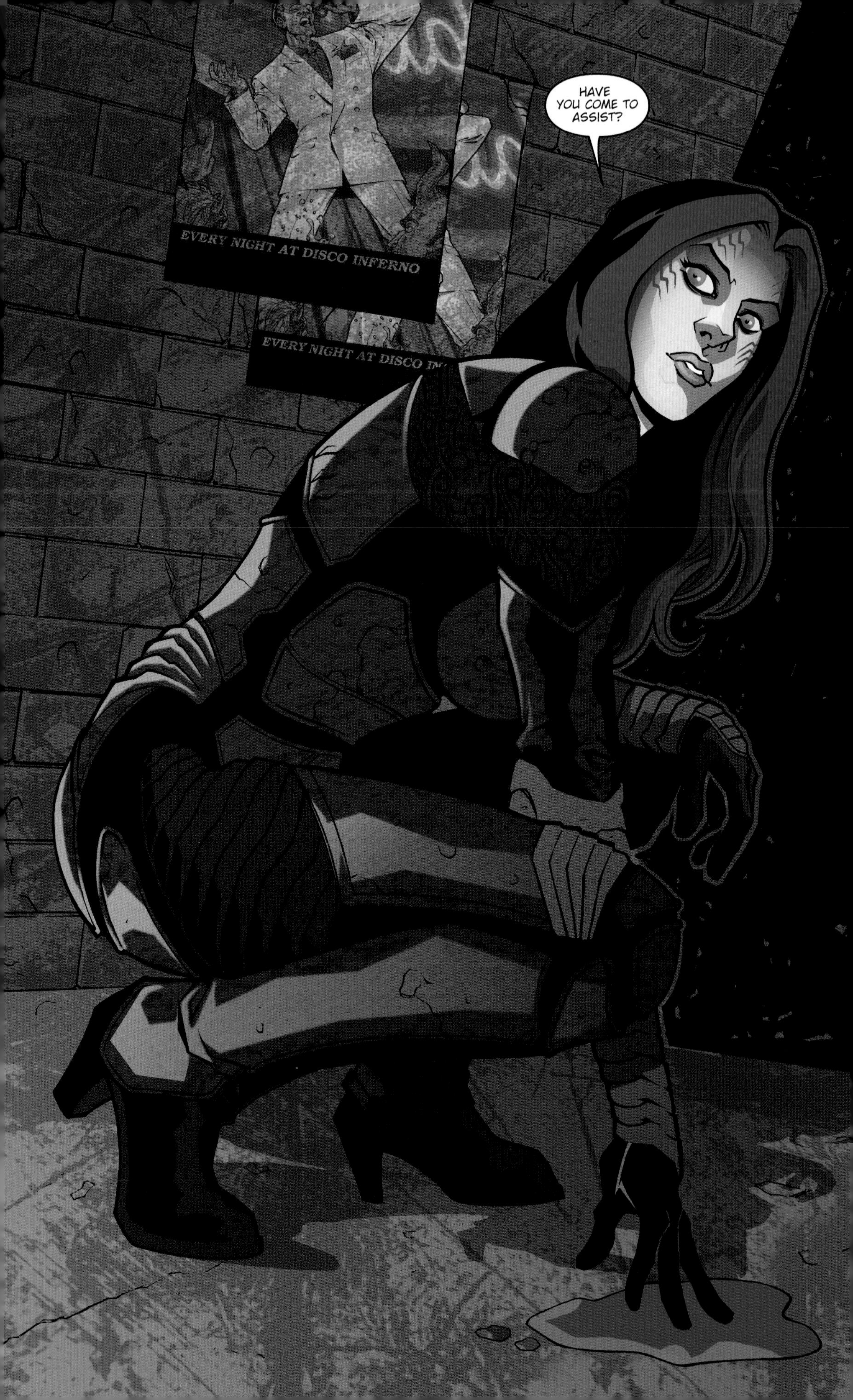
EVERY NIGHT AT DISCO INFERNO
HAVE YOU COME TO ASSIST?

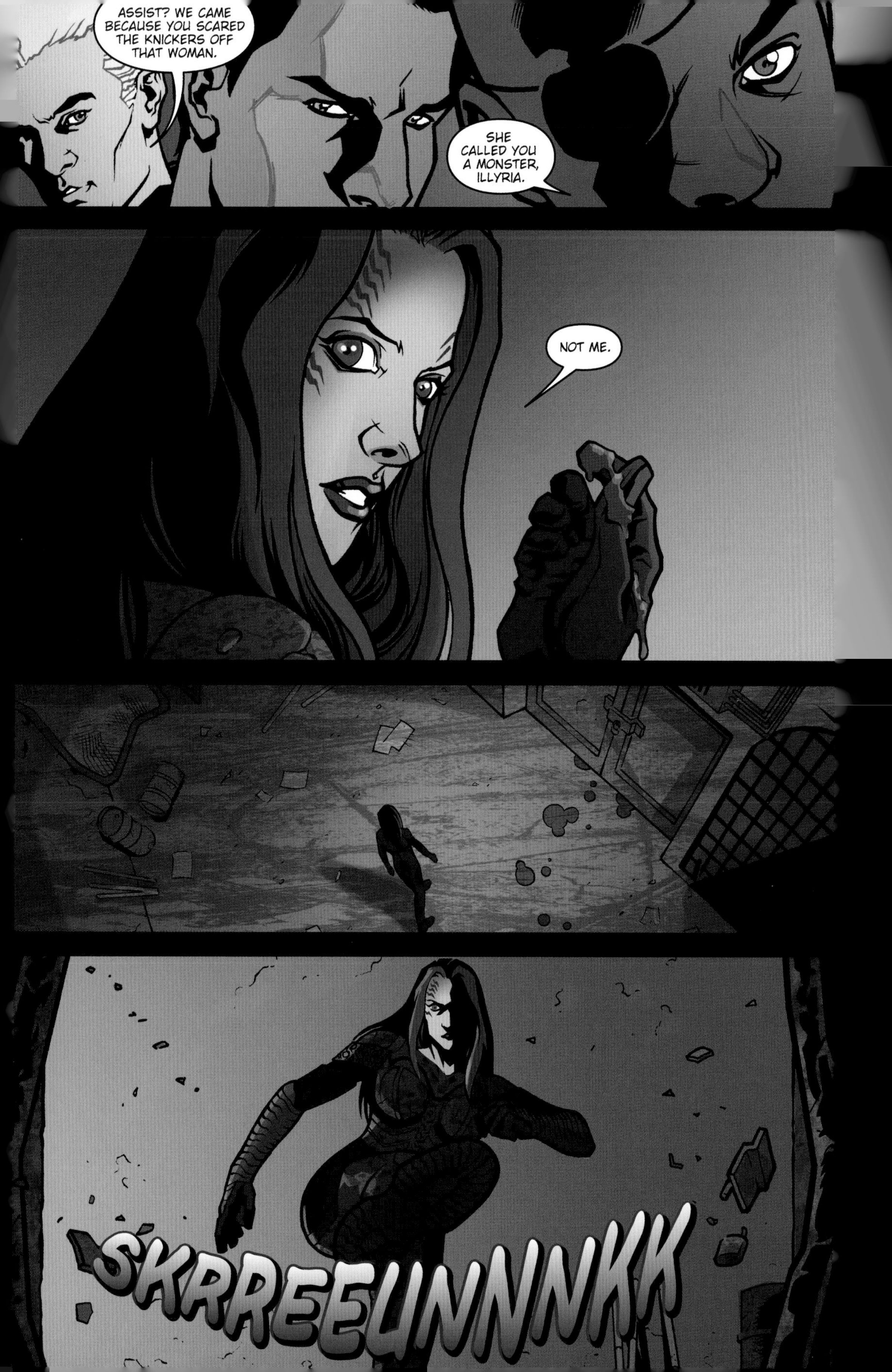
ASSIST? WE CAME BECAUSE YOU SCARED THE KNICKERS OFF THAT WOMAN.
SHE CALLED YOU A MONSTER, ILLYRIA.
NOT ME.
SKRREEUNNNKK

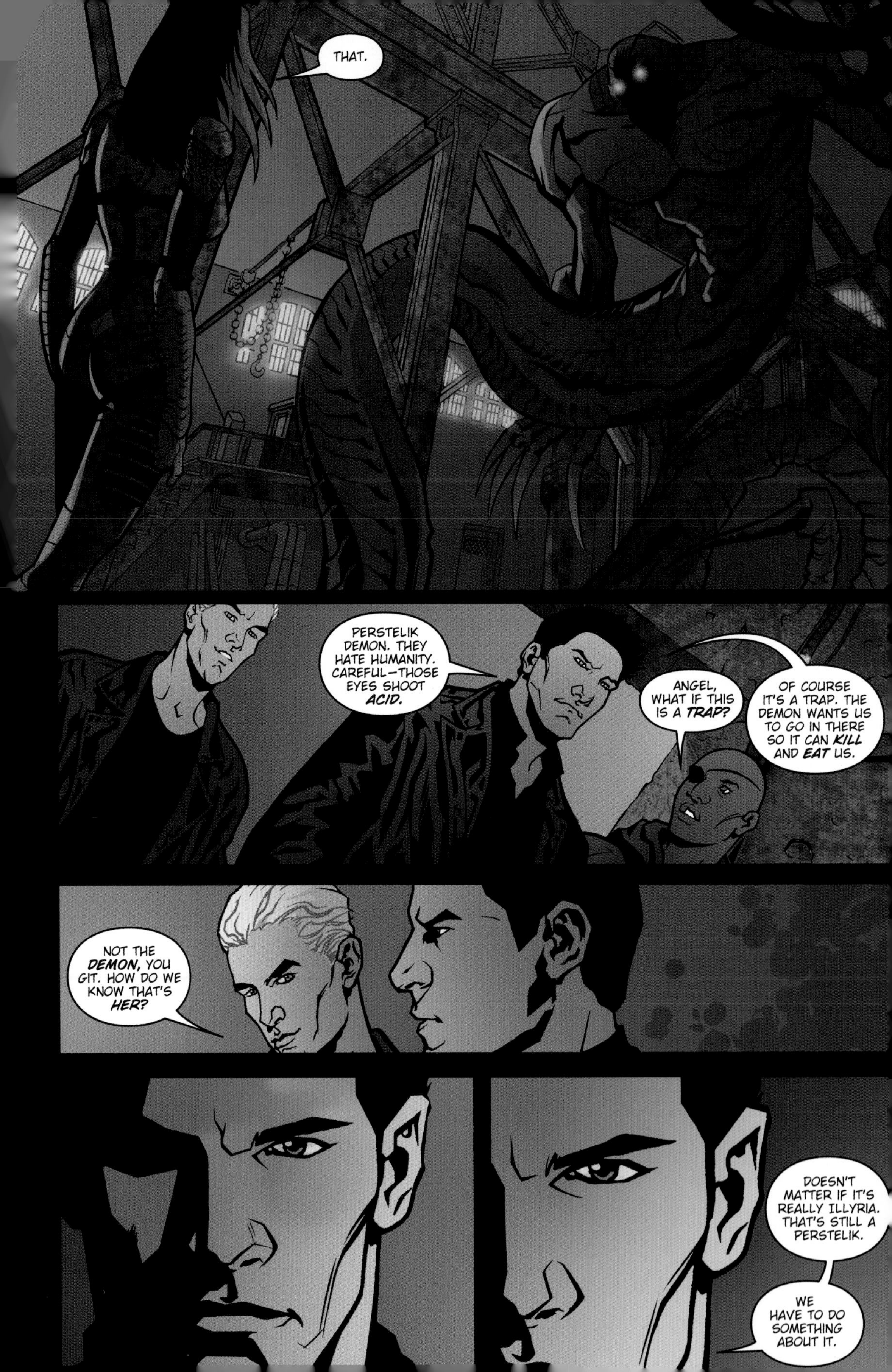
THAT.
PERSTELIK DEMON. THEY HATE HUMANITY. CAREFUL—THOSE EYES SHOOT ACID.
ANGEL, WHAT IF THIS IS A TRAP?
OF COURSE IT'S A TRAP. THE DEMON WANTS US TO GO IN THERE SO IT CAN KILL AND EAT US.
NOT THE DEMON, YOU GIT. HOW DO WE KNOW THAT'S HER?
DOESN'T MATTER IF IT'S REALLY ILLYRIA. THAT'S STILL A PERSTELIK.
WE HAVE TO DO SOMETHING ABOUT IT.

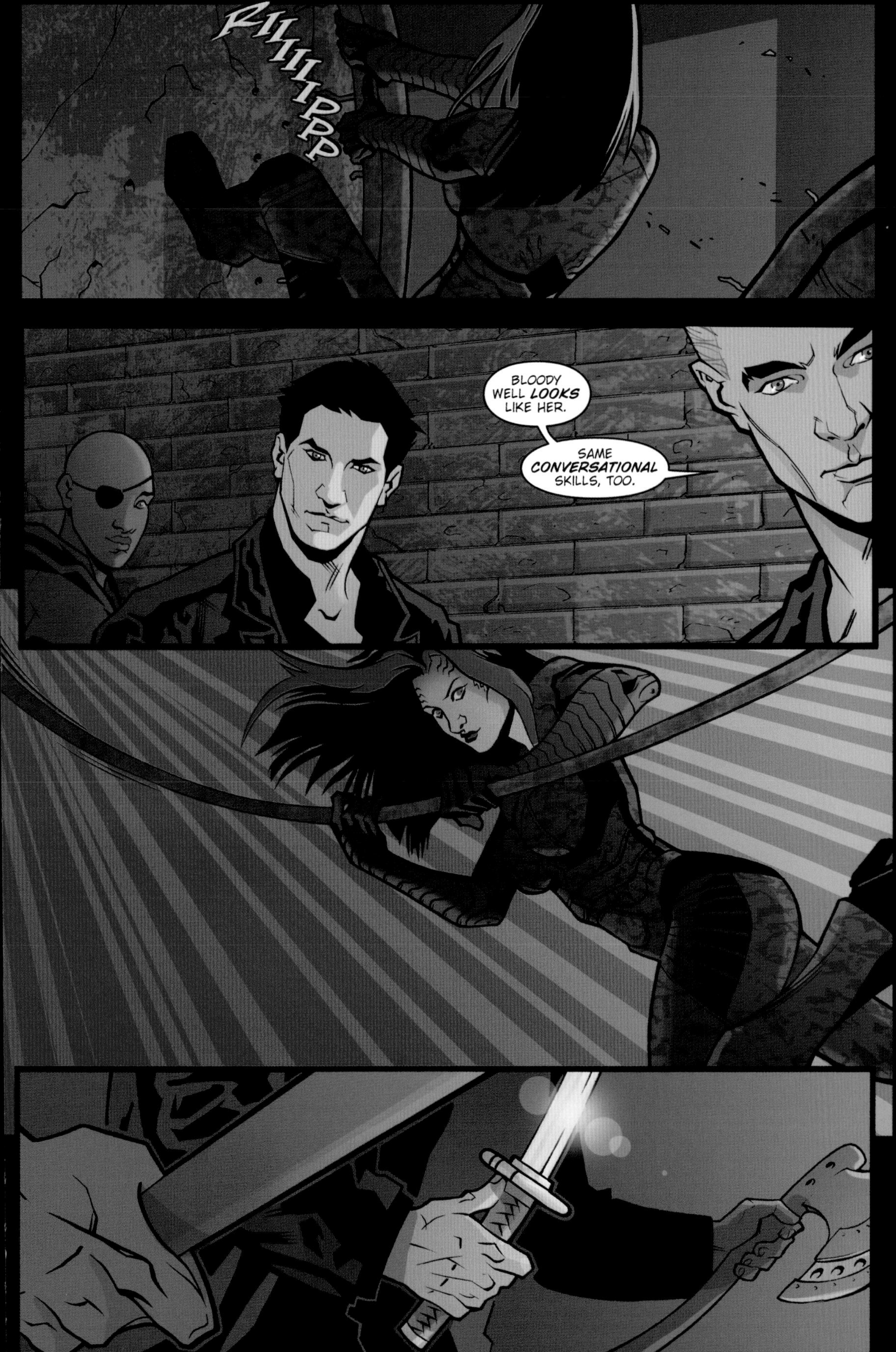
RIIIIIPPP
BLOODY WELL LOOKS LIKE HER.
SAME CONVERSATIONAL SKILLS, TOO.

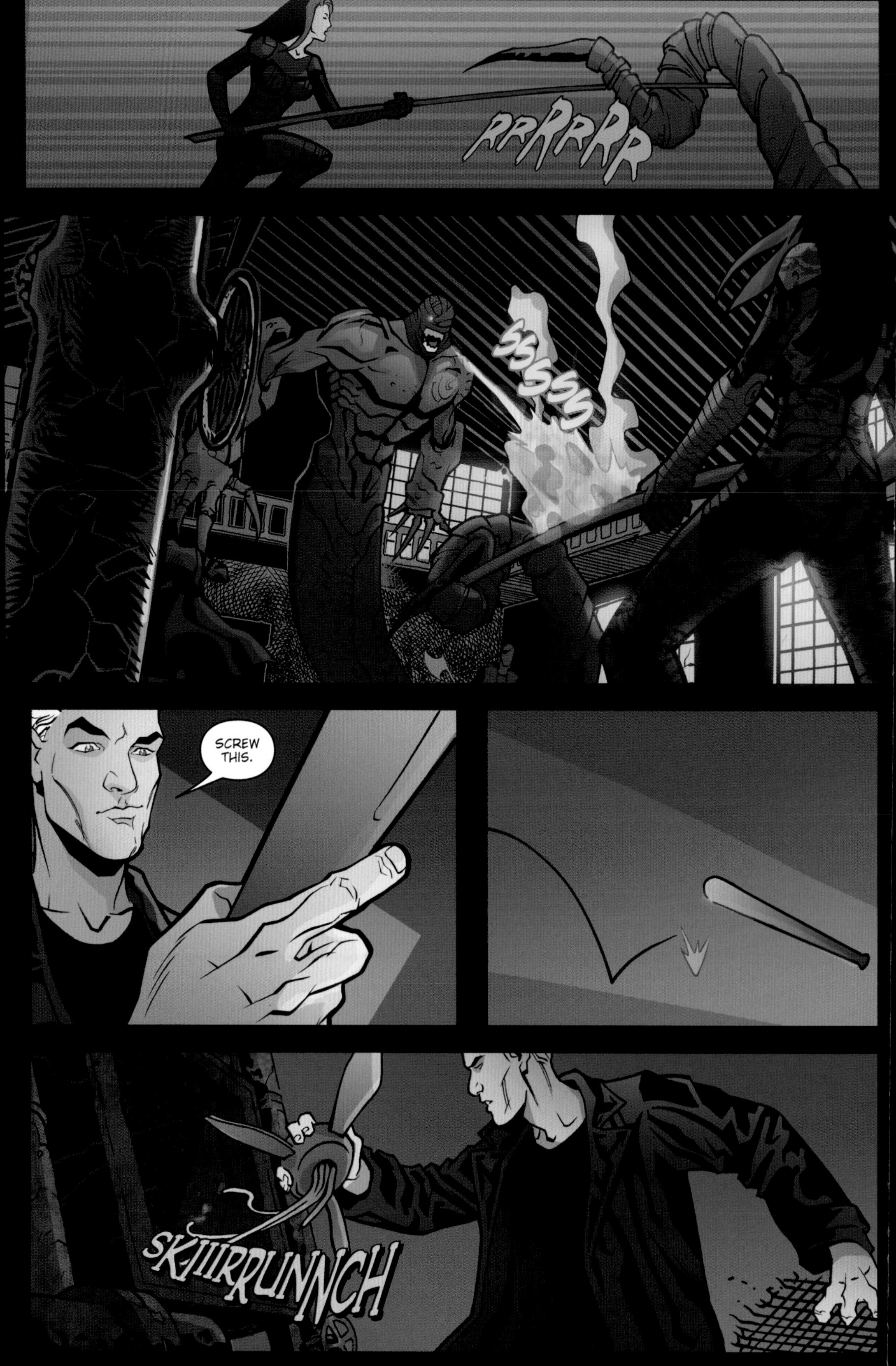
RRRRRR
SSSSSS
SCREW THIS.
SKIIIRRUNNCH

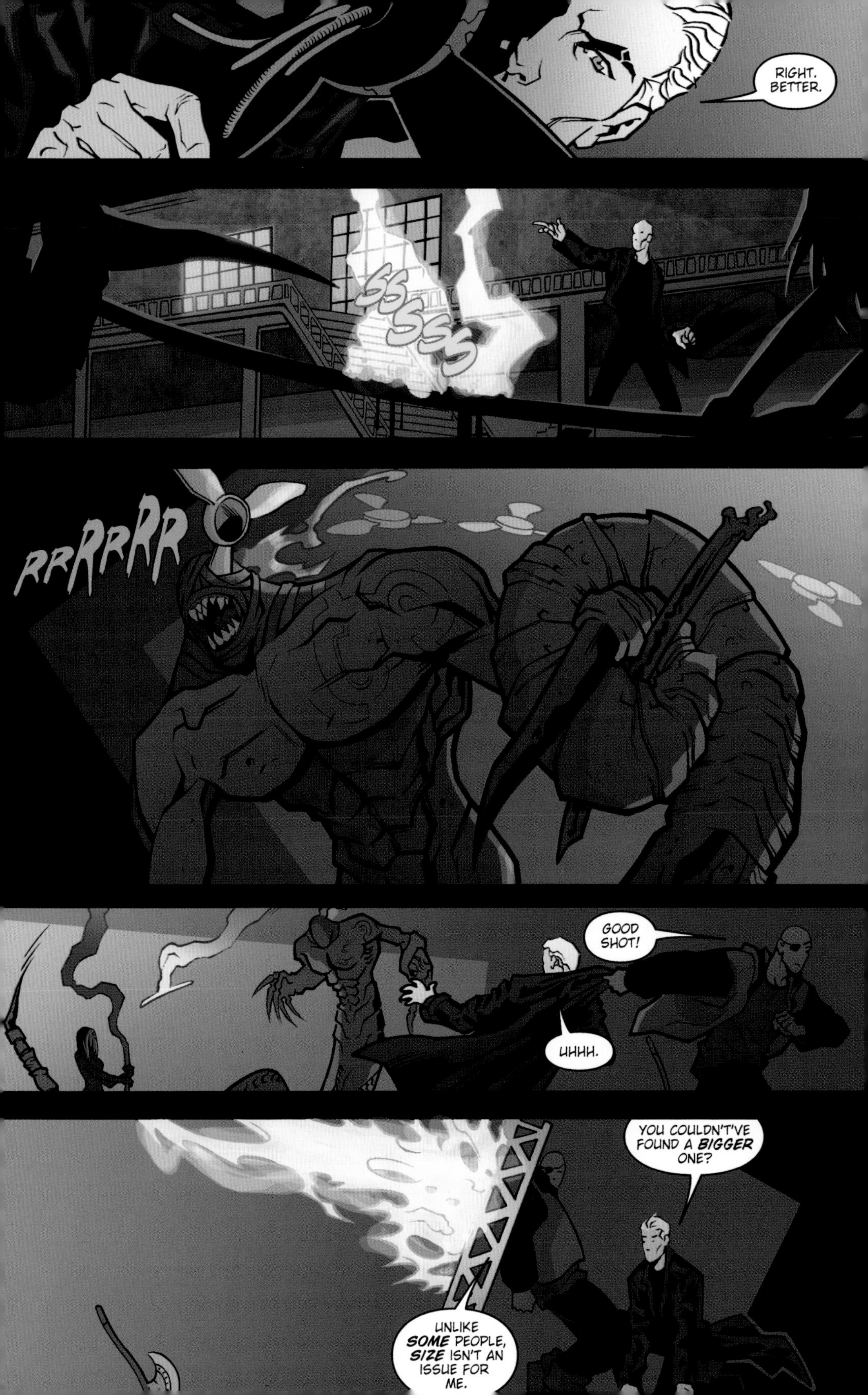
RIGHT. BETTER.
SSSSSS
RRRRRR
GOOD SHOT!
UHHH.
YOU COULDN'T'VE FOUND A **BIGGER** ONE?
UNLIKE **SOME** PEOPLE, **SIZE** ISN'T AN ISSUE FOR ME.

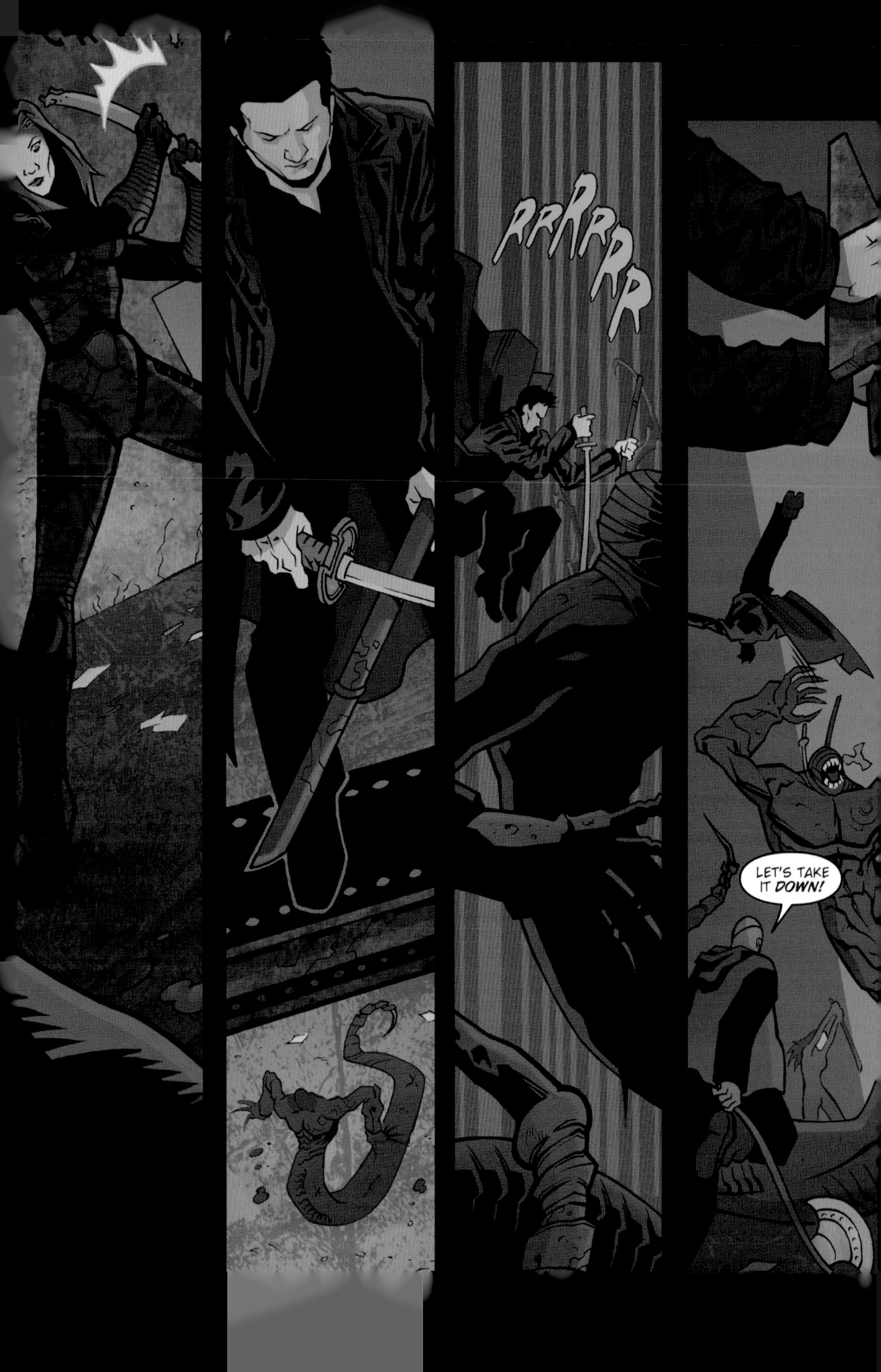
RRRRRRR
LET'S TAKE IT DOWN!

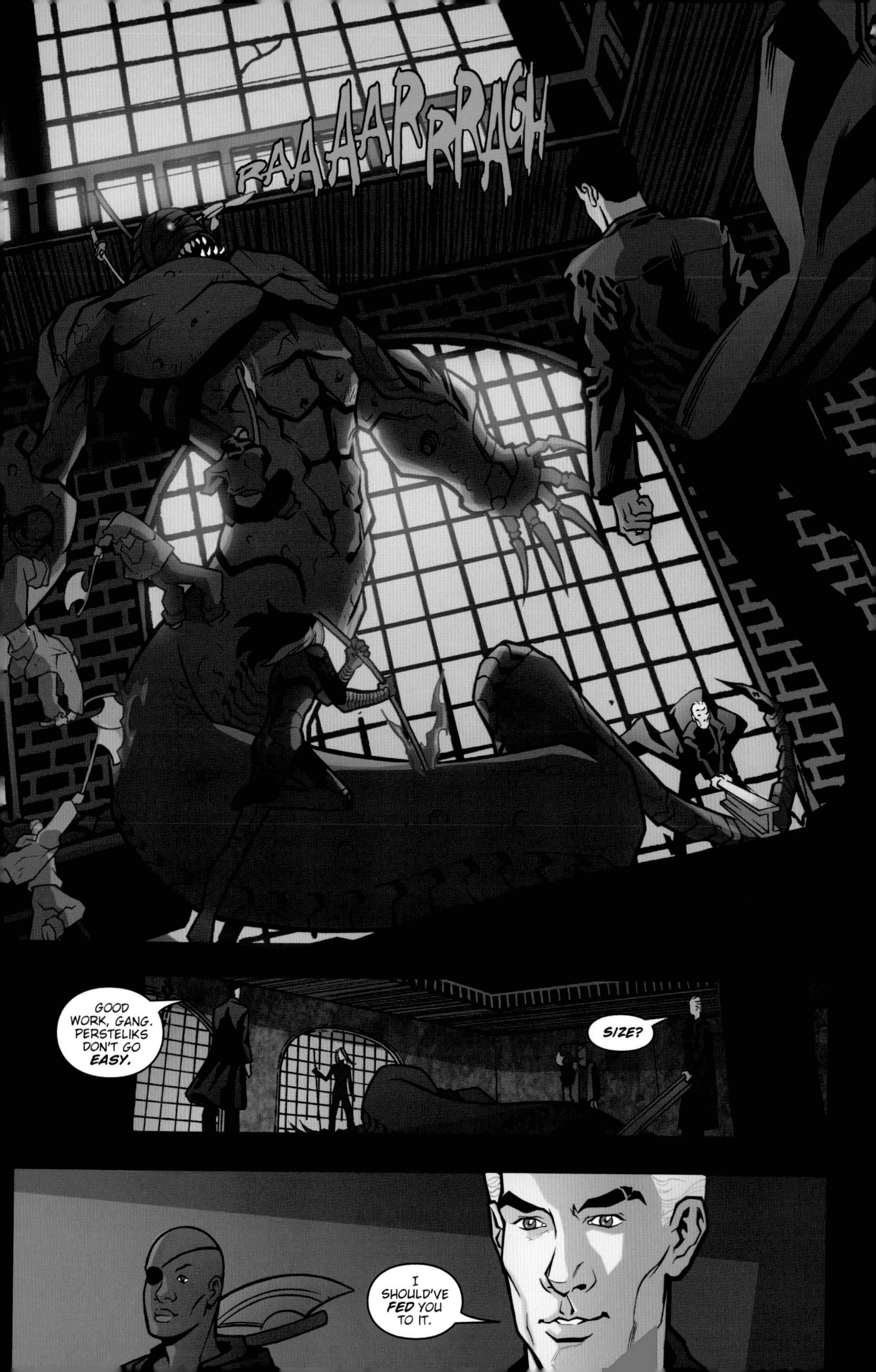
RAAAARRRACH
GOOD WORK, GANG. PERSTELIKS DON'T GO EASY.
SIZE?
I SHOULD'VE FED YOU TO IT.

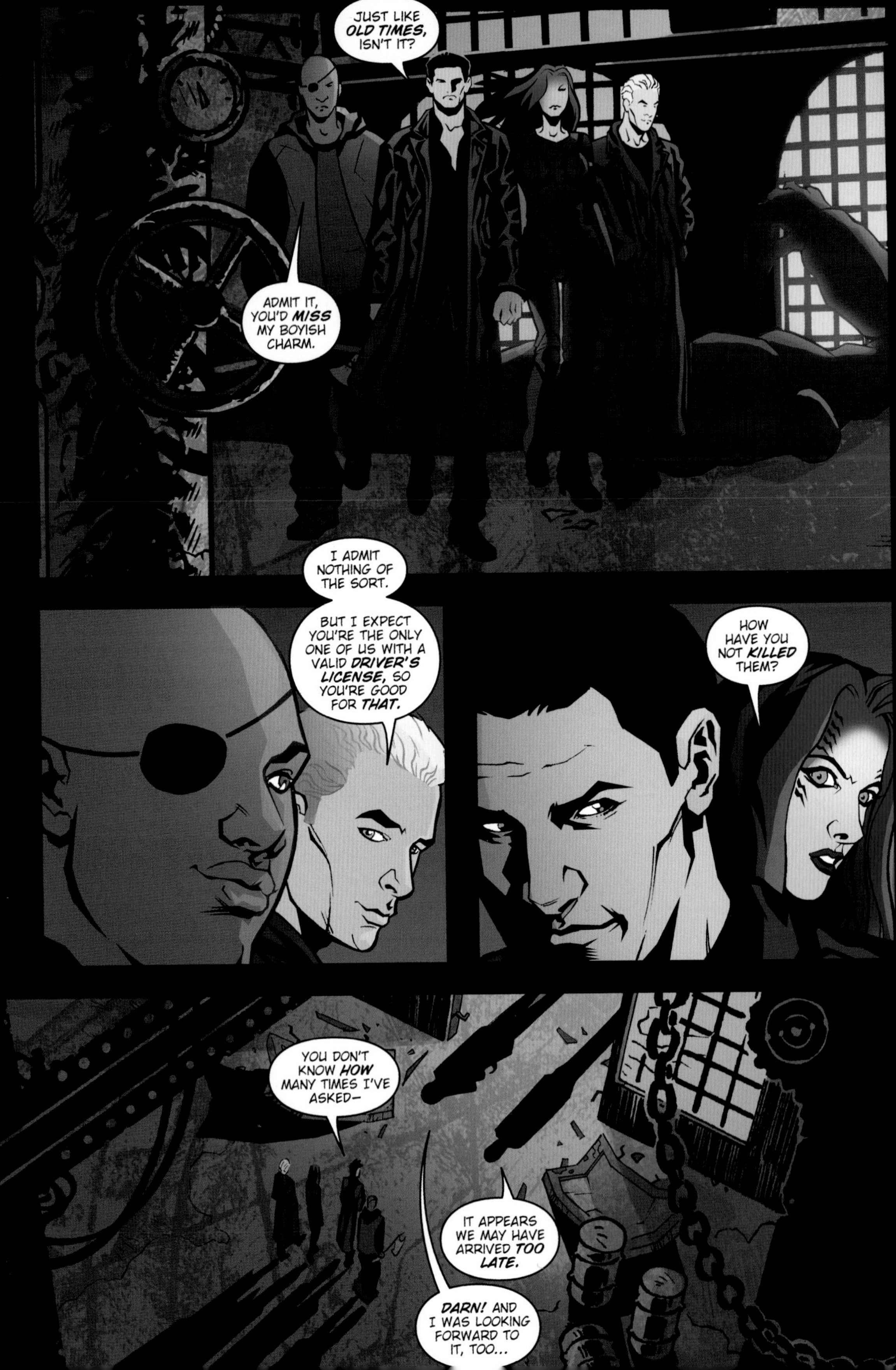
JUST LIKE OLD TIMES, ISN'T IT?
ADMIT IT, YOU'D MISS MY BOYISH CHARM.
I ADMIT NOTHING OF THE SORT.
BUT I EXPECT YOU'RE THE ONLY ONE OF US WITH A VALID DRIVER'S LICENSE, SO YOU'RE GOOD FOR THAT.
HOW HAVE YOU NOT KILLED THEM?
YOU DON'T KNOW HOW MANY TIMES I'VE ASKED—
IT APPEARS WE MAY HAVE ARRIVED TOO LATE.
DARN! AND I WAS LOOKING FORWARD TO IT, TOO...

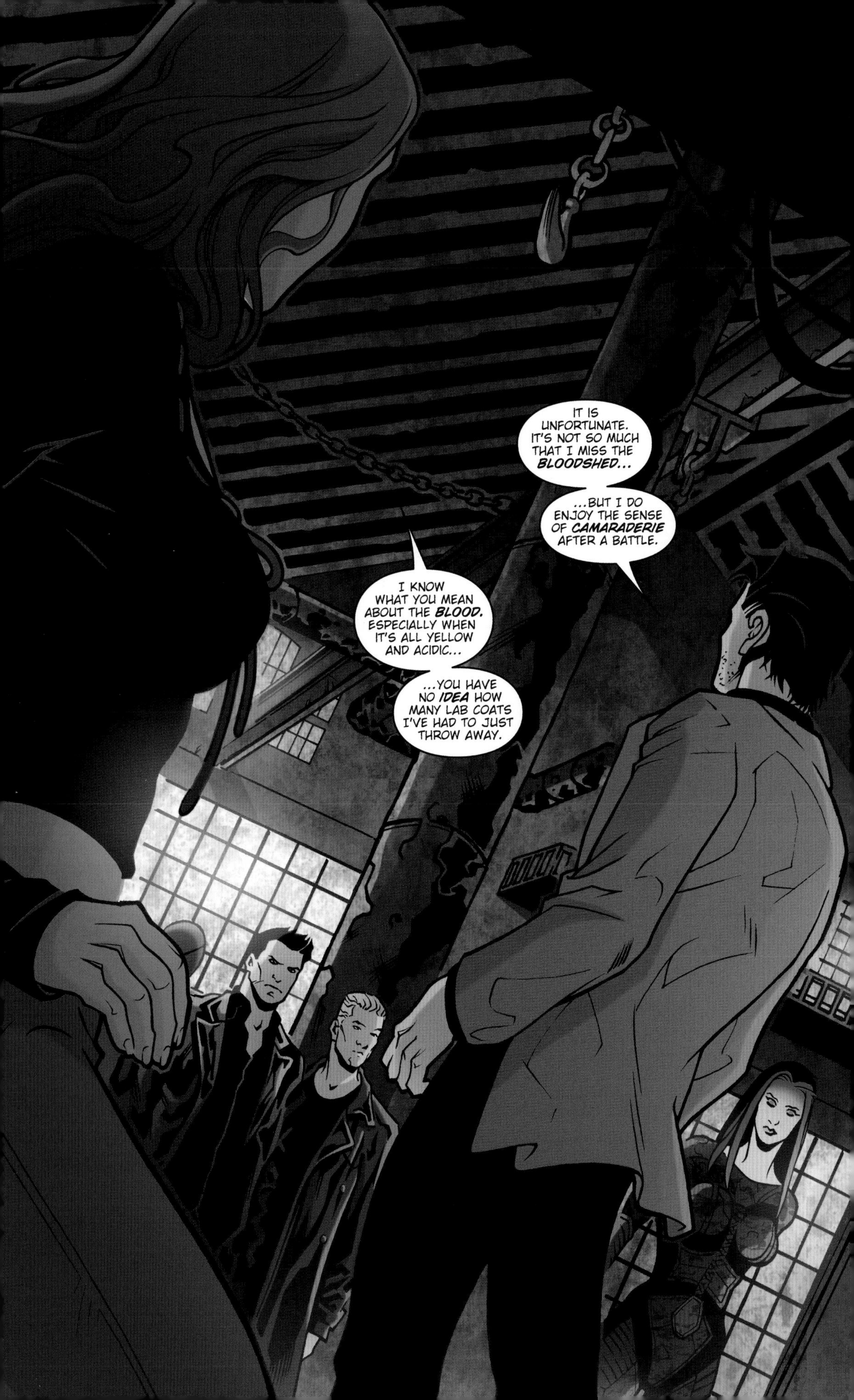
IT IS UNFORTUNATE. IT'S NOT SO MUCH THAT I MISS THE *BLOODSHED*...
...BUT I DO ENJOY THE SENSE OF *CAMARADERIE* AFTER A BATTLE.
I KNOW WHAT YOU MEAN ABOUT THE *BLOOD.* ESPECIALLY WHEN IT'S ALL YELLOW AND ACIDIC...
...YOU HAVE NO *IDEA* HOW MANY LAB COATS I'VE HAD TO JUST THROW AWAY.

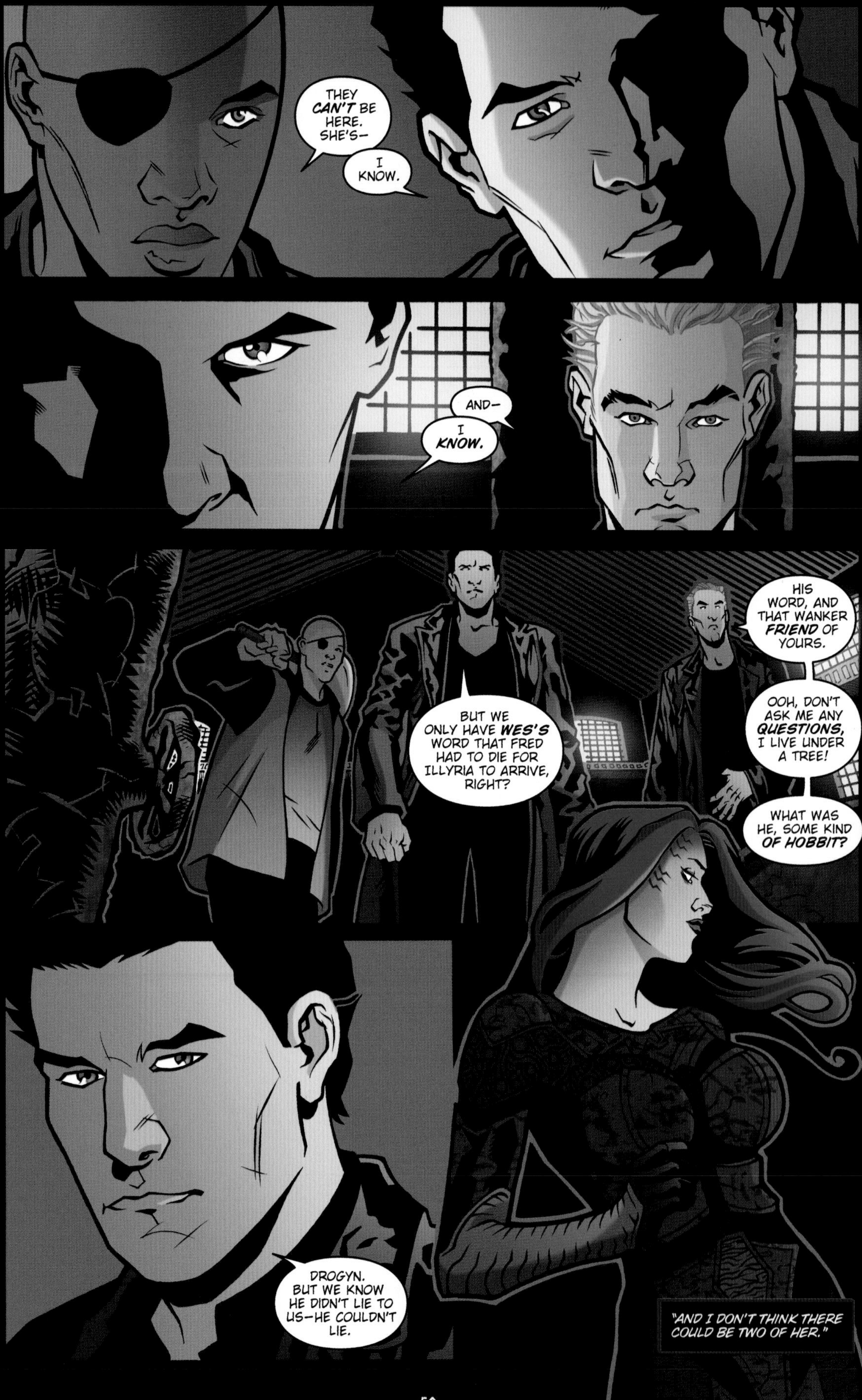
THEY CAN'T BE HERE. SHE'S—
I KNOW.
AND—
I KNOW.
HIS WORD, AND THAT WANKER FRIEND OF YOURS.
BUT WE ONLY HAVE WES'S WORD THAT FRED HAD TO DIE FOR ILLYRIA TO ARRIVE, RIGHT?
OOH, DON'T ASK ME ANY QUESTIONS, I LIVE UNDER A TREE!
WHAT WAS HE, SOME KIND OF HOBBIT?
DROGYN. BUT WE KNOW HE DIDN'T LIE TO US—HE COULDN'T LIE.
"AND I DON'T THINK THERE COULD BE TWO OF HER."

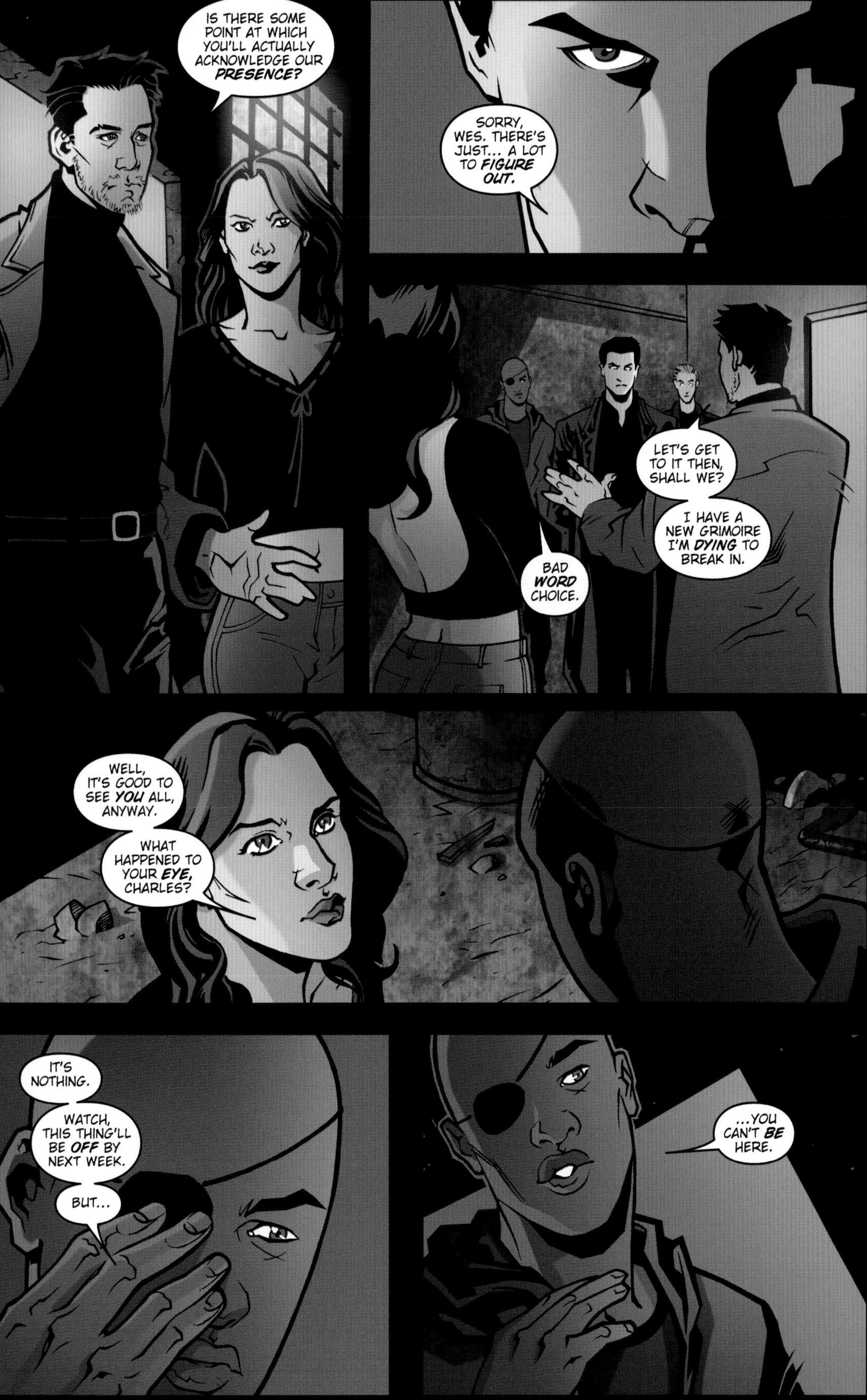
IS THERE SOME POINT AT WHICH YOU'LL ACTUALLY ACKNOWLEDGE OUR PRESENCE?
SORRY, WES. THERE'S JUST... A LOT TO FIGURE OUT.
LET'S GET TO IT THEN, SHALL WE?
I HAVE A NEW GRIMOIRE I'M DYING TO BREAK IN.
BAD WORD CHOICE.
WELL, IT'S GOOD TO SEE YOU ALL, ANYWAY.
WHAT HAPPENED TO YOUR EYE, CHARLES?
IT'S NOTHING.
WATCH, THIS THING'LL BE OFF BY NEXT WEEK.
BUT...
...YOU CAN'T BE HERE.

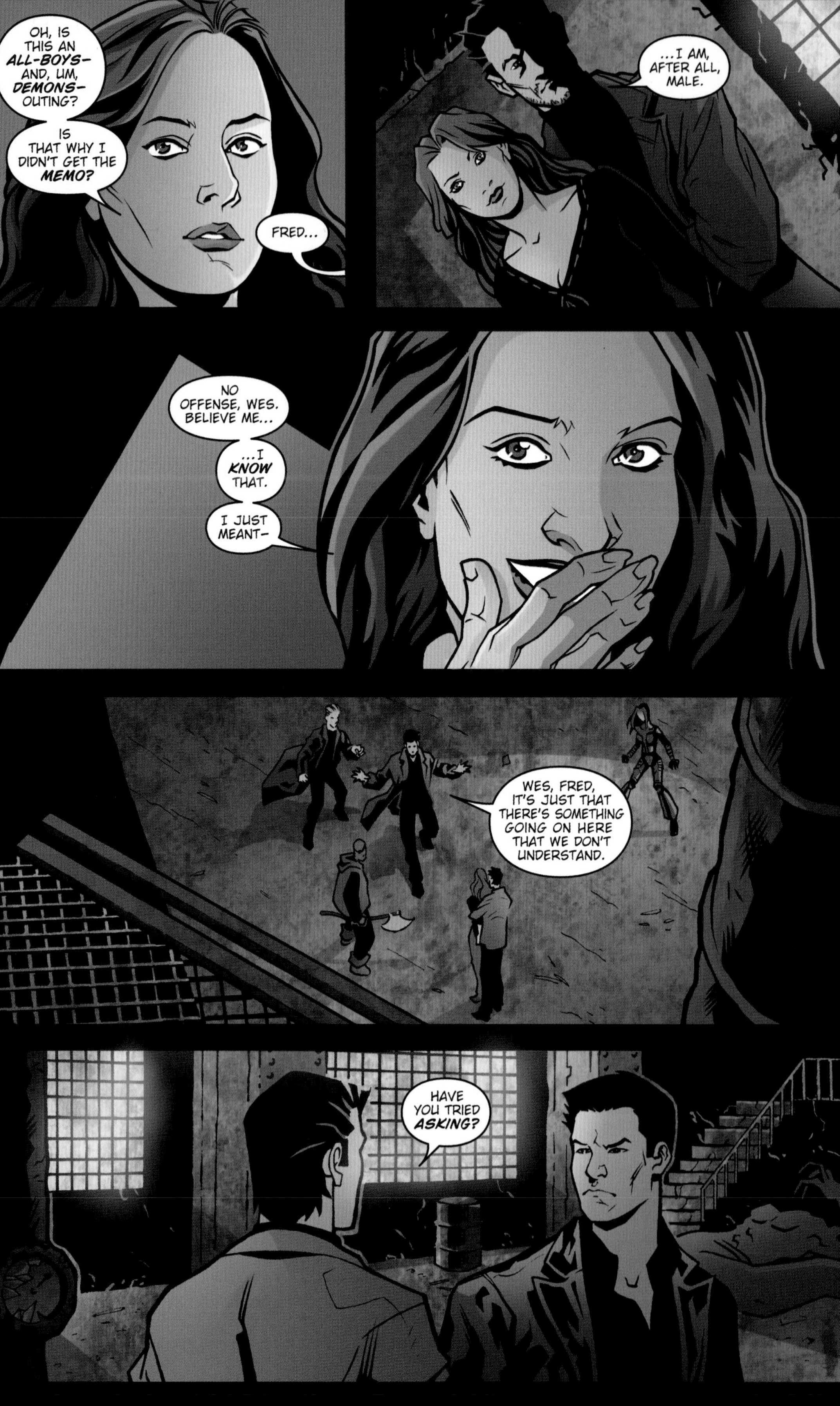
OH, IS THIS AN **ALL-BOYS**- AND, UM, **DEMONS**- OUTING?
IS THAT WHY I DIDN'T GET THE **MEMO?**
FRED...
...I AM, AFTER ALL, MALE.
NO OFFENSE, WES. BELIEVE ME...
...I **KNOW** THAT.
I JUST MEANT-
WES, FRED, IT'S JUST THAT THERE'S SOMETHING GOING ON HERE THAT WE DON'T UNDERSTAND.
HAVE YOU TRIED **ASKING?**

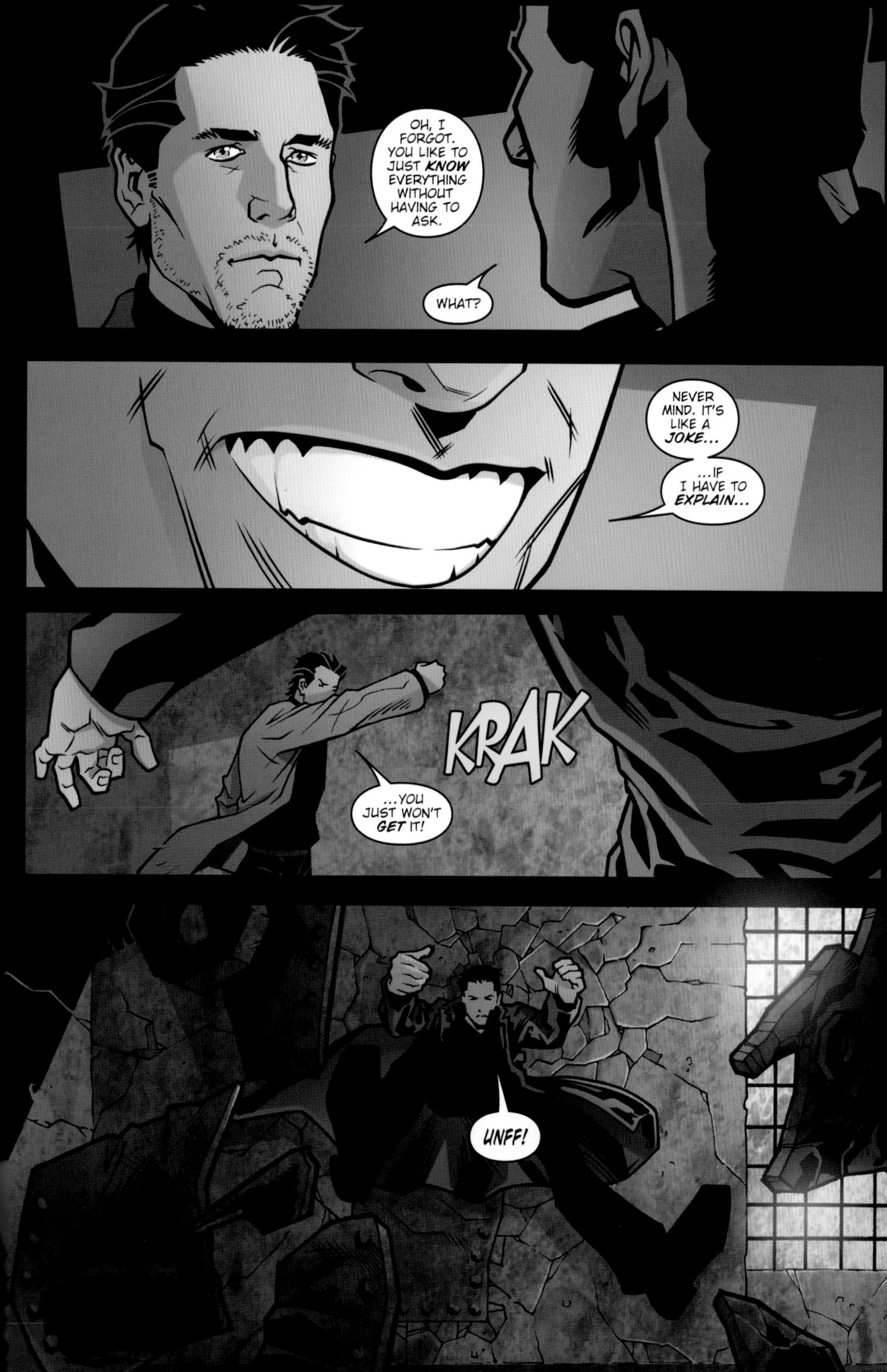
OH, I FORGOT. YOU LIKE TO JUST KNOW EVERYTHING WITHOUT HAVING TO ASK.
WHAT?
NEVER MIND. IT'S LIKE A JOKE...
...IF I HAVE TO EXPLAIN...
KRAK
...YOU JUST WON'T GET IT!
UNFF!

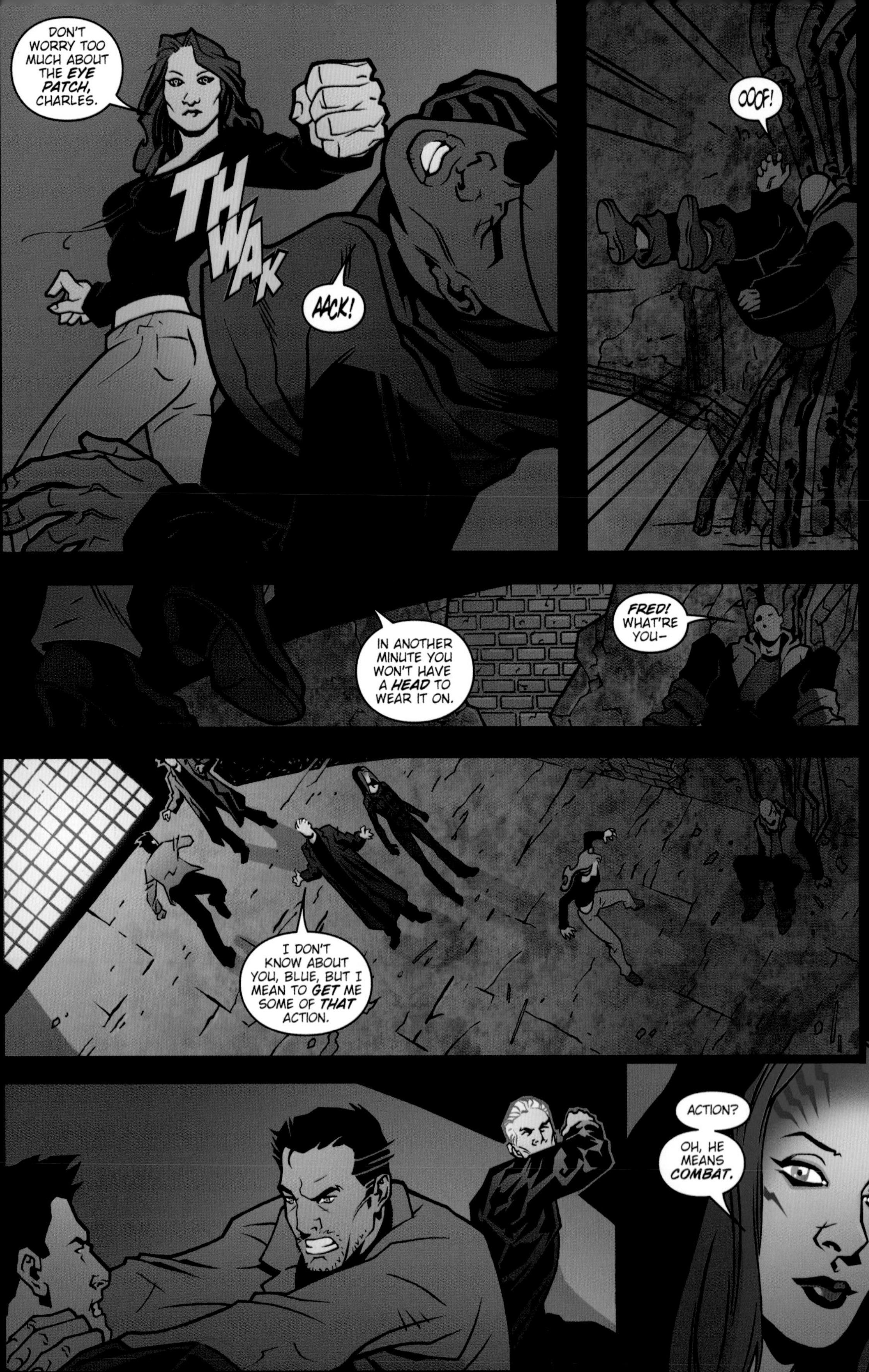

DON'T WORRY TOO MUCH ABOUT THE EYE PATCH, CHARLES.
THWAK
AACK!
OOOF!
IN ANOTHER MINUTE YOU WON'T HAVE A HEAD TO WEAR IT ON.
FRED! WHAT'RE YOU-
I DON'T KNOW ABOUT YOU, BLUE, BUT I MEAN TO GET ME SOME OF THAT ACTION.
ACTION?
OH, HE MEANS COMBAT.

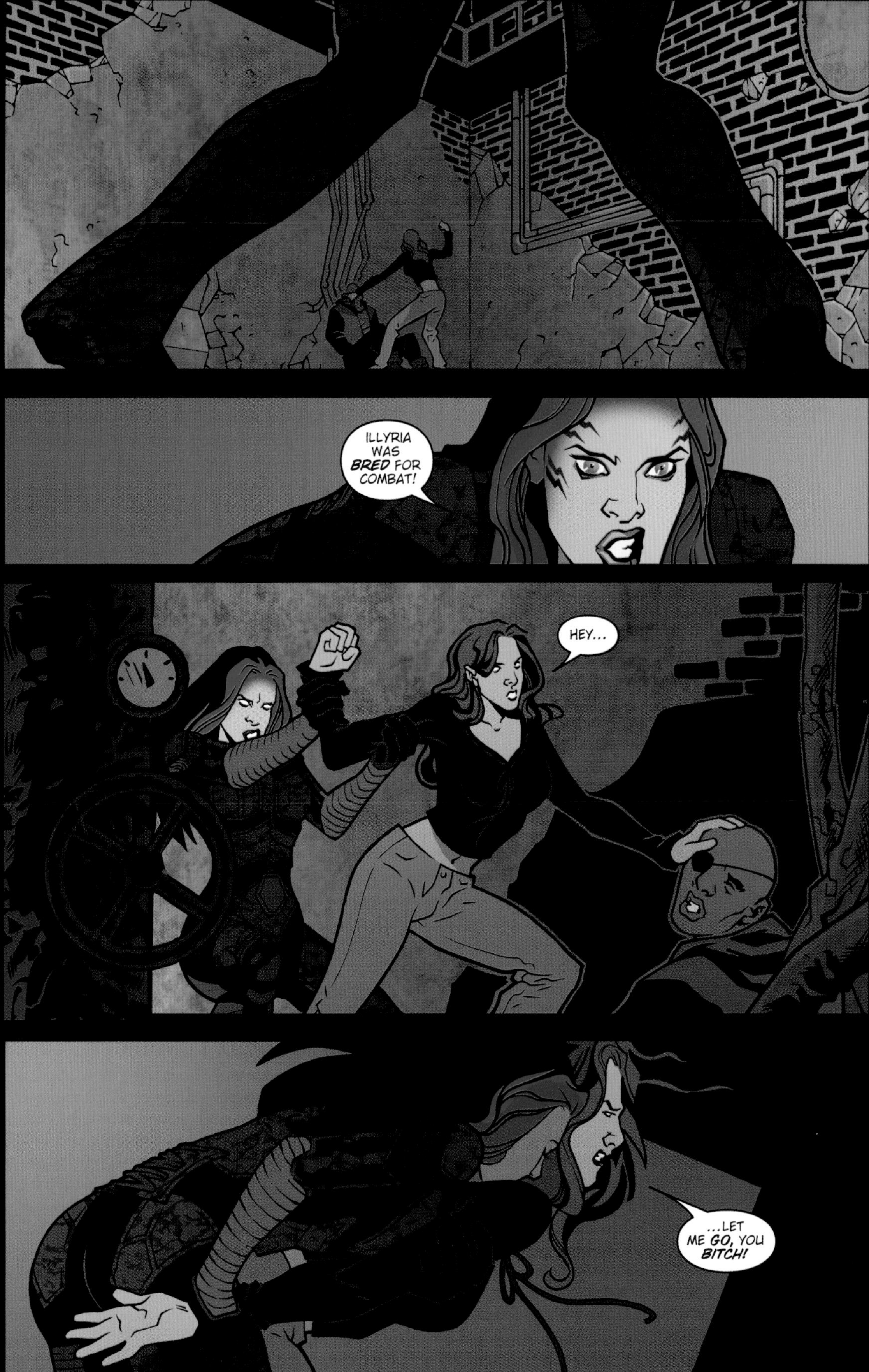
ILLYRIA WAS BRED FOR COMBAT!
HEY...
...LET ME GO, YOU BITCH!

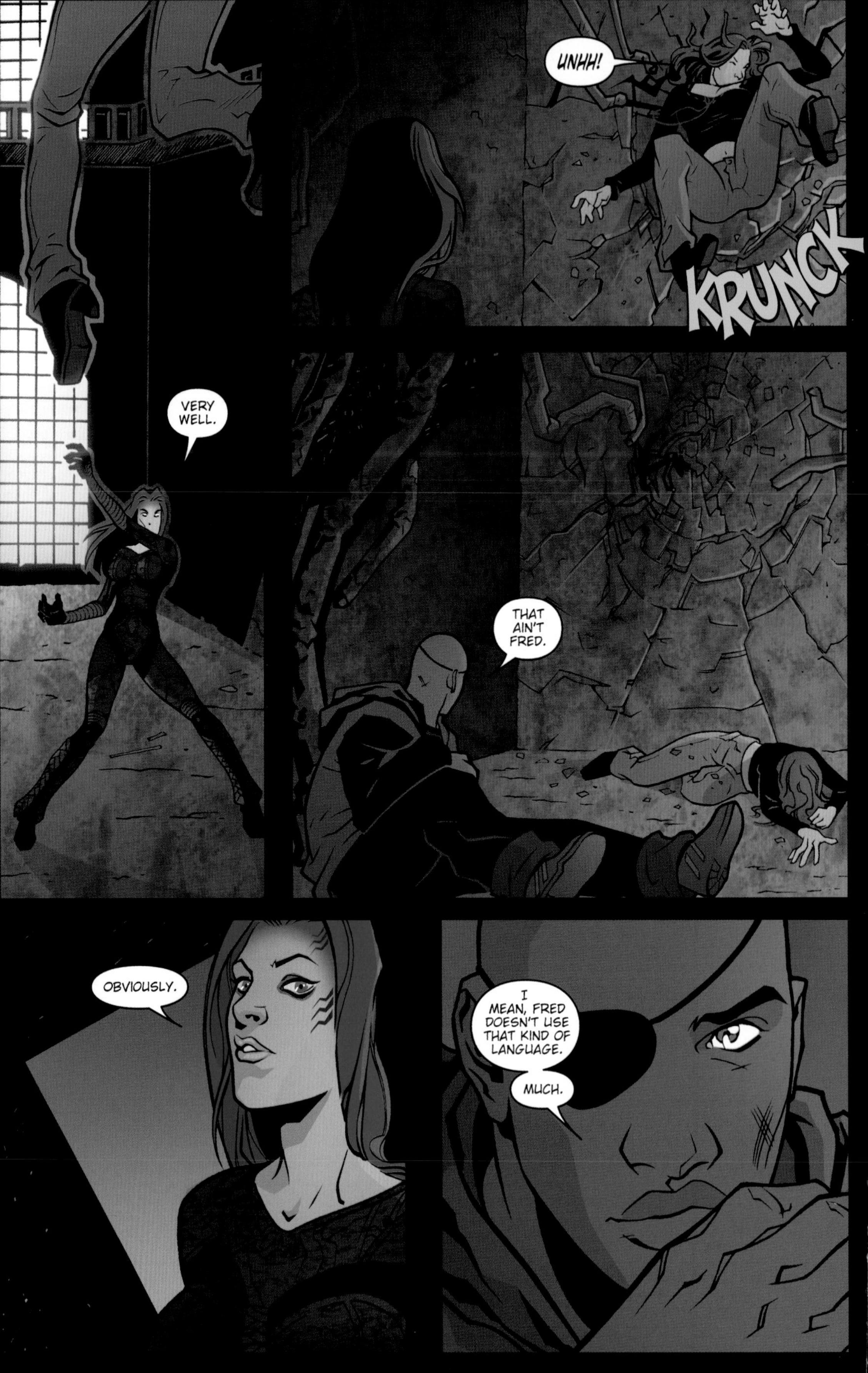
UNHH!
KRUNCK
VERY WELL.
THAT AIN'T FRED.
OBVIOUSLY.
I MEAN, FRED DOESN'T USE THAT KIND OF LANGUAGE.
MUCH.

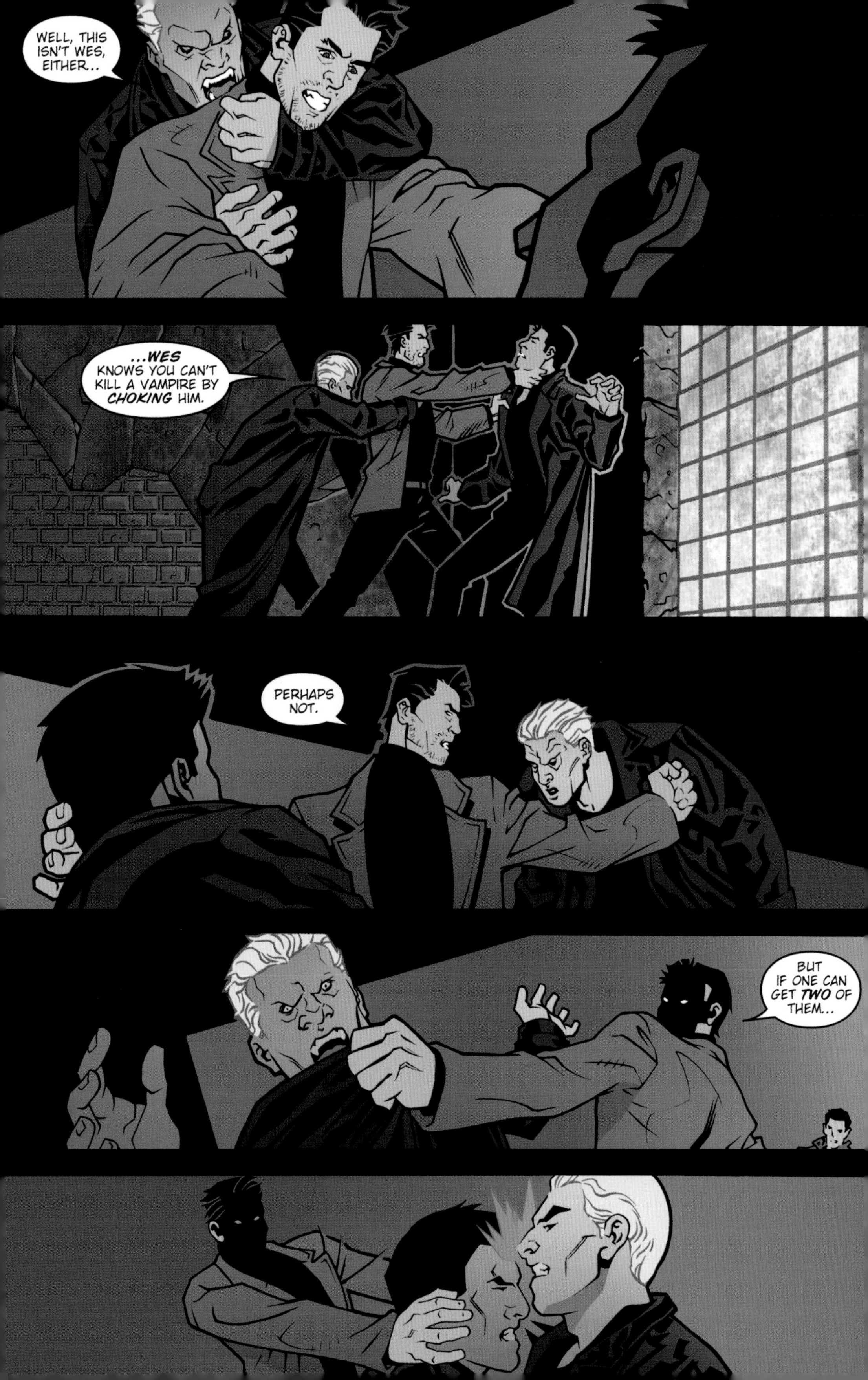
WELL, THIS ISN'T WES, EITHER...
...WES KNOWS YOU CAN'T KILL A VAMPIRE BY CHOKING HIM.
PERHAPS NOT.
BUT IF ONE CAN GET TWO OF THEM...

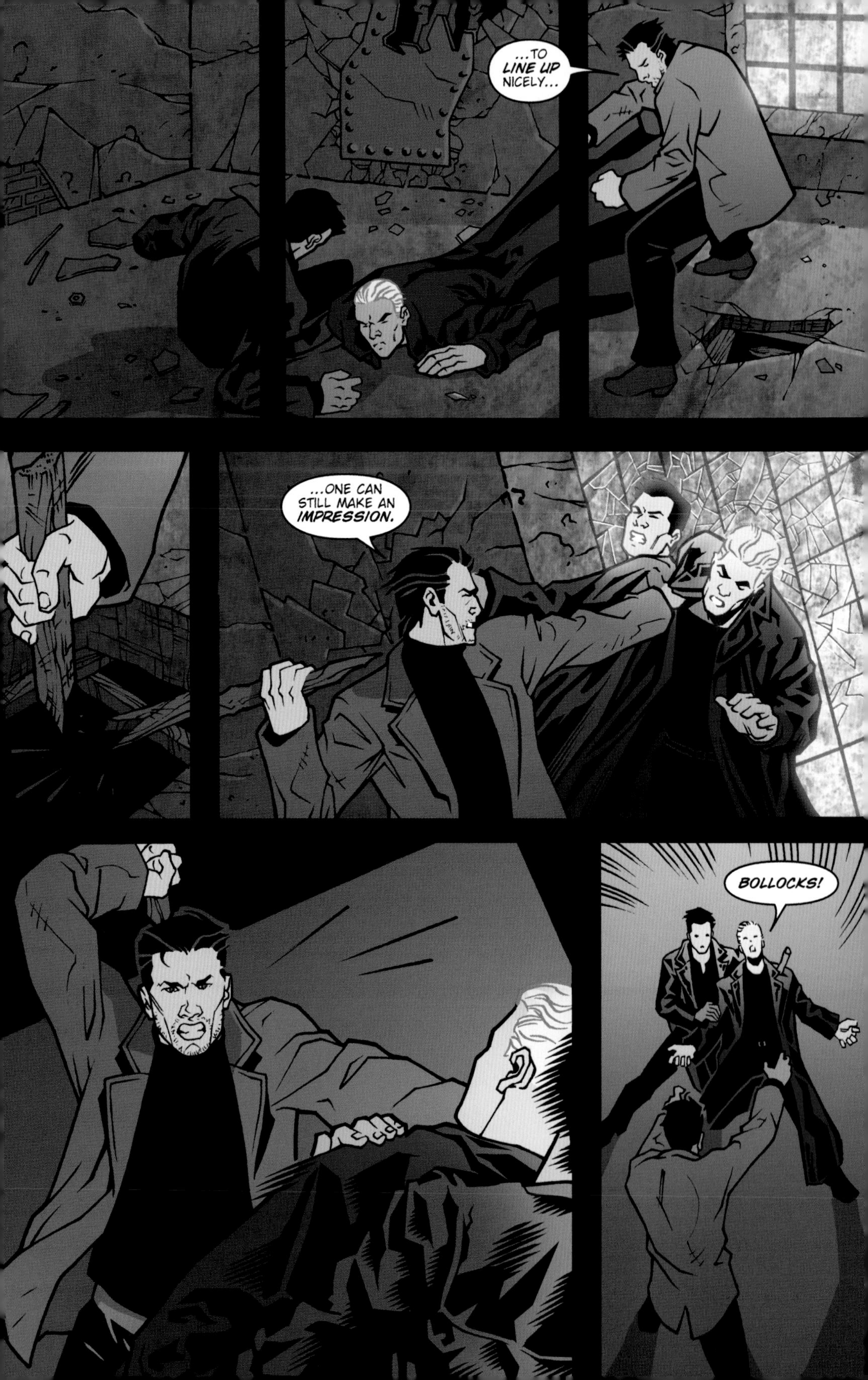
...TO LINE UP NICELY...
...ONE CAN STILL MAKE AN IMPRESSION.
BOLLOCKS!

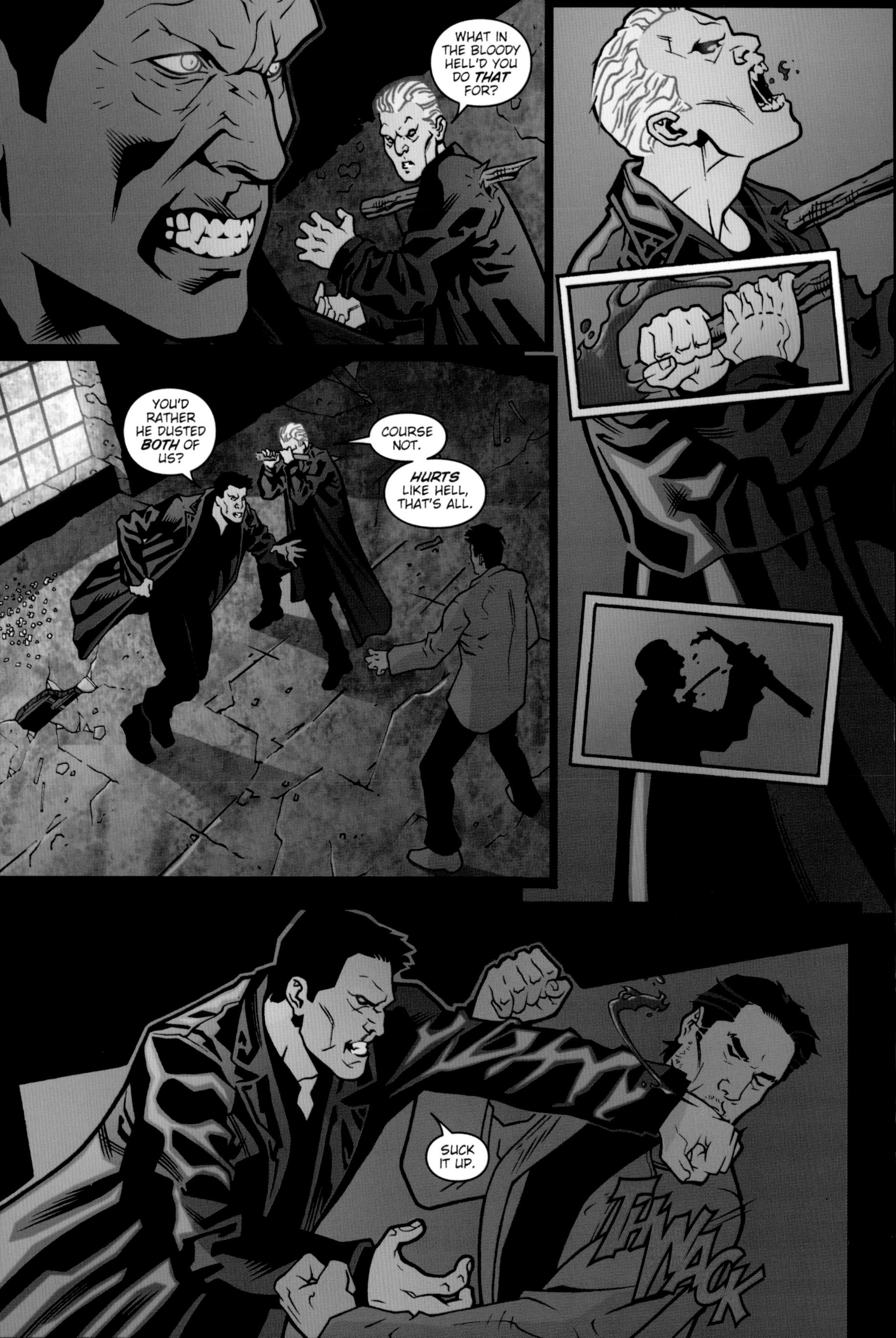
WHAT IN THE BLOODY HELL'D YOU DO *THAT* FOR?
YOU'D RATHER HE DUSTED *BOTH* OF US?
COURSE NOT.
HURTS LIKE HELL, THAT'S ALL.
SUCK IT UP.
THWACK

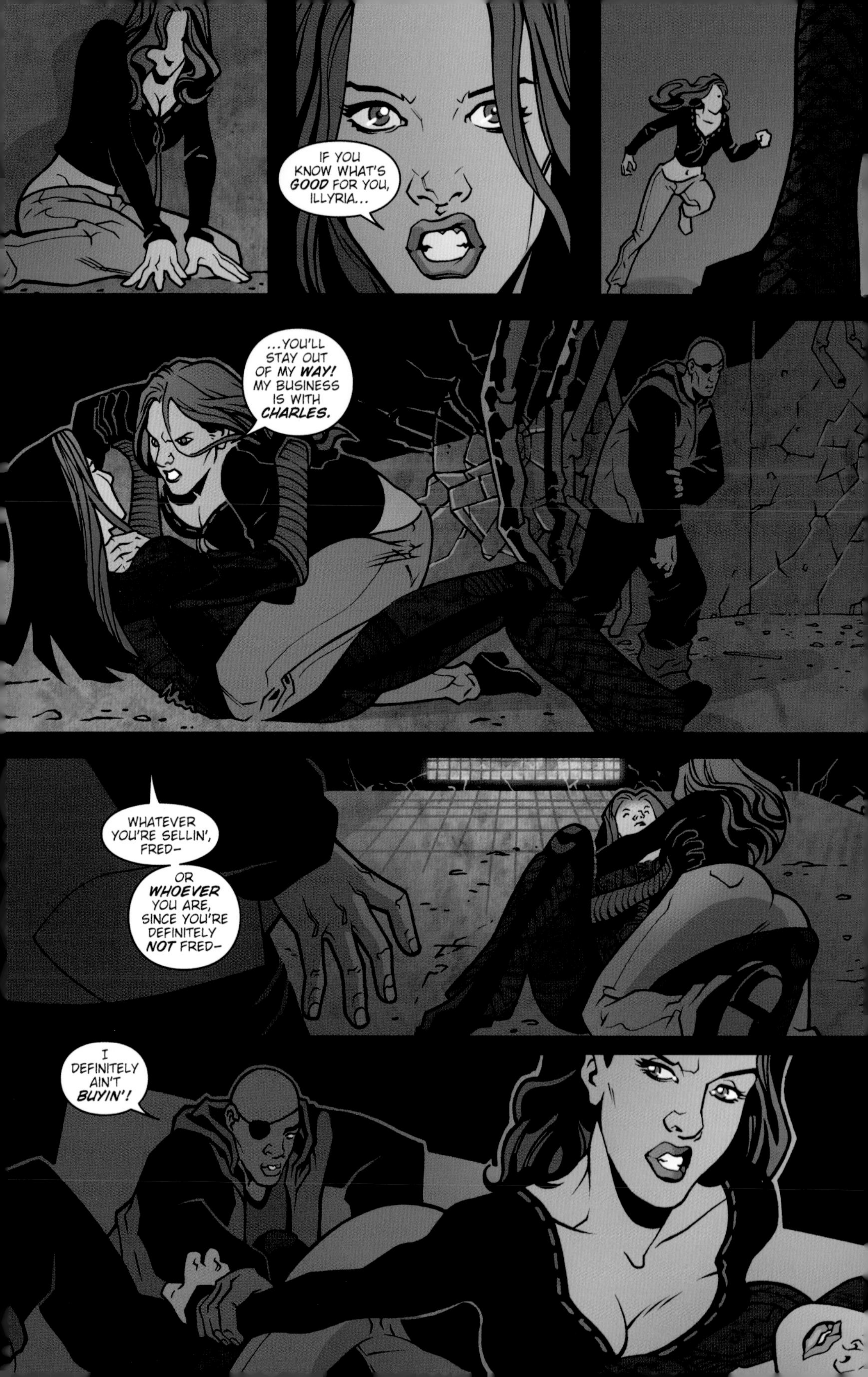
IF YOU KNOW WHAT'S GOOD FOR YOU, ILLYRIA...
...YOU'LL STAY OUT OF MY WAY! MY BUSINESS IS WITH CHARLES.
WHATEVER YOU'RE SELLIN', FRED-
OR WHOEVER YOU ARE, SINCE YOU'RE DEFINITELY NOT FRED-
I DEFINITELY AIN'T BUYIN'!

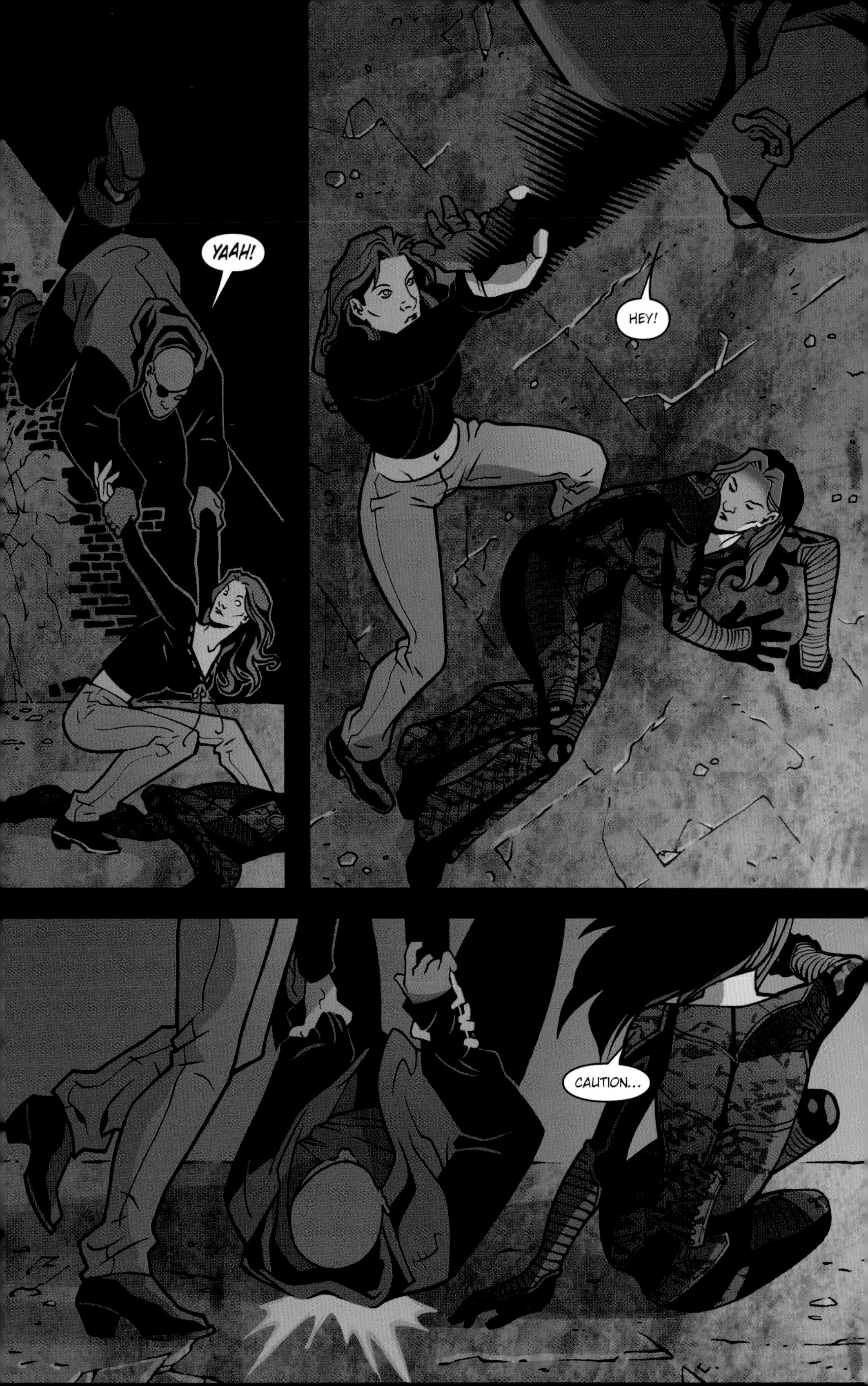
YAAH!
HEY!
CAUTION...

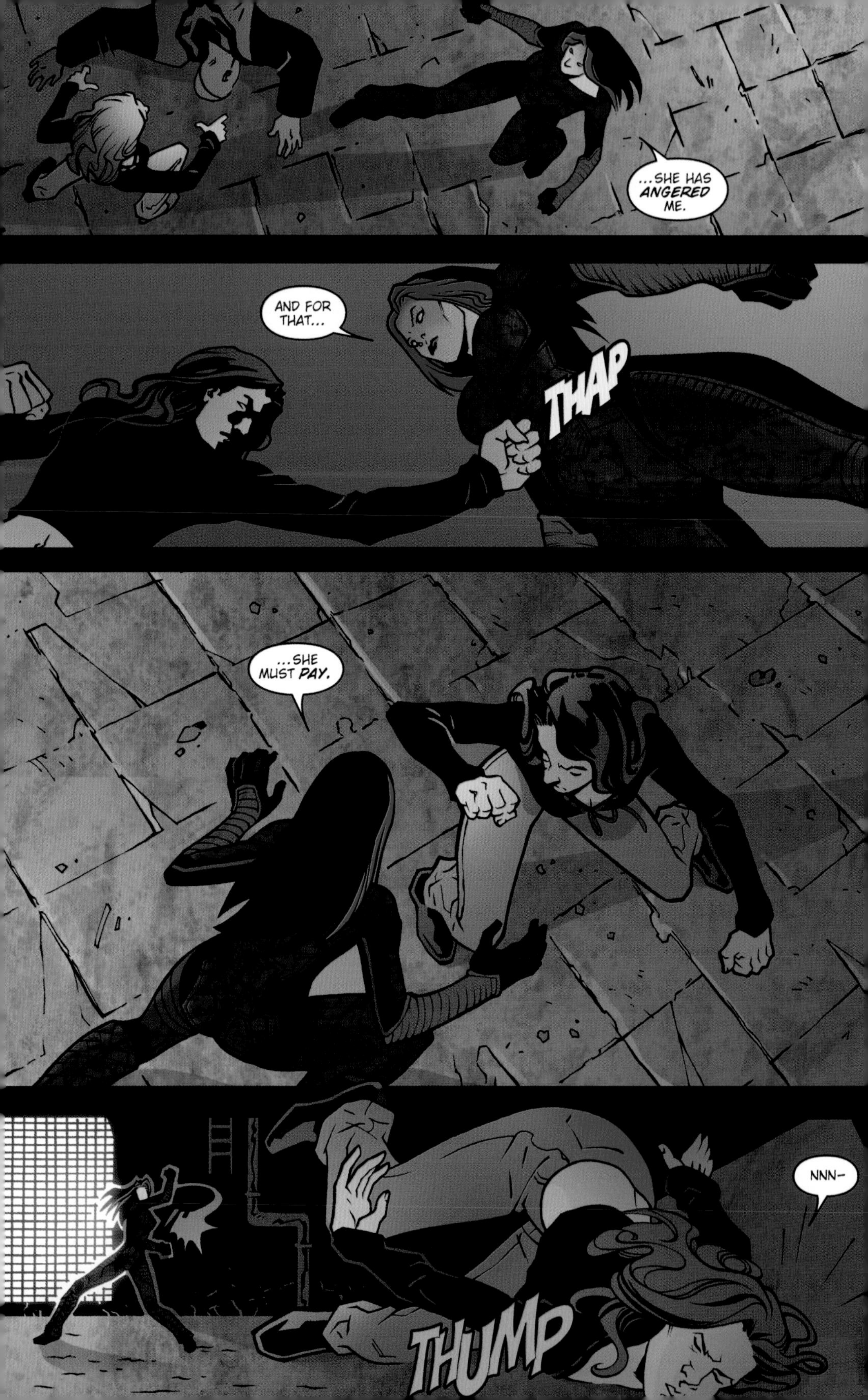
...SHE HAS ANGERED ME.
AND FOR THAT...
THAP
...SHE MUST PAY.
NNN-
THUMP

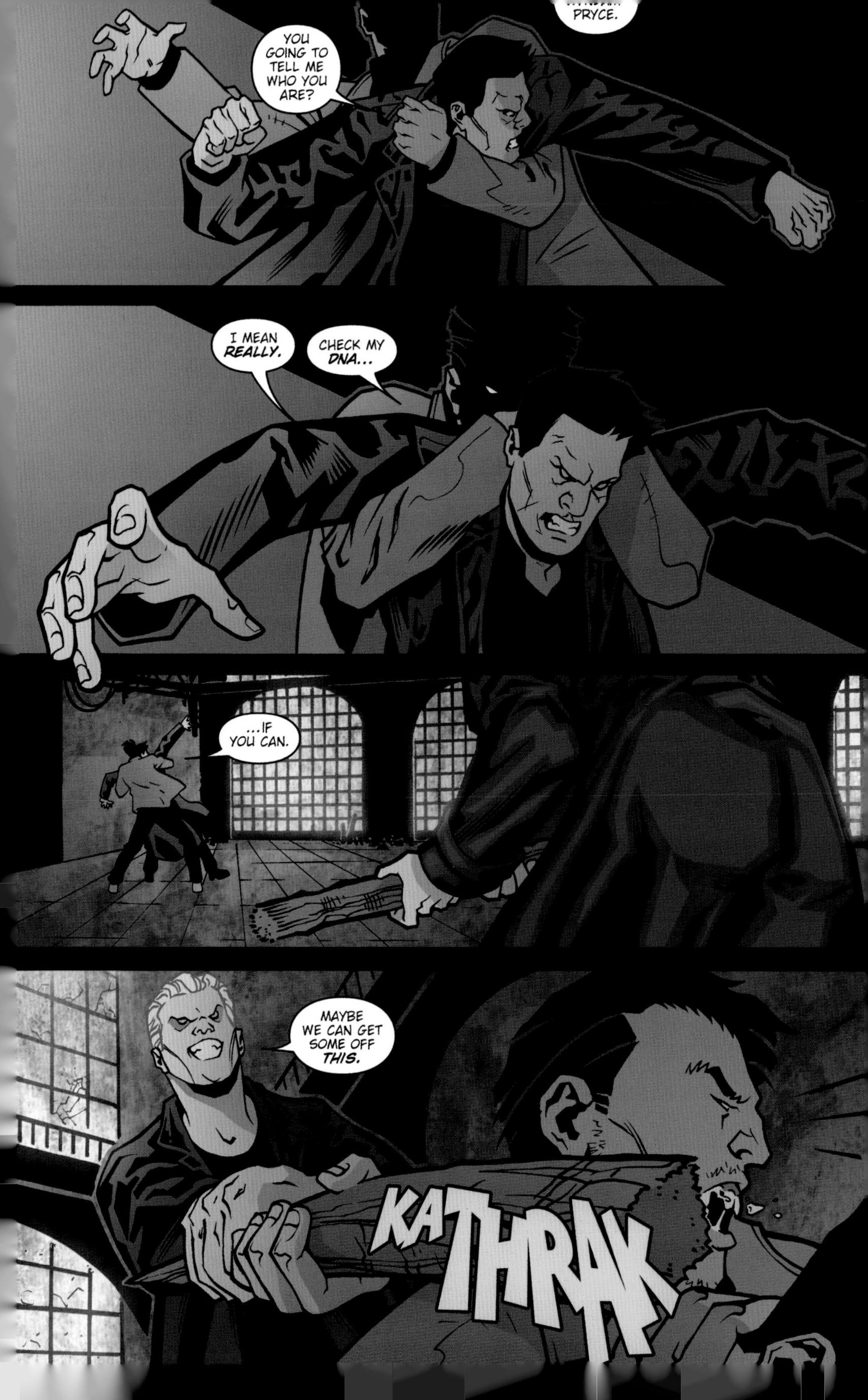
PRYCE.
YOU GOING TO TELL ME WHO YOU ARE?
I MEAN REALLY.
CHECK MY DNA...
...IF YOU CAN.
MAYBE WE CAN GET SOME OFF THIS.
KATHRAK

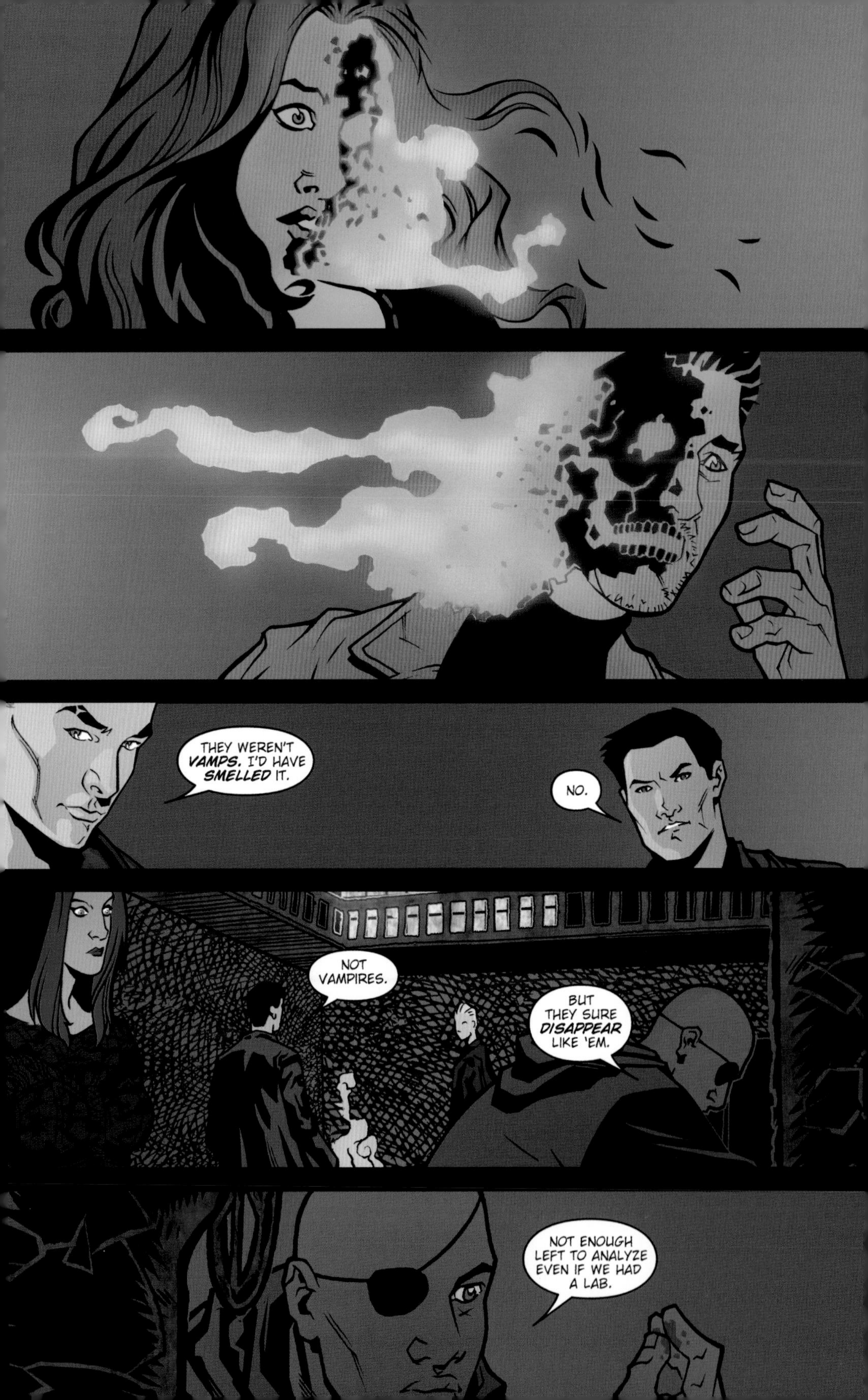
THEY WEREN'T VAMPS. I'D HAVE SMELLED IT.
NO.
NOT VAMPIRES.
BUT THEY SURE DISAPPEAR LIKE 'EM.
NOT ENOUGH LEFT TO ANALYZE EVEN IF WE HAD A LAB.

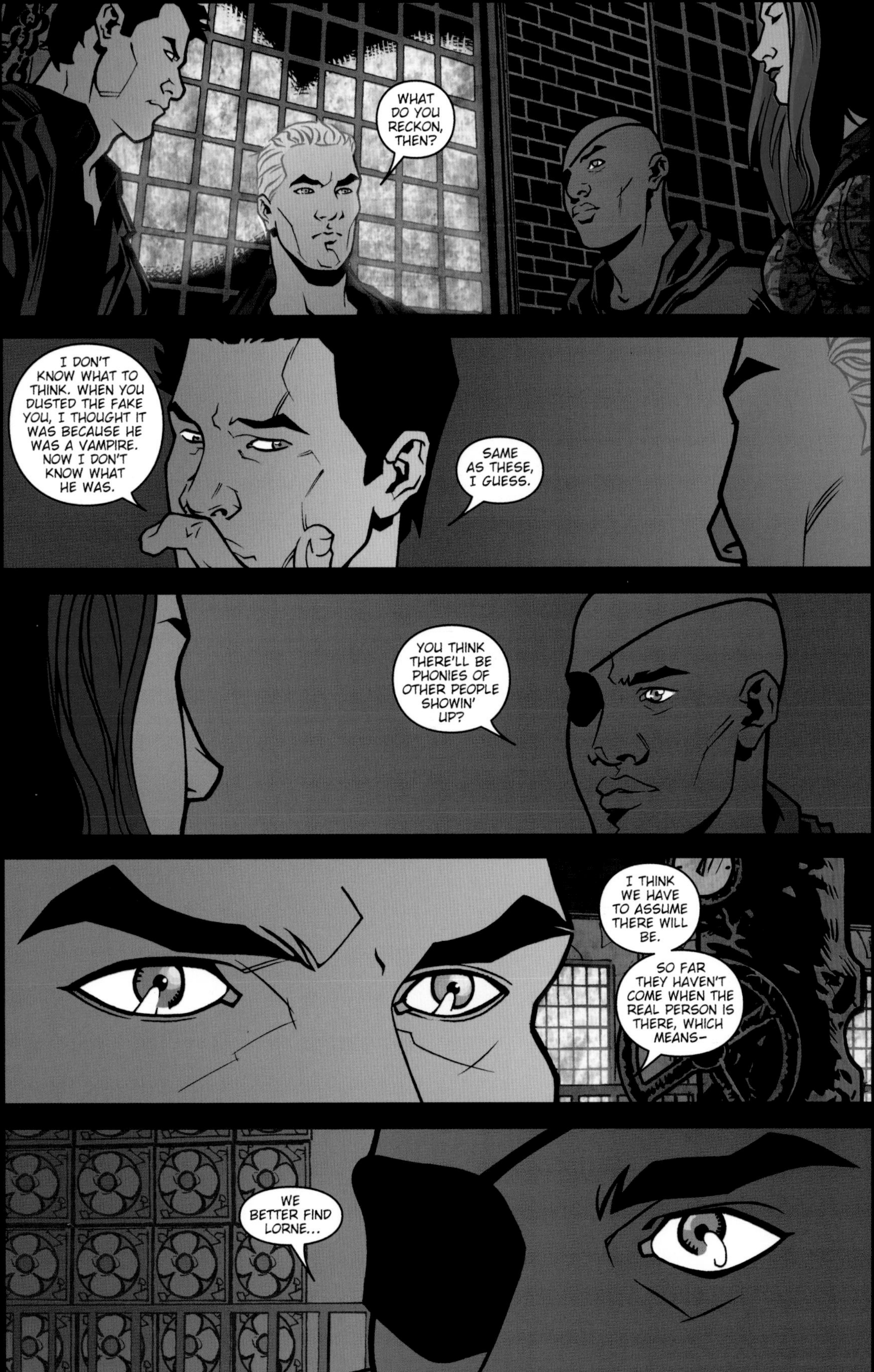
WHAT DO YOU RECKON, THEN?
I DON'T KNOW WHAT TO THINK. WHEN YOU DUSTED THE FAKE YOU, I THOUGHT IT WAS BECAUSE HE WAS A VAMPIRE. NOW I DON'T KNOW WHAT HE WAS.
SAME AS THESE, I GUESS.
YOU THINK THERE'LL BE PHONIES OF OTHER PEOPLE SHOWIN' UP?
I THINK WE HAVE TO ASSUME THERE WILL BE.
SO FAR THEY HAVEN'T COME WHEN THE REAL PERSON IS THERE, WHICH MEANS–
WE BETTER FIND LORNE...

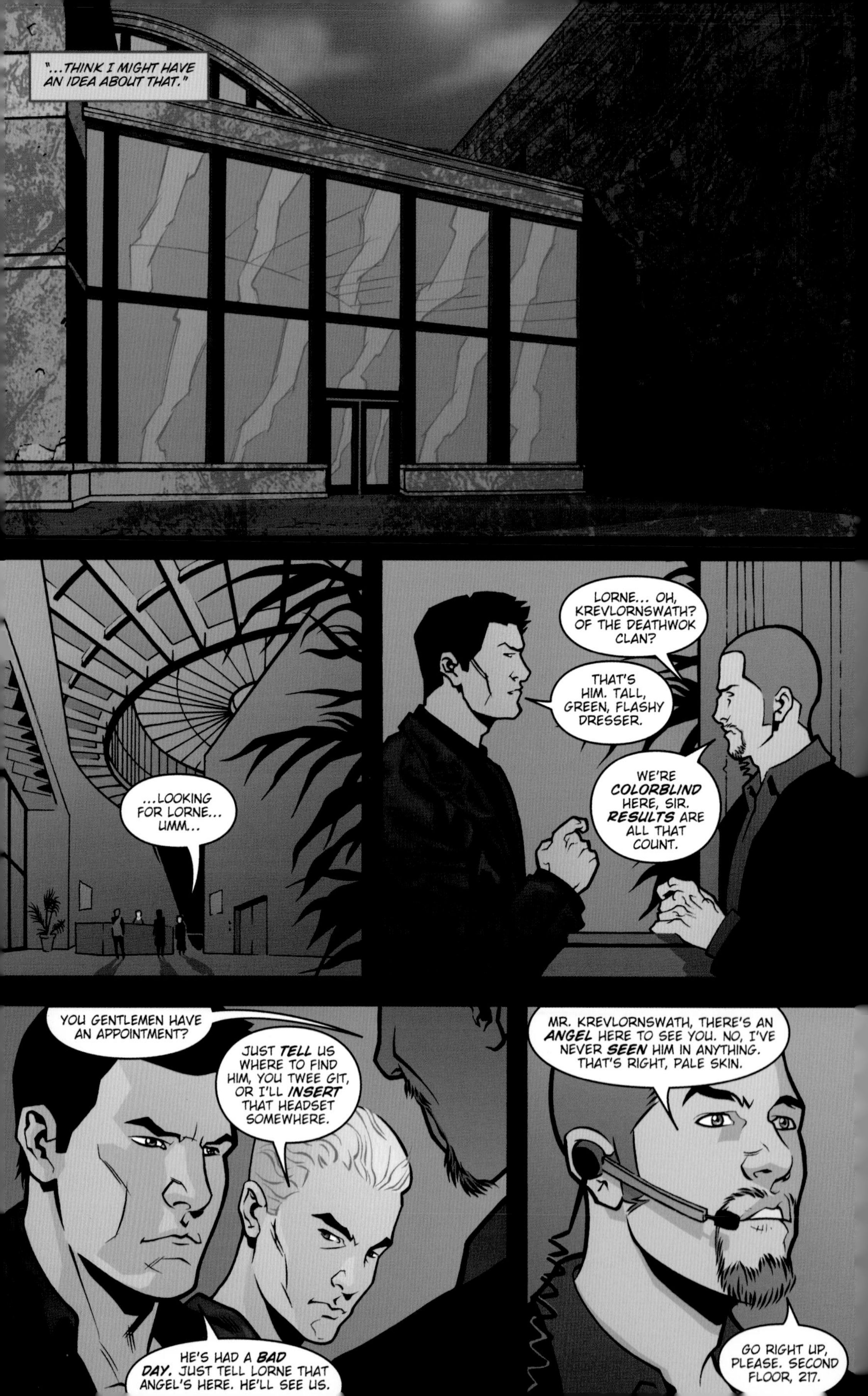
"...THINK I MIGHT HAVE AN IDEA ABOUT THAT."
...LOOKING FOR LORNE... UMM...
LORNE... OH, KREVLORNSWATH? OF THE DEATHWOK CLAN?
THAT'S HIM. TALL, GREEN, FLASHY DRESSER.
WE'RE COLORBLIND HERE, SIR. RESULTS ARE ALL THAT COUNT.
YOU GENTLEMEN HAVE AN APPOINTMENT?
JUST TELL US WHERE TO FIND HIM, YOU TWEE GIT, OR I'LL INSERT THAT HEADSET SOMEWHERE.
HE'S HAD A BAD DAY. JUST TELL LORNE THAT ANGEL'S HERE. HE'LL SEE US.
MR. KREVLORNSWATH, THERE'S AN ANGEL HERE TO SEE YOU. NO, I'VE NEVER SEEN HIM IN ANYTHING. THAT'S RIGHT, PALE SKIN.
GO RIGHT UP, PLEASE. SECOND FLOOR, 217.

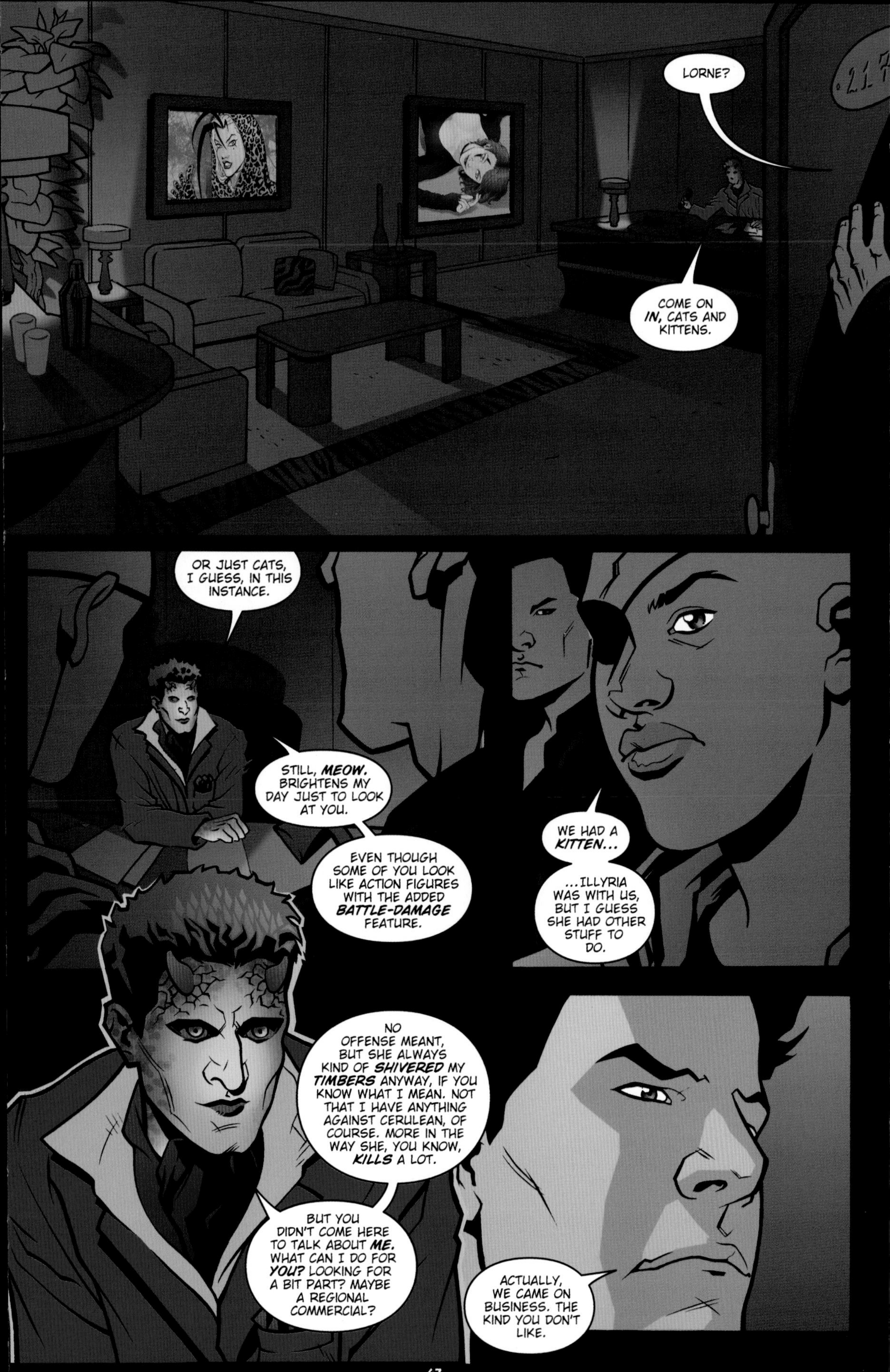
LORNE?
COME ON IN, CATS AND KITTENS.
OR JUST CATS, I GUESS, IN THIS INSTANCE.
STILL, MEOW. BRIGHTENS MY DAY JUST TO LOOK AT YOU.
EVEN THOUGH SOME OF YOU LOOK LIKE ACTION FIGURES WITH THE ADDED BATTLE-DAMAGE FEATURE.
WE HAD A KITTEN...
...ILLYRIA WAS WITH US, BUT I GUESS SHE HAD OTHER STUFF TO DO.
NO OFFENSE MEANT, BUT SHE ALWAYS KIND OF SHIVERED MY TIMBERS ANYWAY, IF YOU KNOW WHAT I MEAN. NOT THAT I HAVE ANYTHING AGAINST CERULEAN, OF COURSE. MORE IN THE WAY SHE, YOU KNOW, KILLS A LOT.
BUT YOU DIDN'T COME HERE TO TALK ABOUT ME. WHAT CAN I DO FOR YOU? LOOKING FOR A BIT PART? MAYBE A REGIONAL COMMERCIAL?
ACTUALLY, WE CAME ON BUSINESS. THE KIND YOU DON'T LIKE.

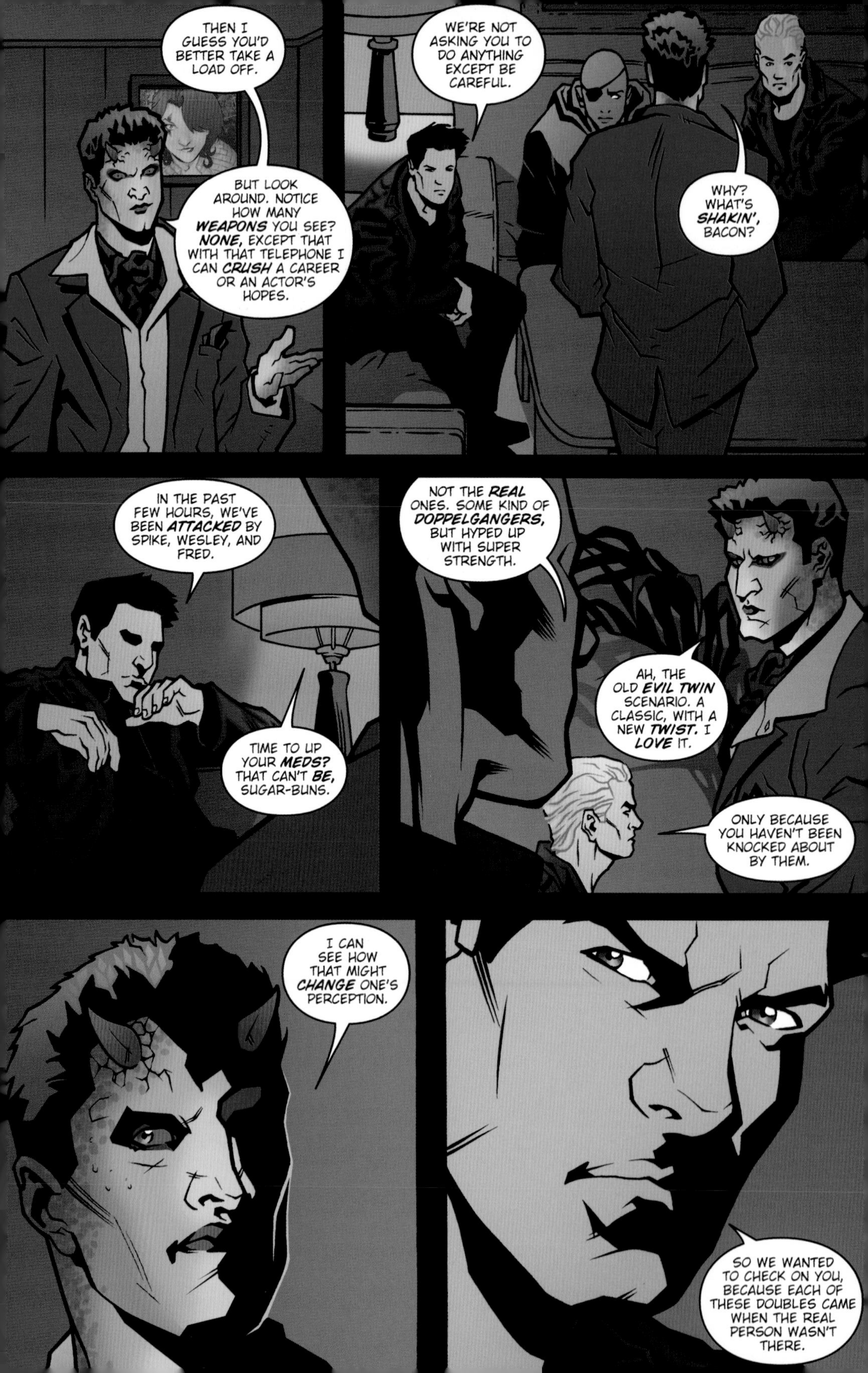

THEN I GUESS YOU'D BETTER TAKE A LOAD OFF.
BUT LOOK AROUND. NOTICE HOW MANY WEAPONS YOU SEE? NONE, EXCEPT THAT WITH THAT TELEPHONE I CAN CRUSH A CAREER OR AN ACTOR'S HOPES.
WE'RE NOT ASKING YOU TO DO ANYTHING EXCEPT BE CAREFUL.
WHY? WHAT'S SHAKIN', BACON?
IN THE PAST FEW HOURS, WE'VE BEEN ATTACKED BY SPIKE, WESLEY, AND FRED.
TIME TO UP YOUR MEDS? THAT CAN'T BE, SUGAR-BUNS.
NOT THE REAL ONES. SOME KIND OF DOPPELGANGERS, BUT HYPED UP WITH SUPER STRENGTH.
AH, THE OLD EVIL TWIN SCENARIO. A CLASSIC, WITH A NEW TWIST. I LOVE IT.
ONLY BECAUSE YOU HAVEN'T BEEN KNOCKED ABOUT BY THEM.
I CAN SEE HOW THAT MIGHT CHANGE ONE'S PERCEPTION.
SO WE WANTED TO CHECK ON YOU, BECAUSE EACH OF THESE DOUBLES CAME WHEN THE REAL PERSON WASN'T THERE.

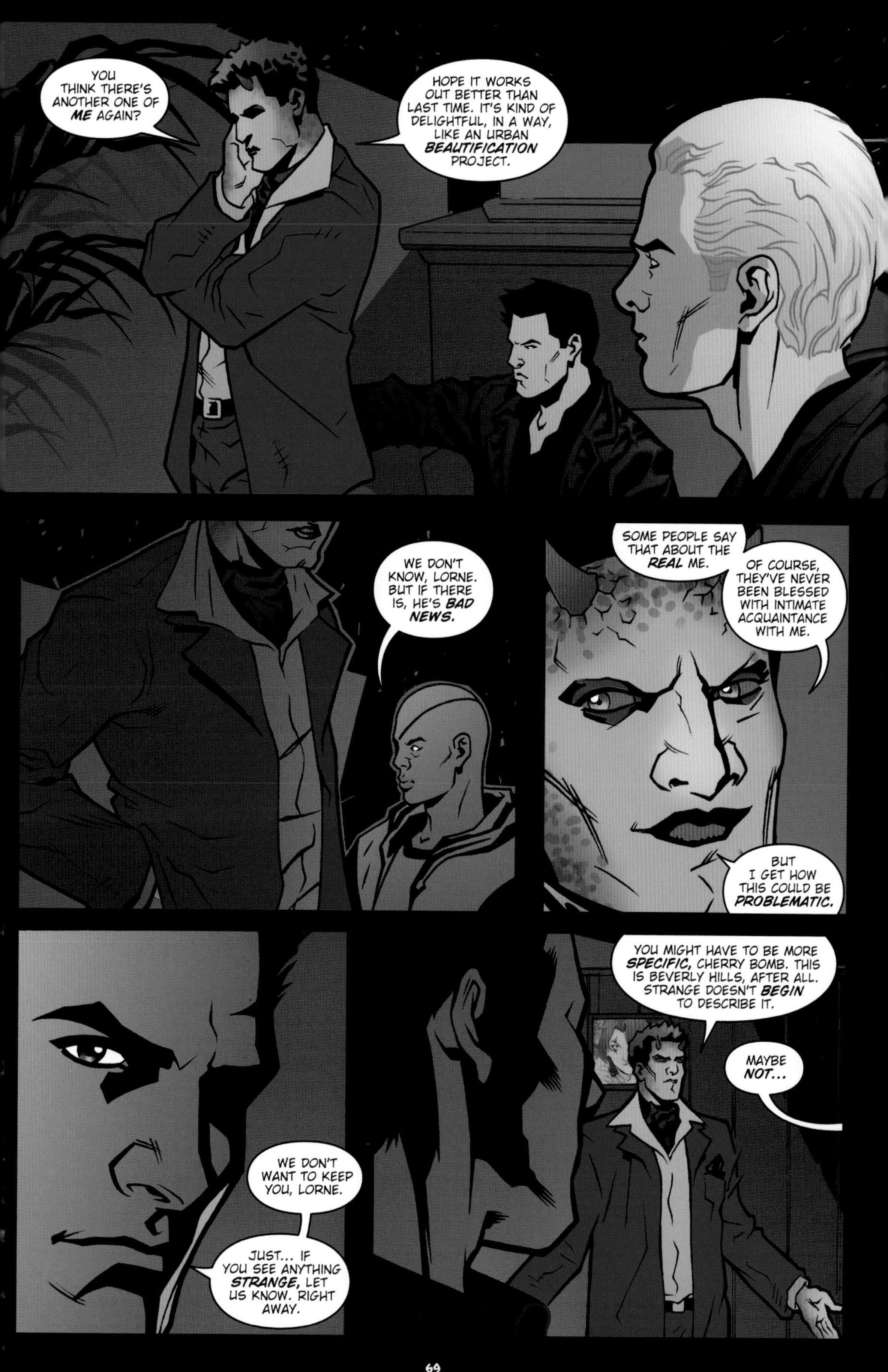
YOU THINK THERE'S ANOTHER ONE OF ME AGAIN?
HOPE IT WORKS OUT BETTER THAN LAST TIME. IT'S KIND OF DELIGHTFUL, IN A WAY, LIKE AN URBAN BEAUTIFICATION PROJECT.
WE DON'T KNOW, LORNE. BUT IF THERE IS, HE'S BAD NEWS.
SOME PEOPLE SAY THAT ABOUT THE REAL ME.
OF COURSE, THEY'VE NEVER BEEN BLESSED WITH INTIMATE ACQUAINTANCE WITH ME.
BUT I GET HOW THIS COULD BE PROBLEMATIC.
WE DON'T WANT TO KEEP YOU, LORNE.
JUST... IF YOU SEE ANYTHING STRANGE, LET US KNOW. RIGHT AWAY.
YOU MIGHT HAVE TO BE MORE SPECIFIC, CHERRY BOMB. THIS IS BEVERLY HILLS, AFTER ALL. STRANGE DOESN'T BEGIN TO DESCRIBE IT.
MAYBE NOT...

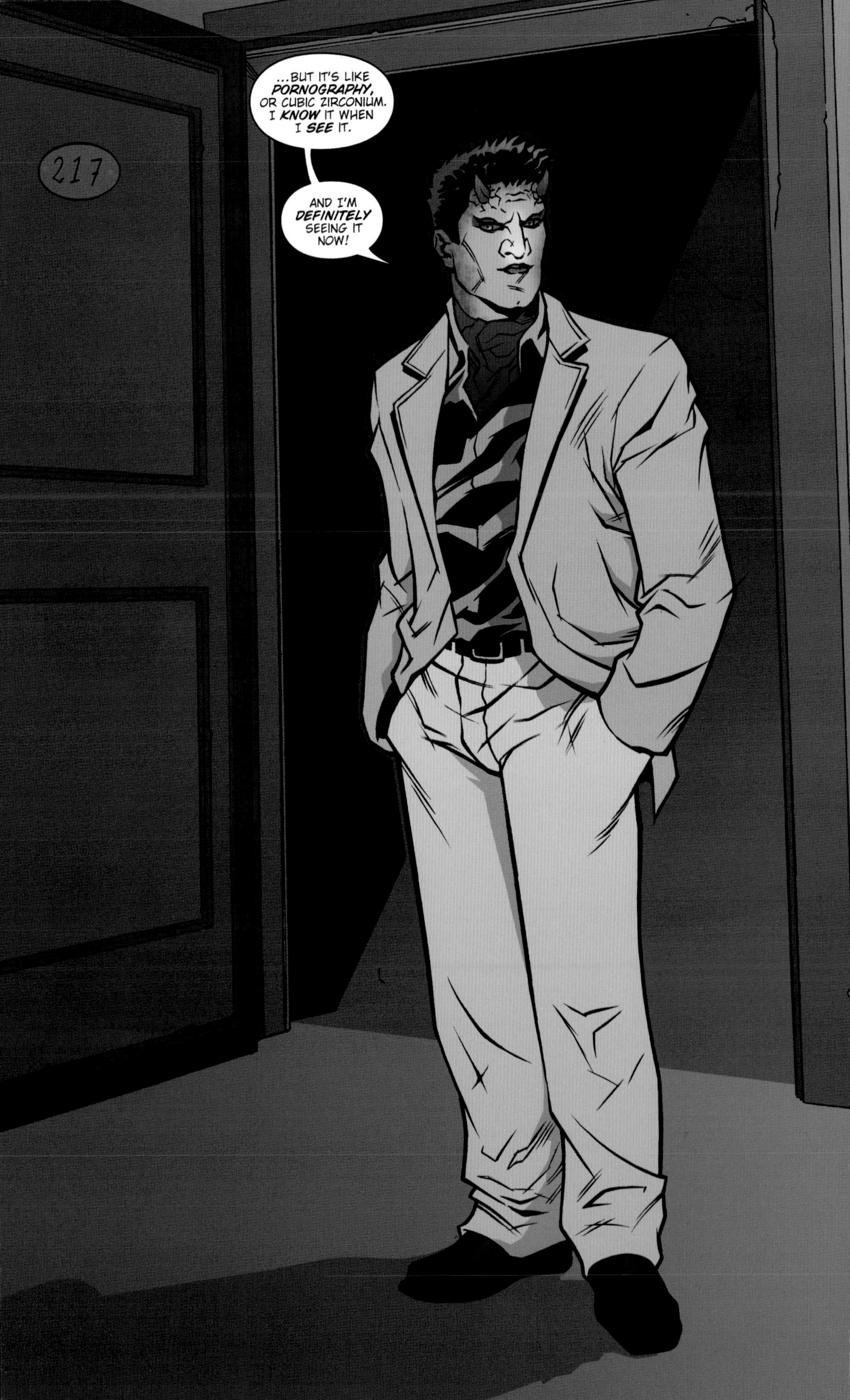
...BUT IT'S LIKE PORNOGRAPHY, OR CUBIC ZIRCONIUM. I KNOW IT WHEN I SEE IT.
AND I'M DEFINITELY SEEING IT NOW!
217

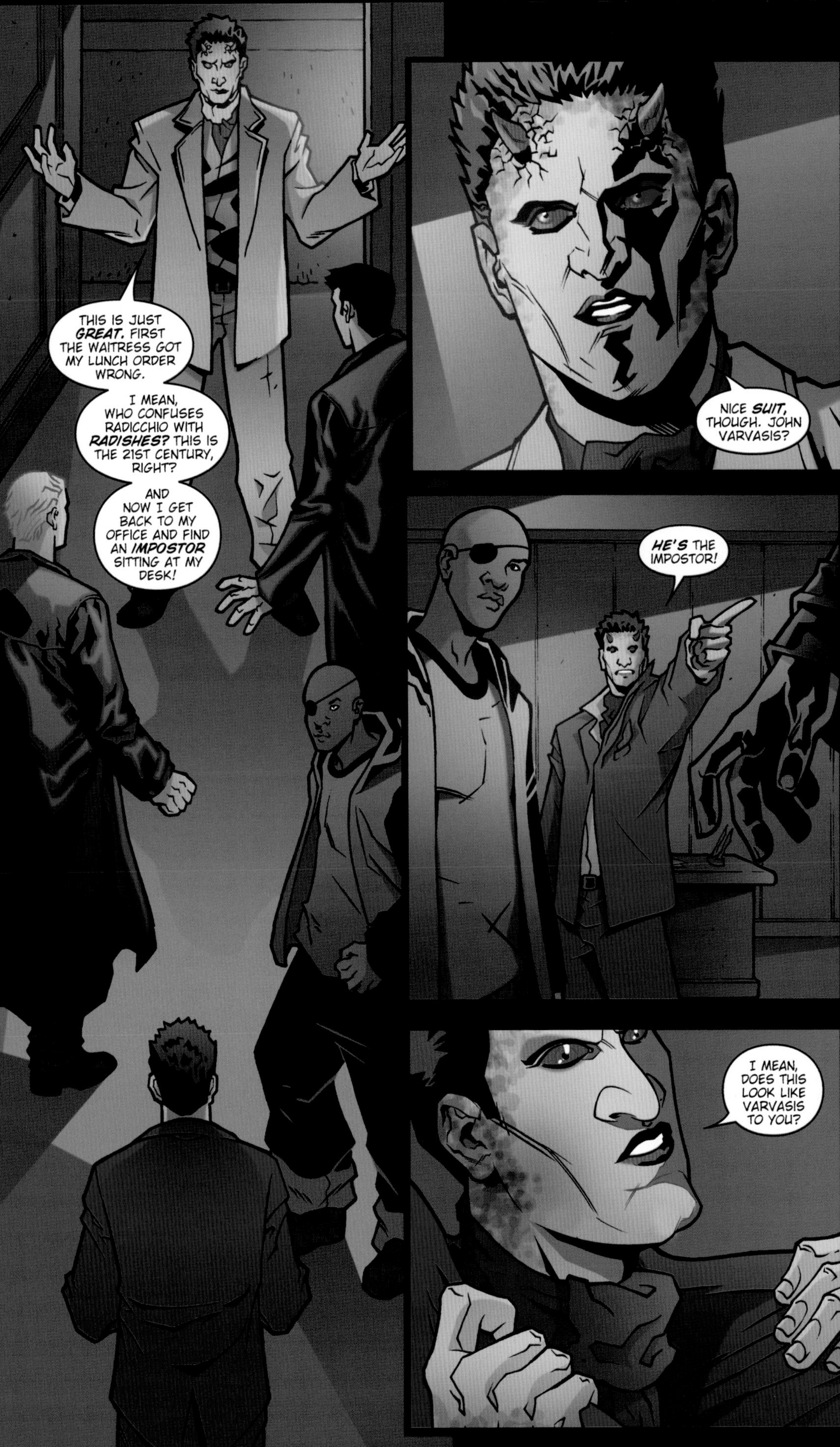
THIS IS JUST GREAT. FIRST THE WAITRESS GOT MY LUNCH ORDER WRONG.
I MEAN, WHO CONFUSES RADICCHIO WITH RADISHES? THIS IS THE 21ST CENTURY, RIGHT?
AND NOW I GET BACK TO MY OFFICE AND FIND AN IMPOSTOR SITTING AT MY DESK!
NICE SUIT, THOUGH. JOHN VARVASIS?
HE'S THE IMPOSTOR!
I MEAN, DOES THIS LOOK LIKE VARVASIS TO YOU?

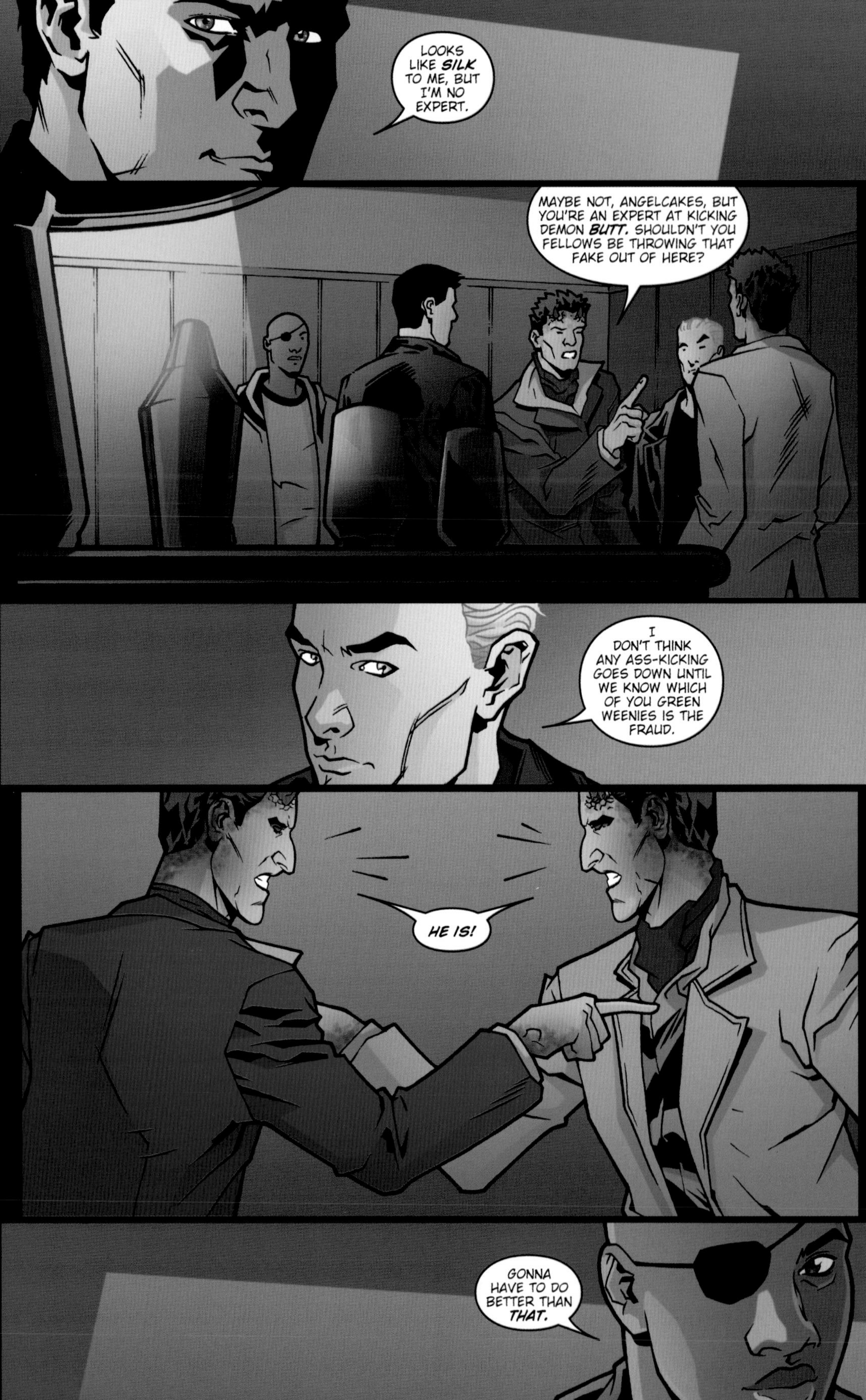
LOOKS LIKE SILK TO ME, BUT I'M NO EXPERT.
MAYBE NOT, ANGELCAKES, BUT YOU'RE AN EXPERT AT KICKING DEMON BUTT. SHOULDN'T YOU FELLOWS BE THROWING THAT FAKE OUT OF HERE?
I DON'T THINK ANY ASS-KICKING GOES DOWN UNTIL WE KNOW WHICH OF YOU GREEN WEENIES IS THE FRAUD.
HE IS!
GONNA HAVE TO DO BETTER THAN THAT.

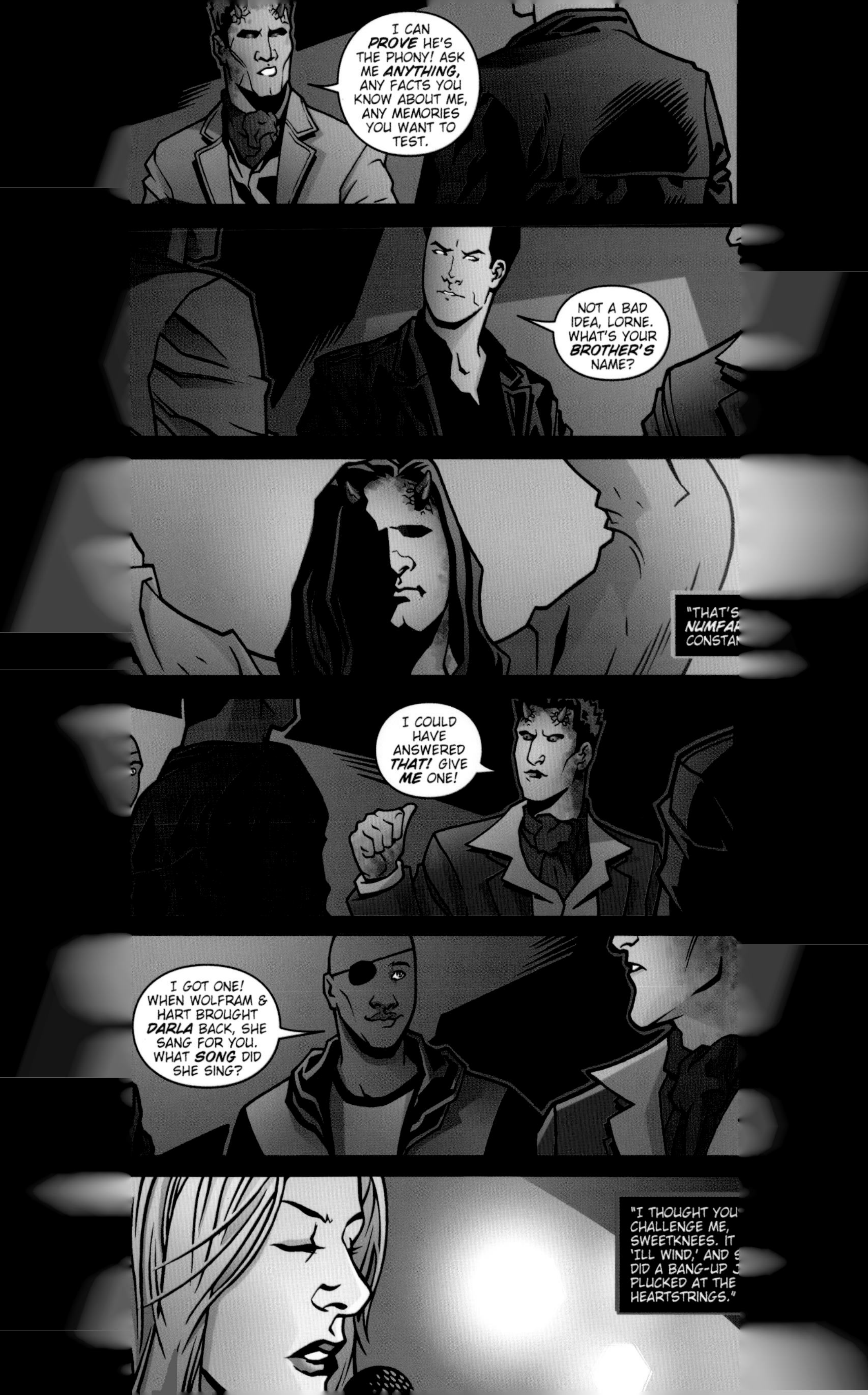
I CAN PROVE HE'S THE PHONY! ASK ME ANYTHING, ANY FACTS YOU KNOW ABOUT ME, ANY MEMORIES YOU WANT TO TEST.
NOT A BAD IDEA, LORNE. WHAT'S YOUR BROTHER'S NAME?
"THAT'S
NUMFAR
CONSTAN
I COULD HAVE ANSWERED THAT! GIVE ME ONE!
I GOT ONE! WHEN WOLFRAM & HART BROUGHT DARLA BACK, SHE SANG FOR YOU. WHAT SONG DID SHE SING?
"I THOUGHT YOU
CHALLENGE ME,
SWEETKNEES. IT
'ILL WIND,' AND S
DID A BANG-UP J
PLUCKED AT THE
HEARTSTRINGS."

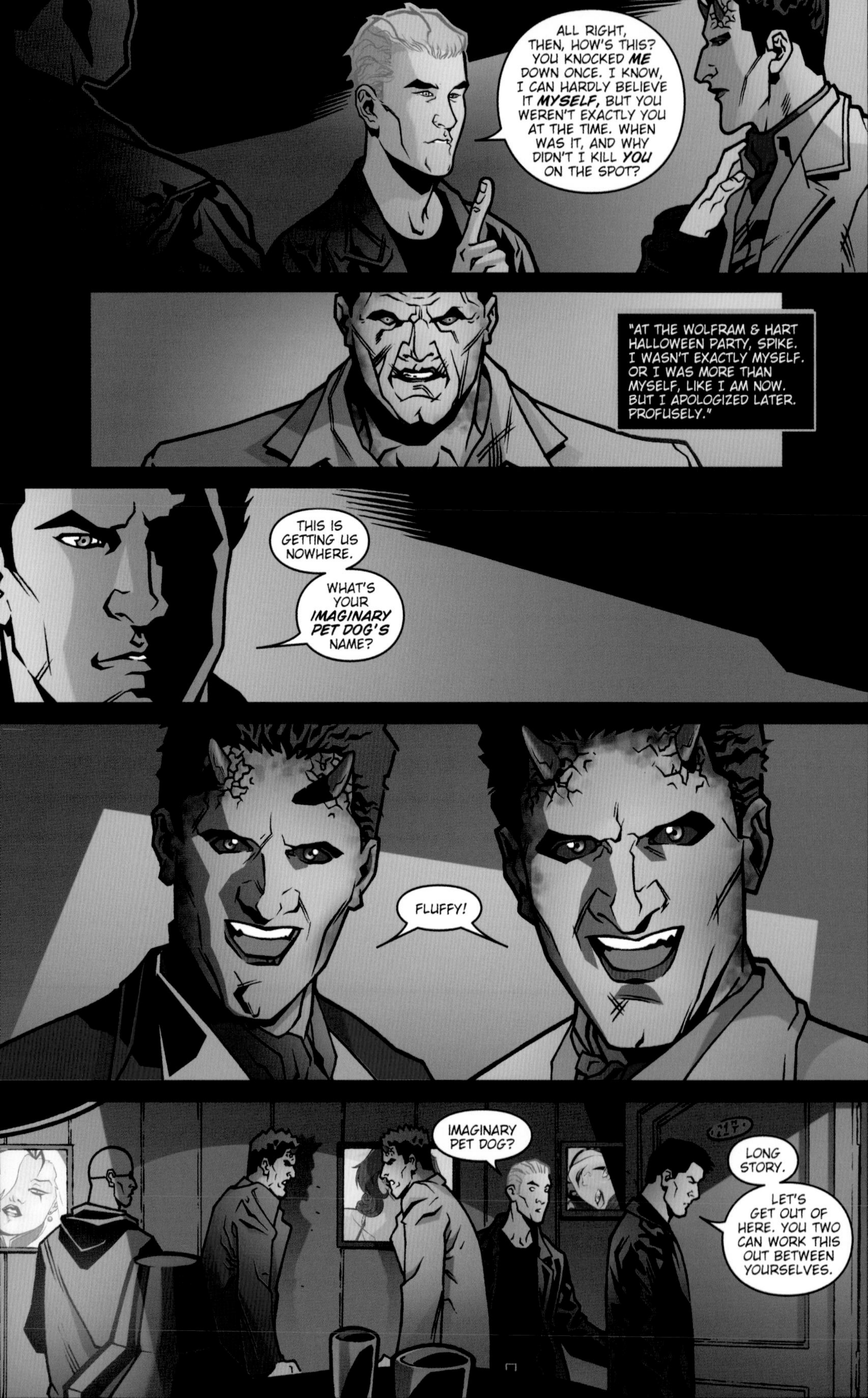
ALL RIGHT, THEN, HOW'S THIS? YOU KNOCKED ME DOWN ONCE. I KNOW, I CAN HARDLY BELIEVE IT MYSELF, BUT YOU WEREN'T EXACTLY YOU AT THE TIME. WHEN WAS IT, AND WHY DIDN'T I KILL YOU ON THE SPOT?
"AT THE WOLFRAM & HART HALLOWEEN PARTY, SPIKE. I WASN'T EXACTLY MYSELF. OR I WAS MORE THAN MYSELF, LIKE I AM NOW. BUT I APOLOGIZED LATER. PROFUSELY."
THIS IS GETTING US NOWHERE.
WHAT'S YOUR IMAGINARY PET DOG'S NAME?
FLUFFY!
IMAGINARY PET DOG?
LONG STORY.
LET'S GET OUT OF HERE. YOU TWO CAN WORK THIS OUT BETWEEN YOURSELVES.

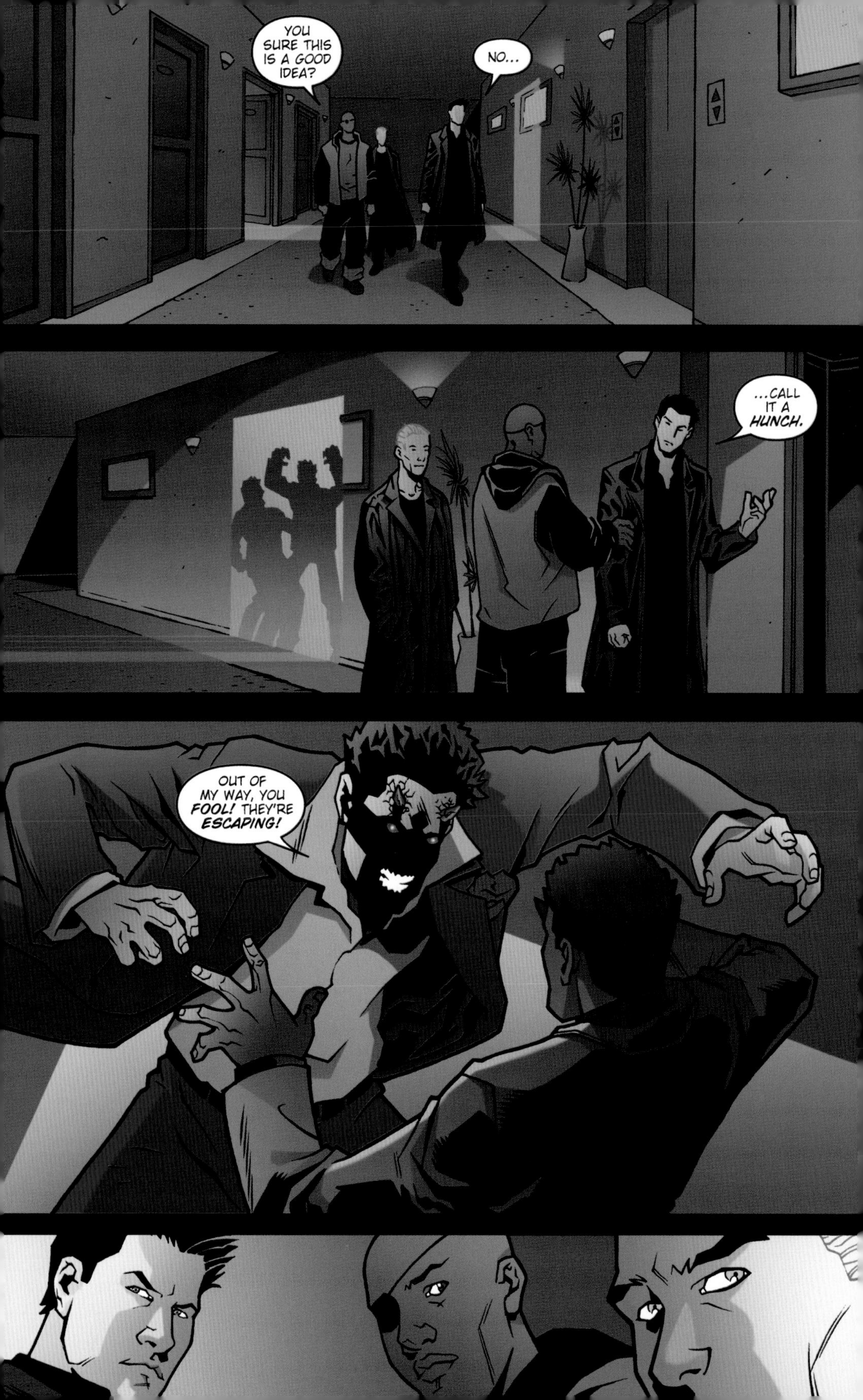
YOU SURE THIS IS A GOOD IDEA?
NO...
...CALL IT A *HUNCH.*
OUT OF MY WAY, YOU *FOOL!* THEY'RE *ESCAPING!*

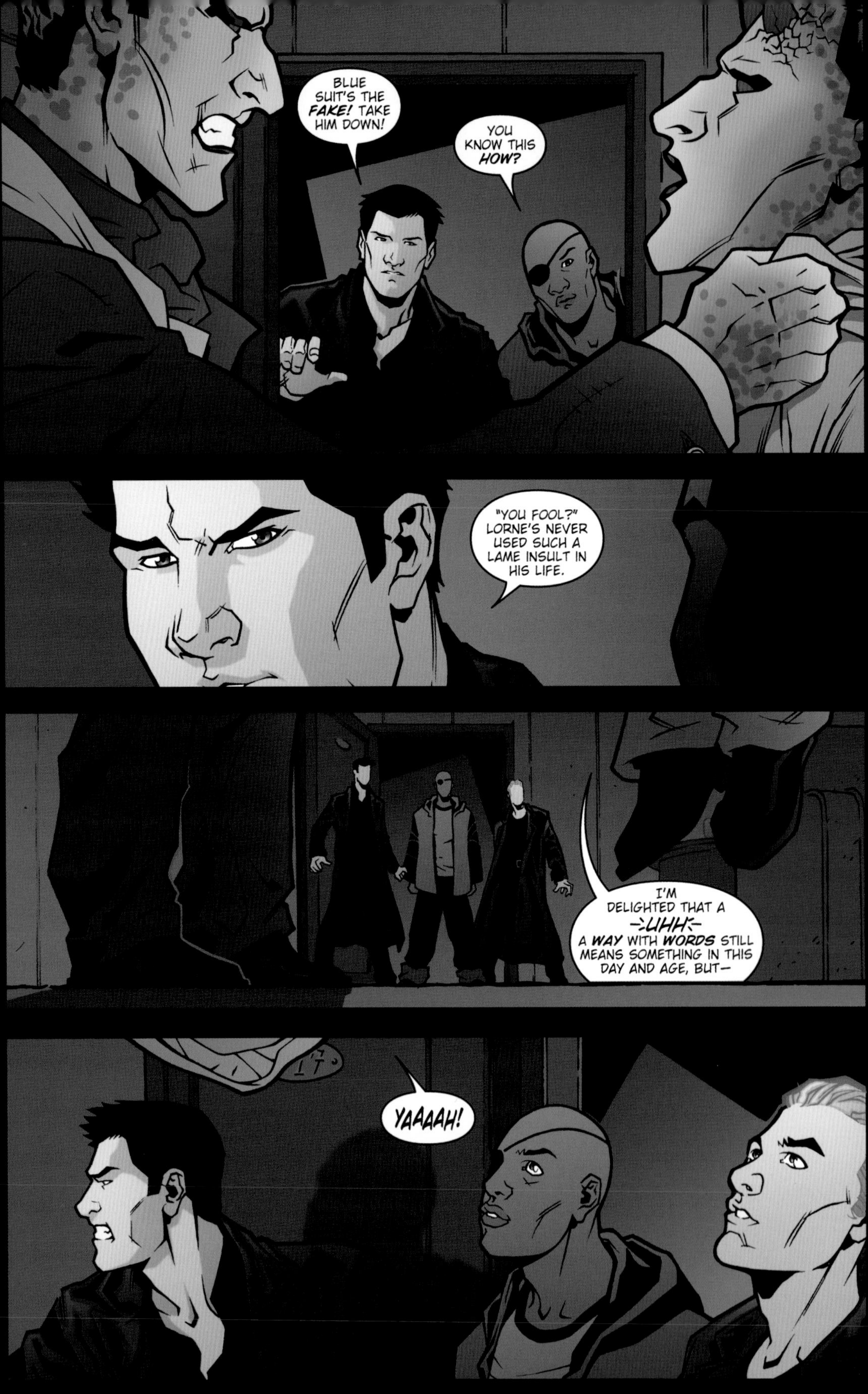

BLUE SUIT'S THE FAKE! TAKE HIM DOWN!
YOU KNOW THIS HOW?
"YOU FOOL?" LORNE'S NEVER USED SUCH A LAME INSULT IN HIS LIFE.
I'M DELIGHTED THAT A -UHH- A WAY WITH WORDS STILL MEANS SOMETHING IN THIS DAY AND AGE, BUT—
YAAAAH!

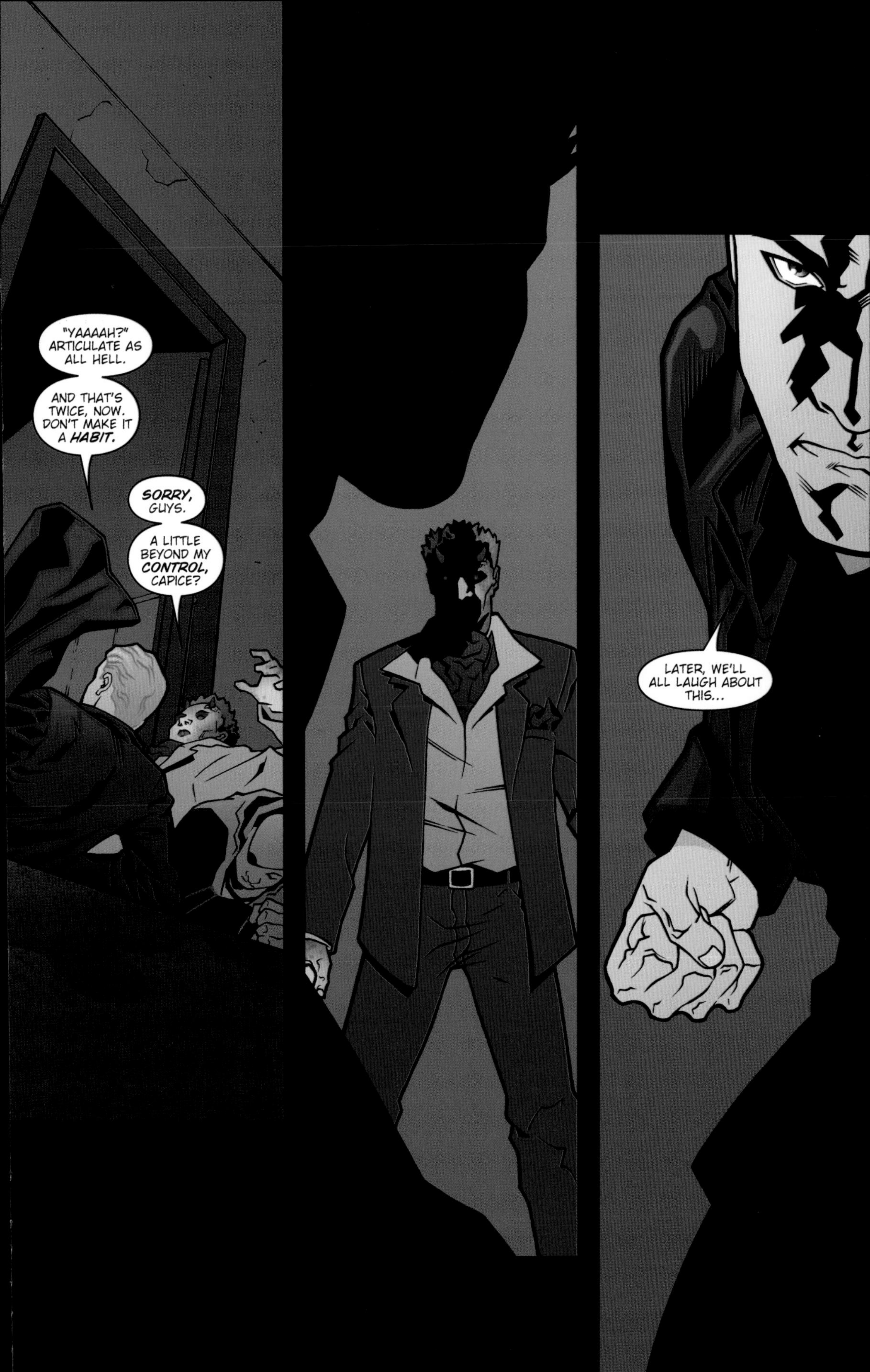
"YAAAAH?" ARTICULATE AS ALL HELL.
AND THAT'S TWICE, NOW. DON'T MAKE IT A *HABIT*.
SORRY, GUYS.
A LITTLE BEYOND MY *CONTROL,* CAPICE?
LATER, WE'LL ALL LAUGH ABOUT THIS...

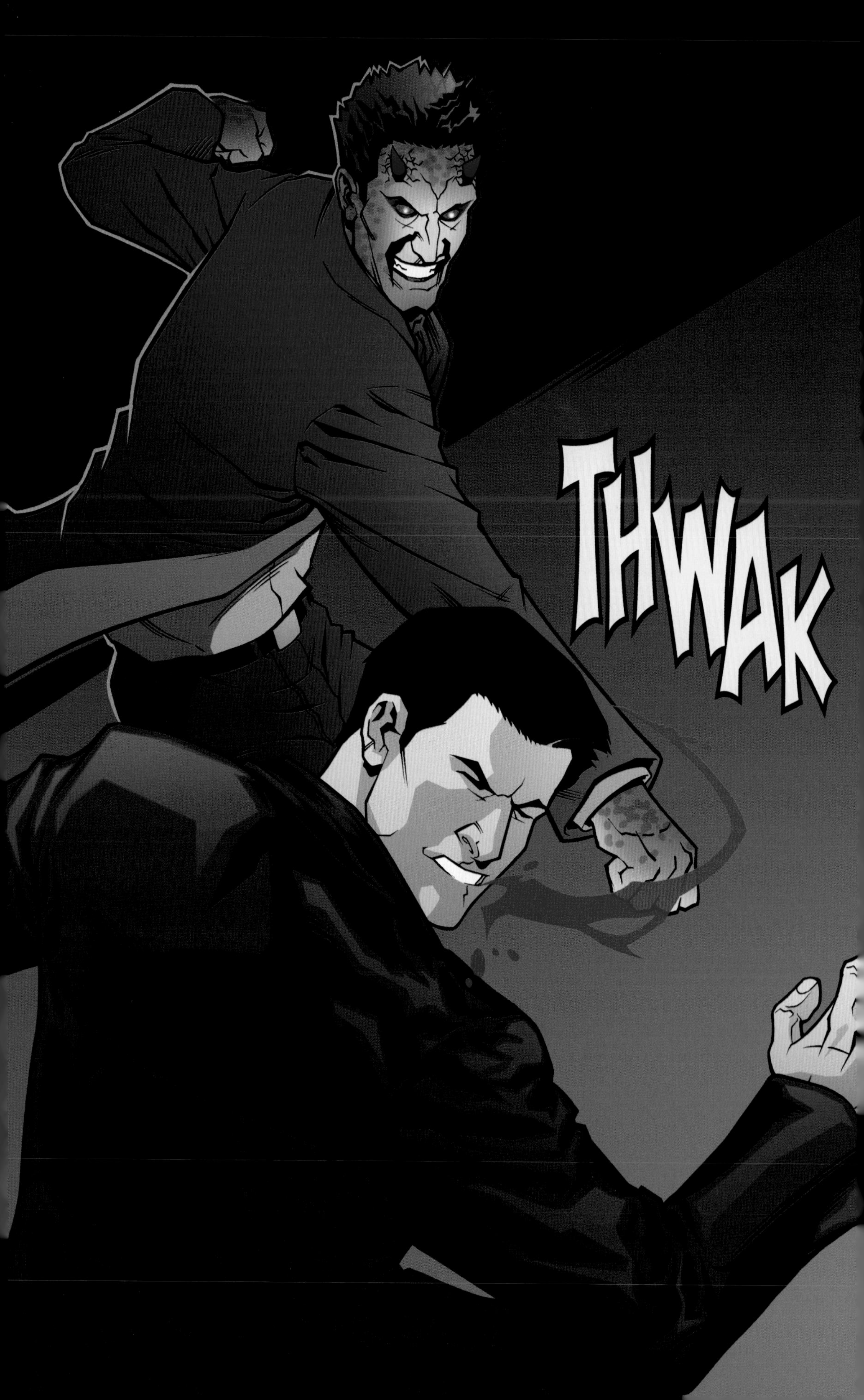
THWAK

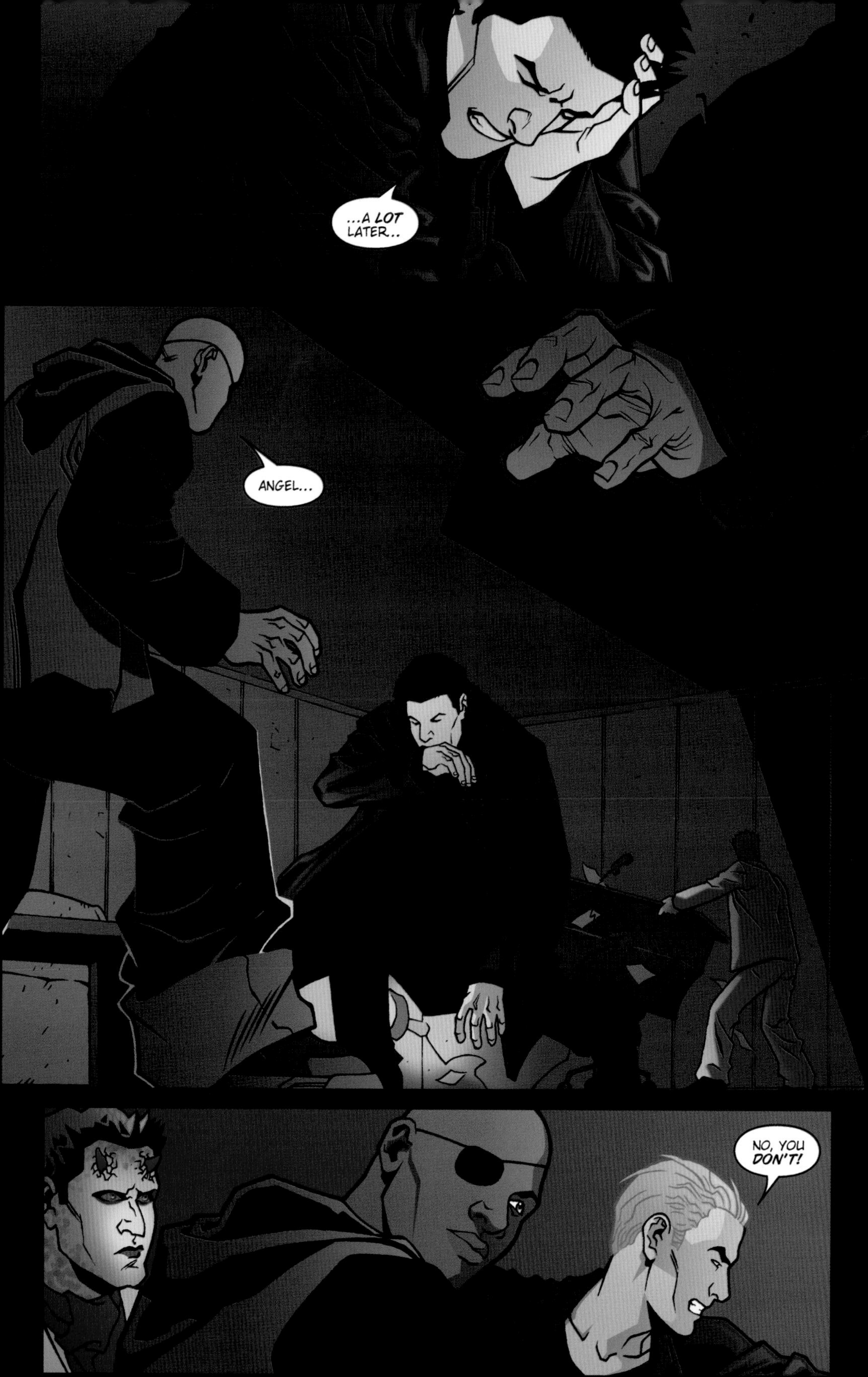
...A LOT LATER...
ANGEL...
NO, YOU DON'T!

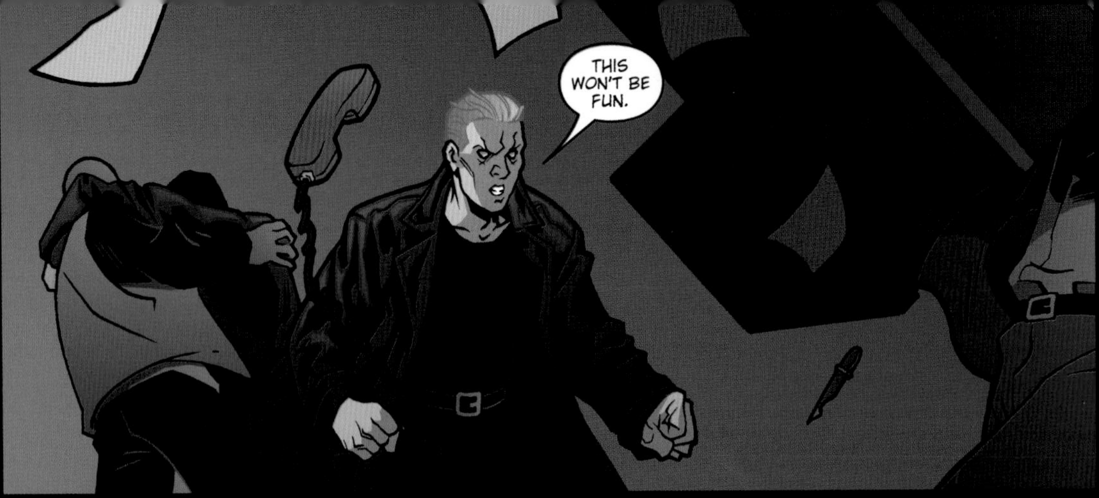
THIS WON'T BE FUN.

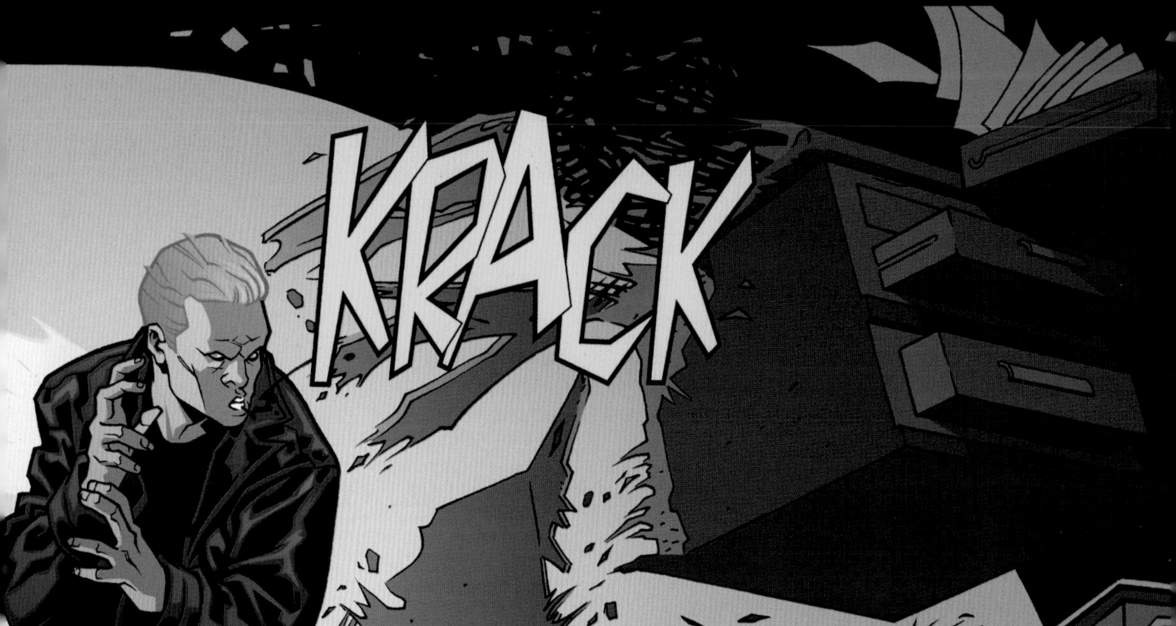
KRACK

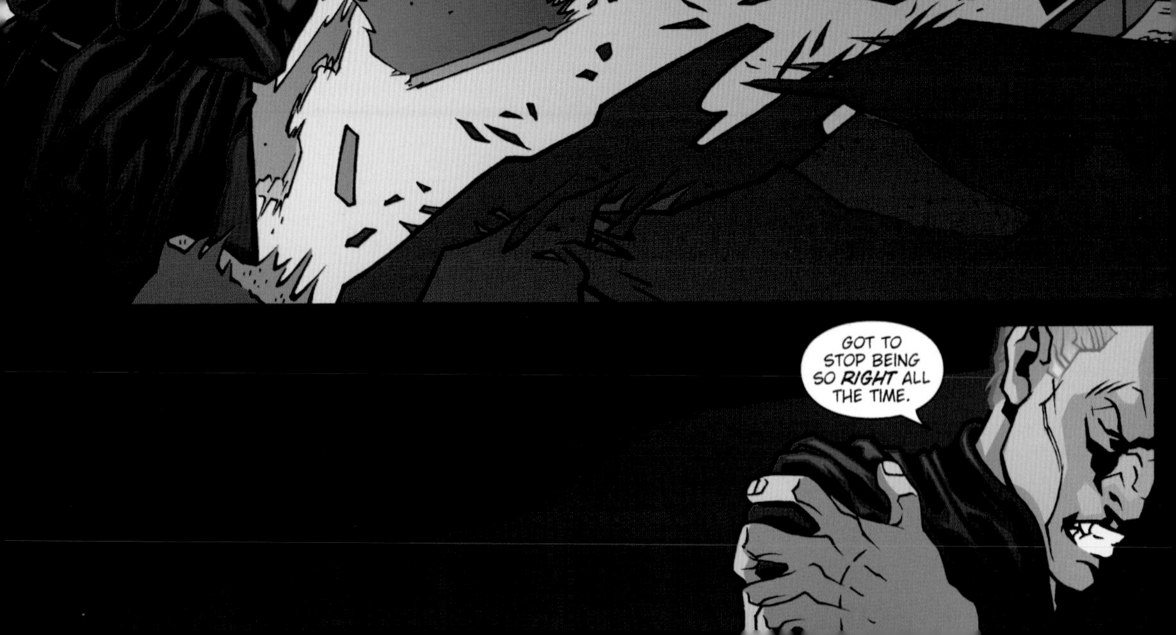
GOT TO STOP BEING SO ***RIGHT*** ALL THE TIME.

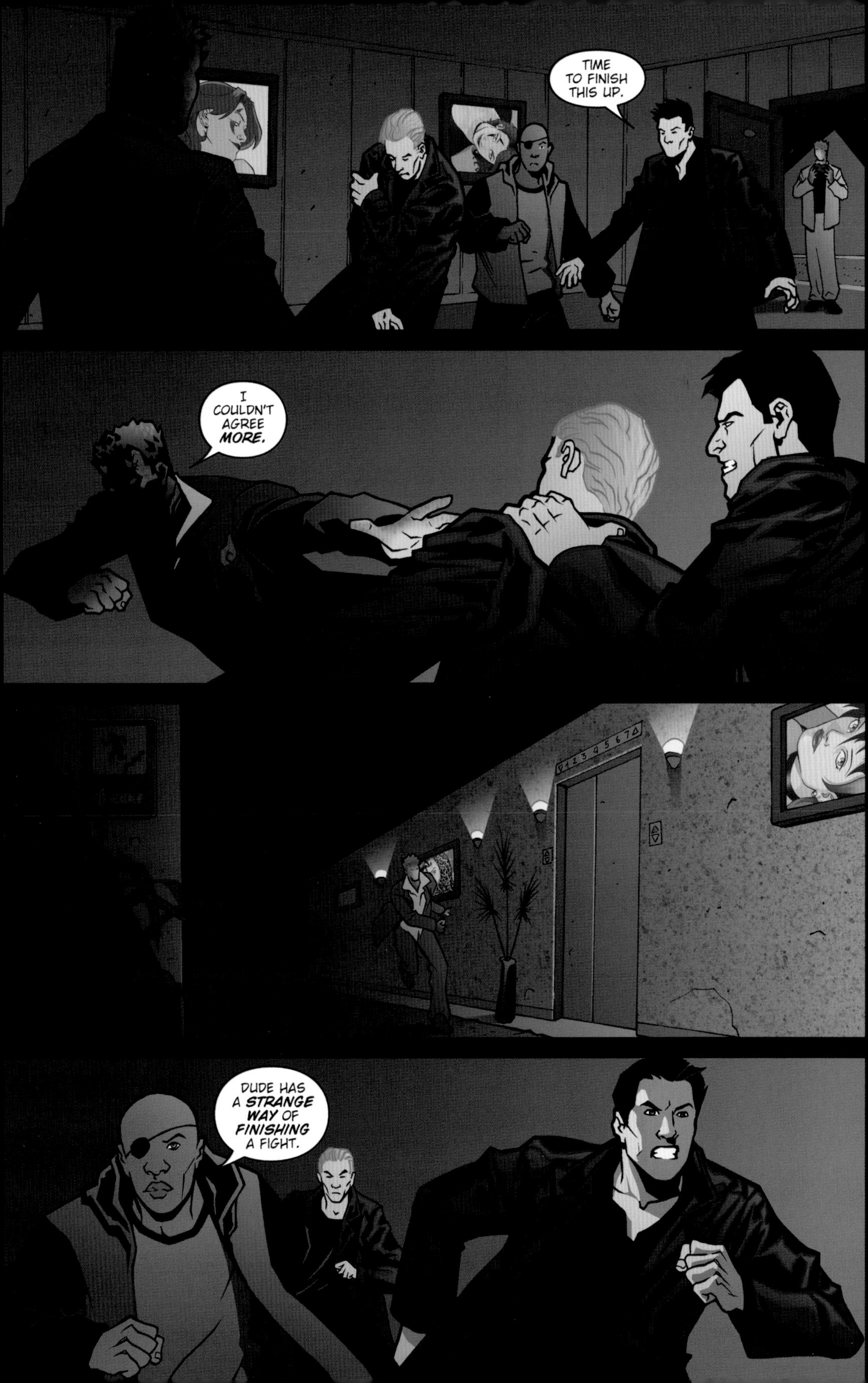
TIME TO FINISH THIS UP.
I COULDN'T AGREE MORE.
DUDE HAS A STRANGE WAY OF FINISHING A FIGHT.

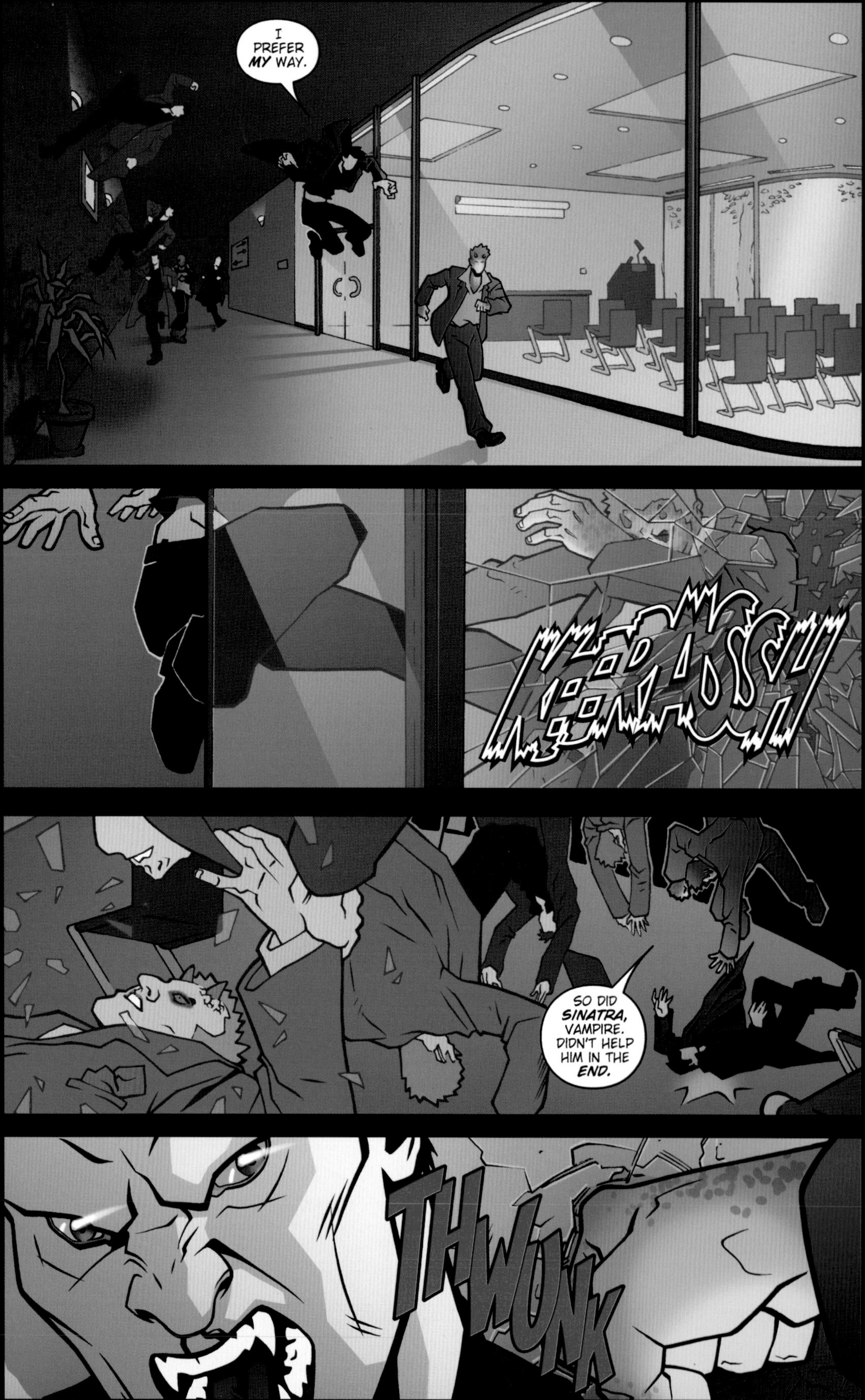

I PREFER MY WAY.
KERASCH
SO DID SINATRA, VAMPIRE. DIDN'T HELP HIM IN THE END.
THWUNK

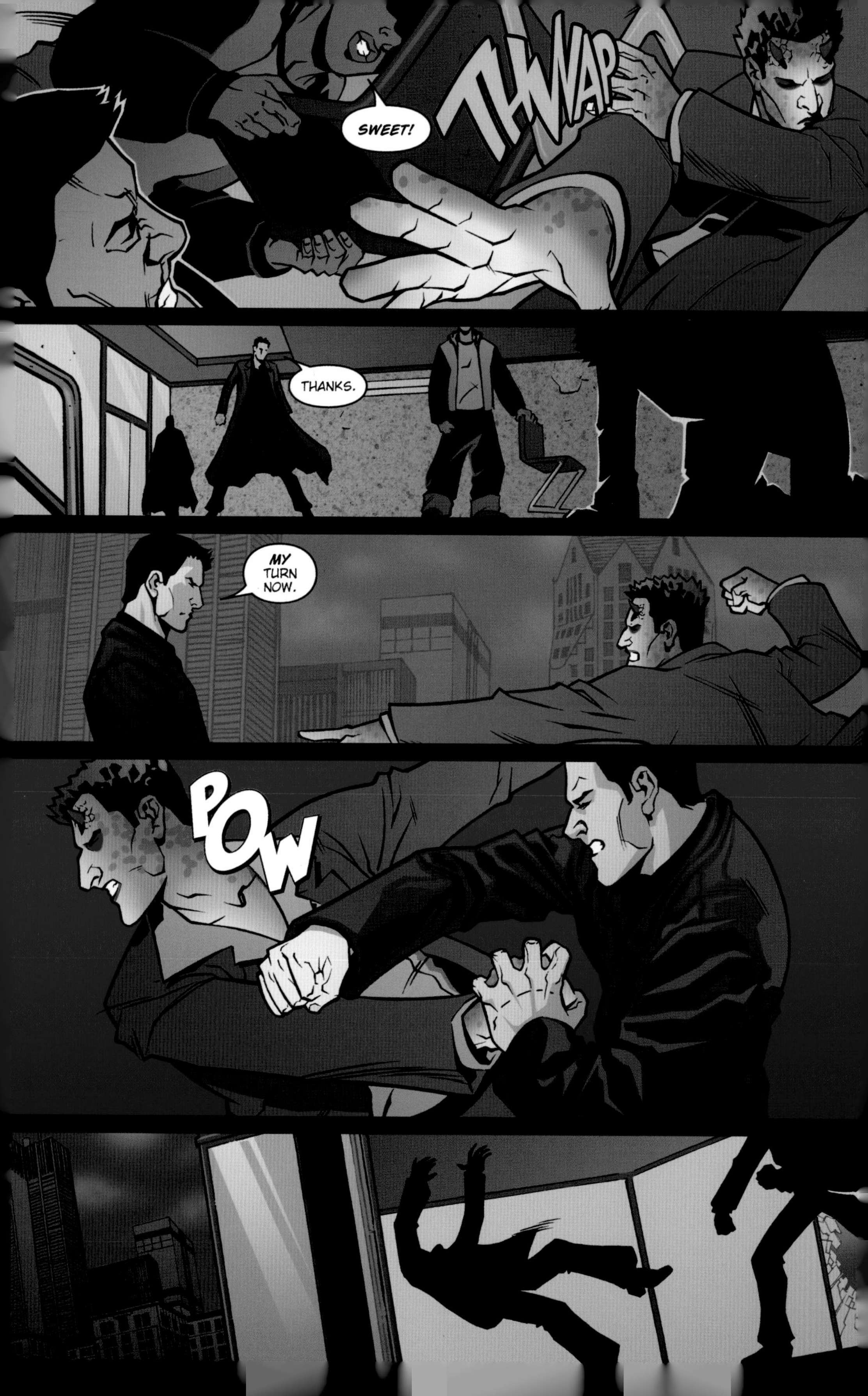
SWEET!
THWAP
THANKS.
MY TURN NOW.
POW

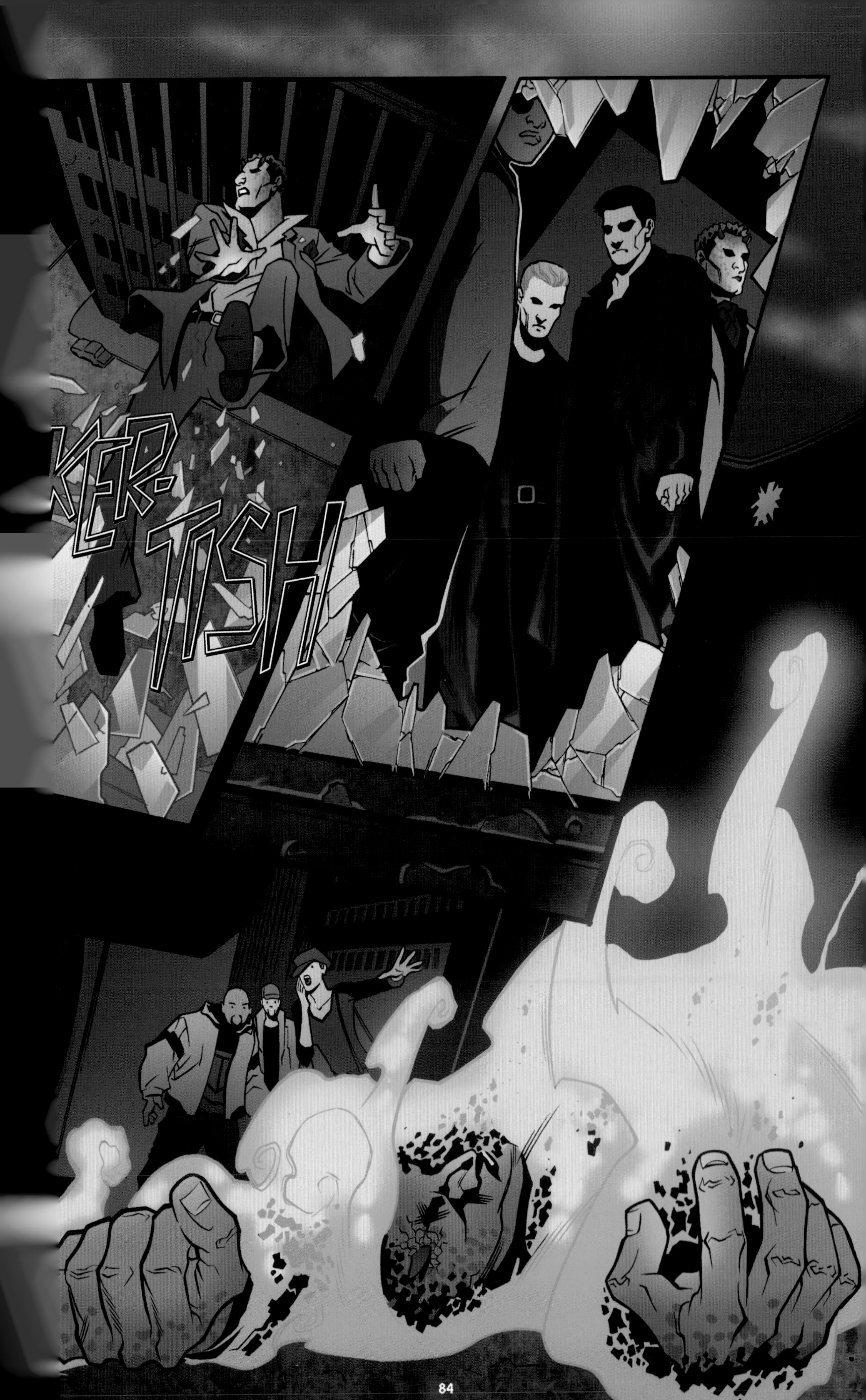
KER-TISH

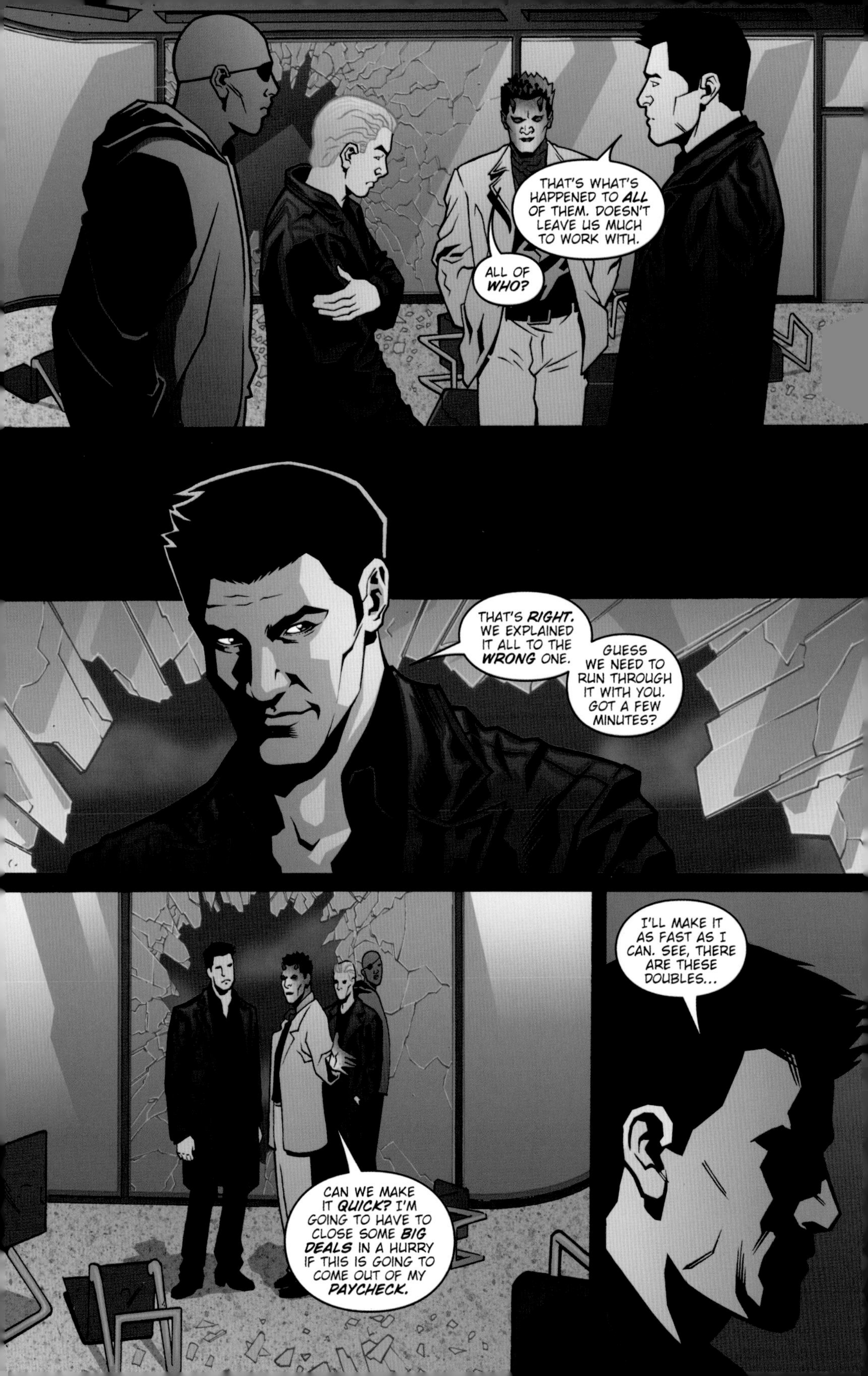
THAT'S WHAT'S HAPPENED TO ALL OF THEM. DOESN'T LEAVE US MUCH TO WORK WITH.
ALL OF WHO?
THAT'S RIGHT. WE EXPLAINED IT ALL TO THE WRONG ONE.
GUESS WE NEED TO RUN THROUGH IT WITH YOU. GOT A FEW MINUTES?
CAN WE MAKE IT QUICK? I'M GOING TO HAVE TO CLOSE SOME BIG DEALS IN A HURRY IF THIS IS GOING TO COME OUT OF MY PAYCHECK.
I'LL MAKE IT AS FAST AS I CAN. SEE, THERE ARE THESE DOUBLES...

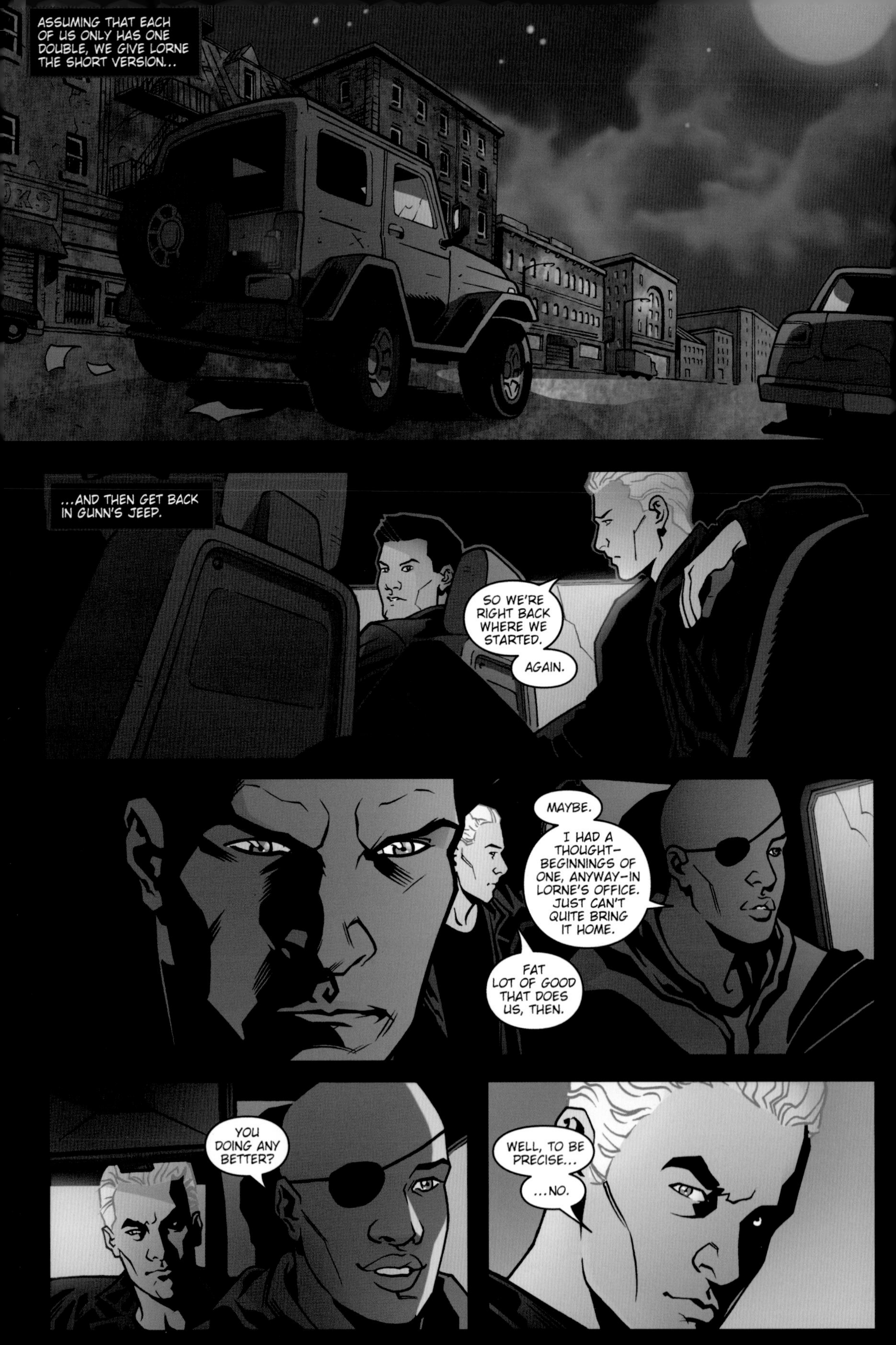
ASSUMING THAT EACH OF US ONLY HAS ONE DOUBLE, WE GIVE LORNE THE SHORT VERSION...
...AND THEN GET BACK IN GUNN'S JEEP.
SO WE'RE RIGHT BACK WHERE WE STARTED.
AGAIN.
MAYBE.
I HAD A THOUGHT--BEGINNINGS OF ONE, ANYWAY--IN LORNE'S OFFICE. JUST CAN'T QUITE BRING IT HOME.
FAT LOT OF GOOD THAT DOES US, THEN.
YOU DOING ANY BETTER?
WELL, TO BE PRECISE...
...NO.

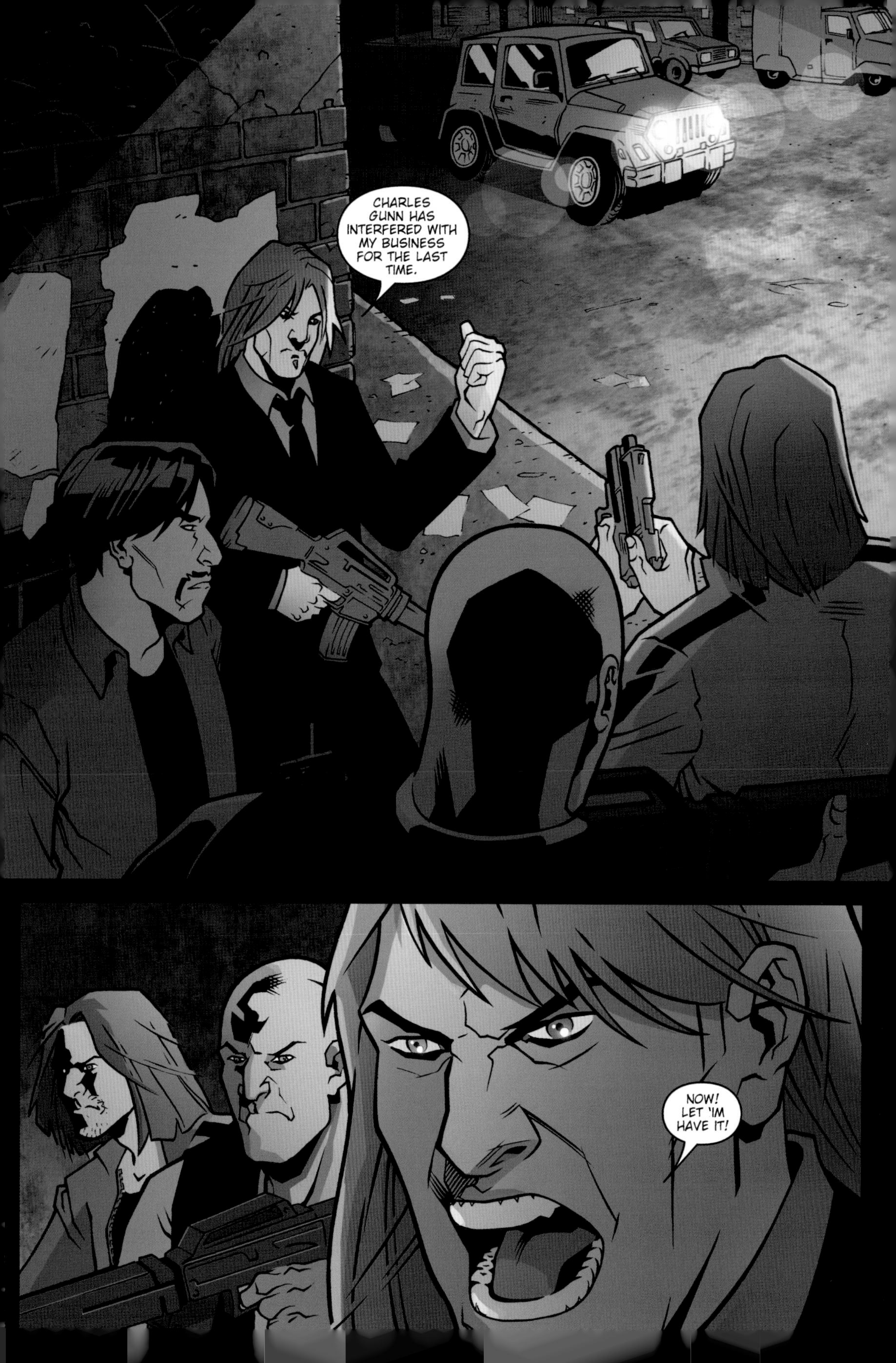
CHARLES GUNN HAS INTERFERED WITH MY BUSINESS FOR THE LAST TIME.
NOW! LET 'IM HAVE IT!

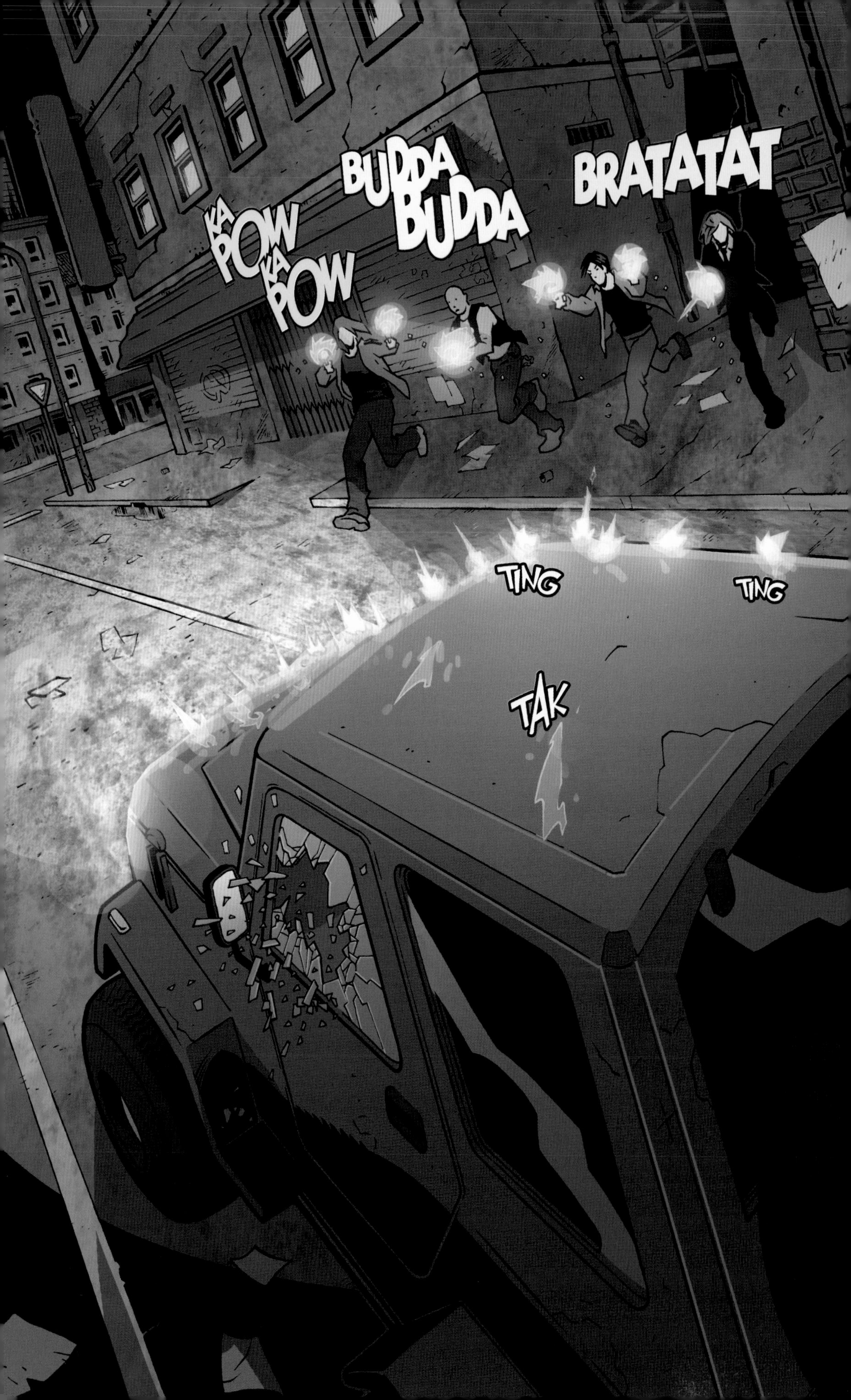
KA POW KA POW
BUDDA BUDDA
BRATATAT
TING
TING
TAK

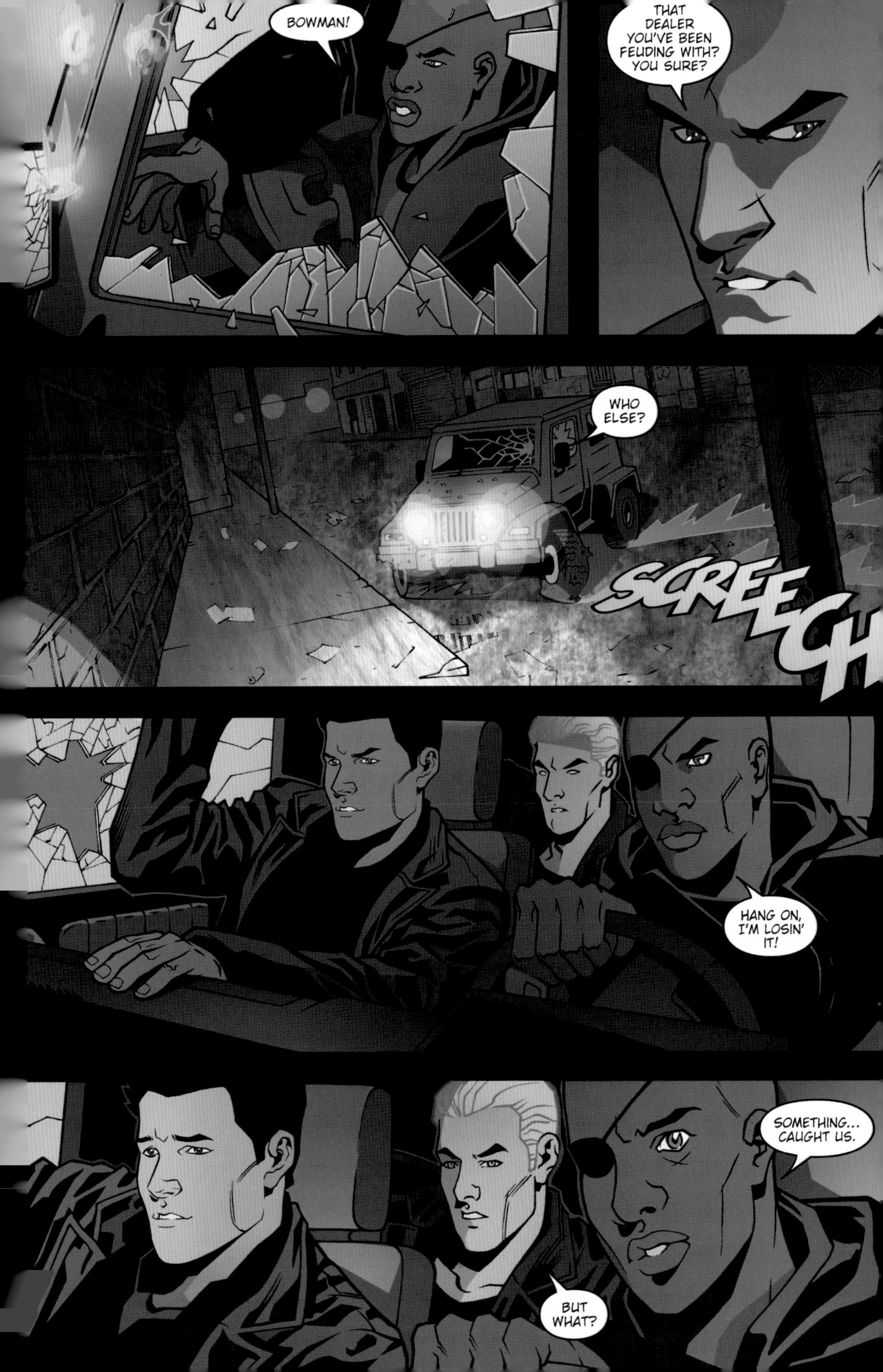
BOWMAN!
THAT DEALER YOU'VE BEEN FEUDING WITH? YOU SURE?
WHO ELSE?
SCREECH
HANG ON, I'M LOSIN' IT!
SOMETHING... CAUGHT US.
BUT WHAT?

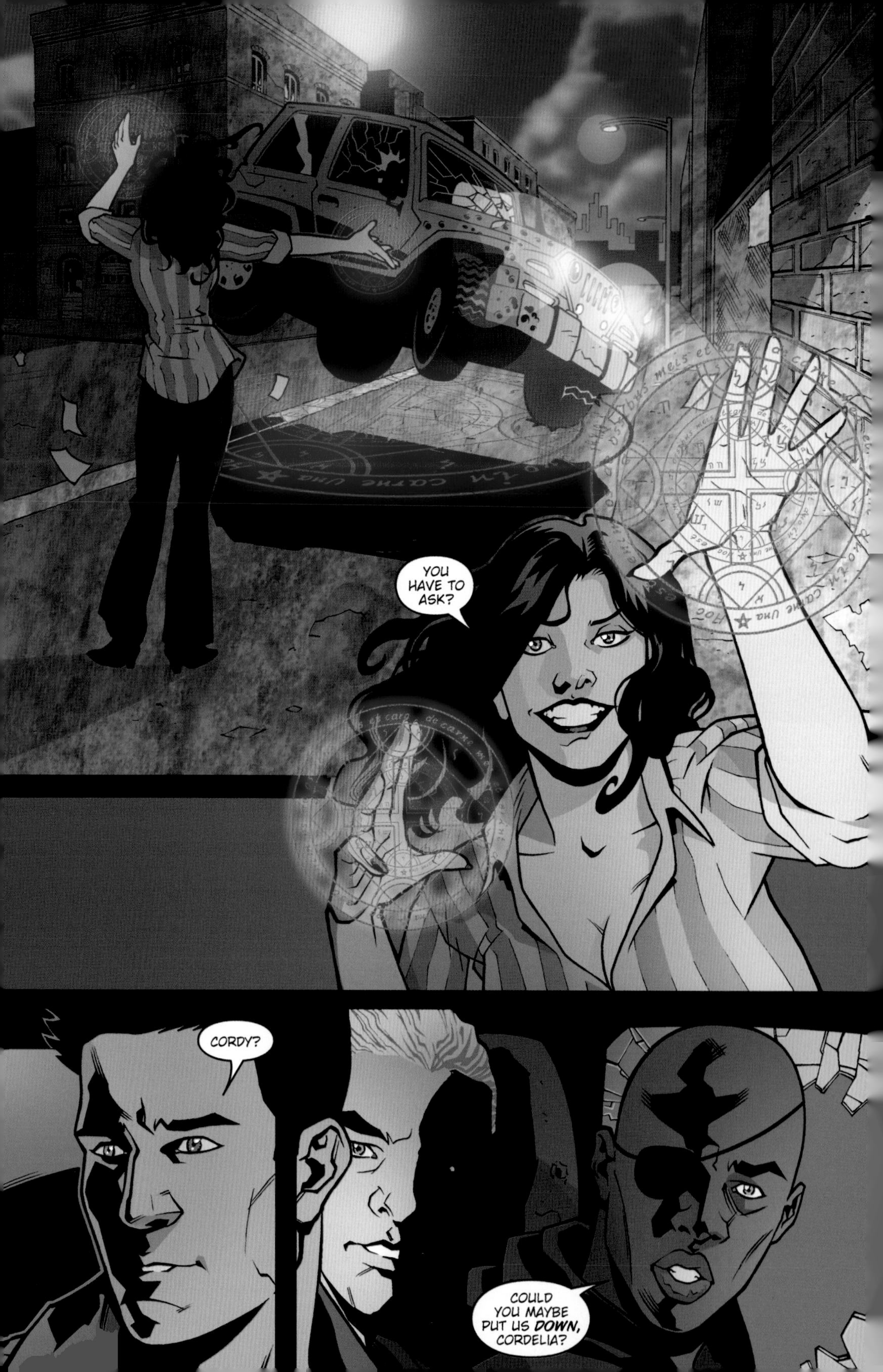

YOU HAVE TO ASK?
CORDY?
COULD YOU MAYBE PUT US *DOWN*, CORDELIA?

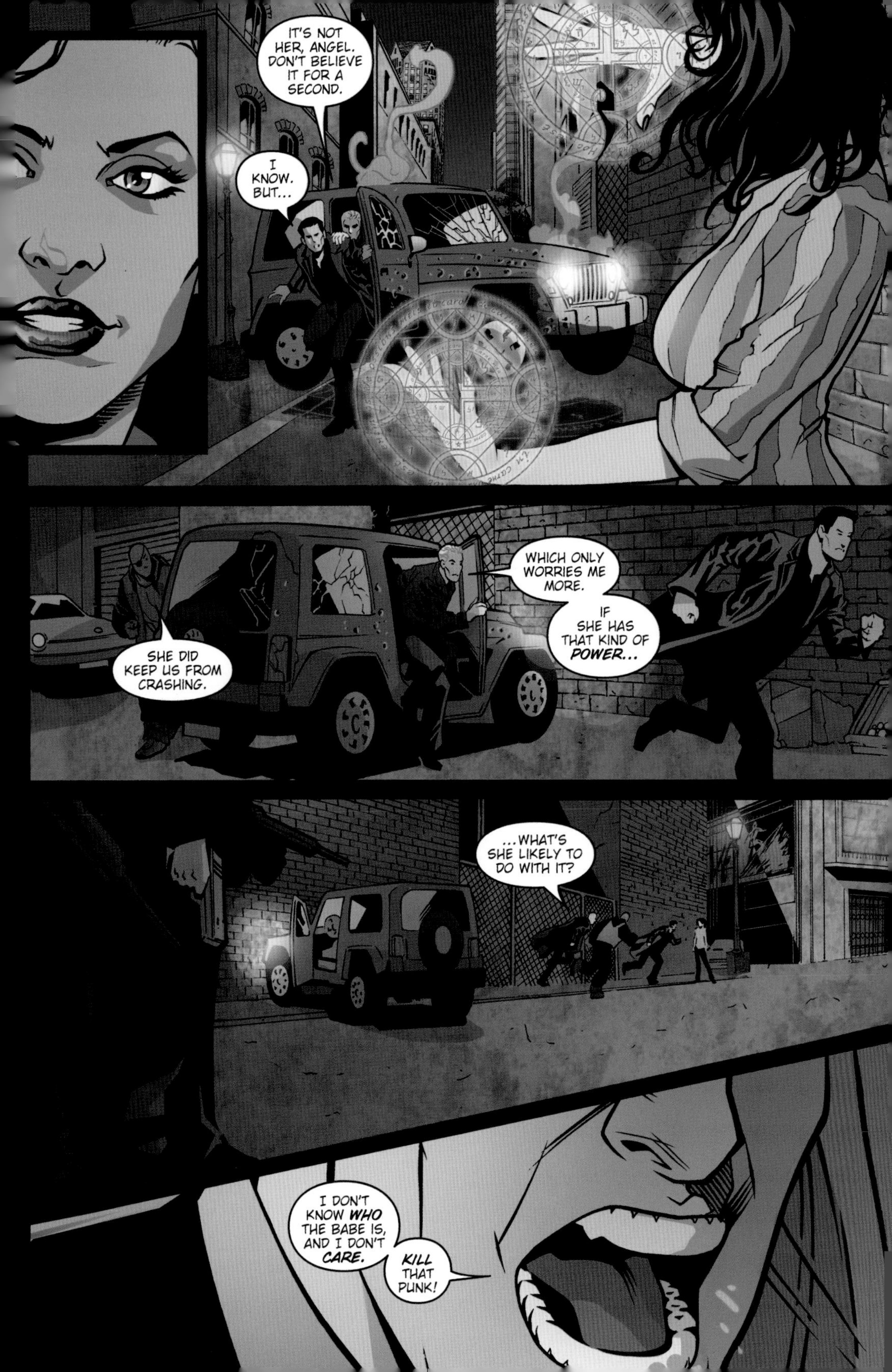
IT'S NOT HER, ANGEL. DON'T BELIEVE IT FOR A SECOND.
I KNOW. BUT...
WHICH ONLY WORRIES ME MORE.
SHE DID KEEP US FROM CRASHING.
IF SHE HAS THAT KIND OF POWER...
...WHAT'S SHE LIKELY TO DO WITH IT?
I DON'T KNOW WHO THE BABE IS, AND I DON'T CARE.
KILL THAT PUNK!

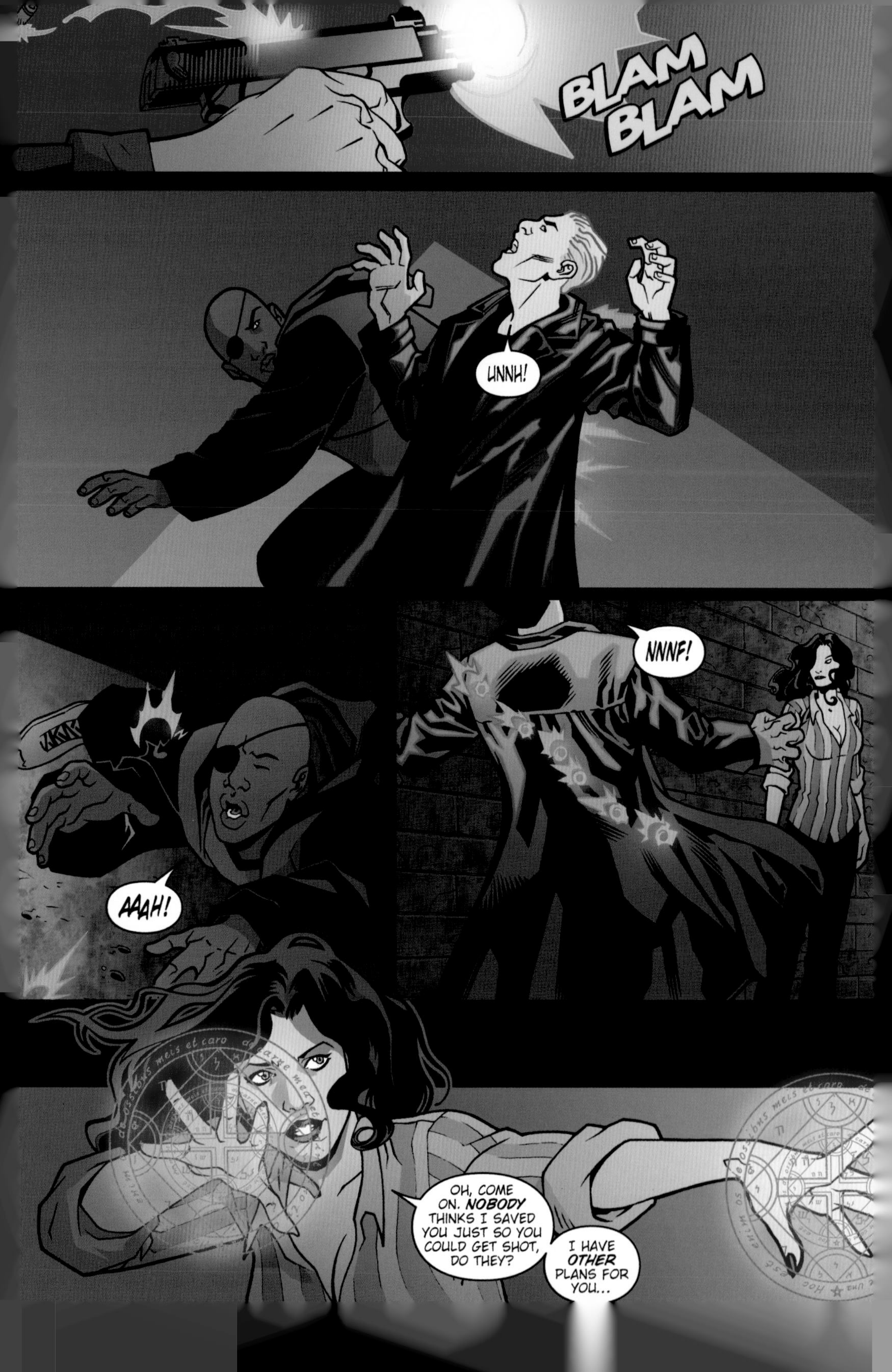
BLAM BLAM
UNNH!
AAAH!
NNNF!
OH, COME ON. **NOBODY** THINKS I SAVED YOU JUST SO YOU COULD GET SHOT, DO THEY?
I HAVE ***OTHER*** PLANS FOR YOU...

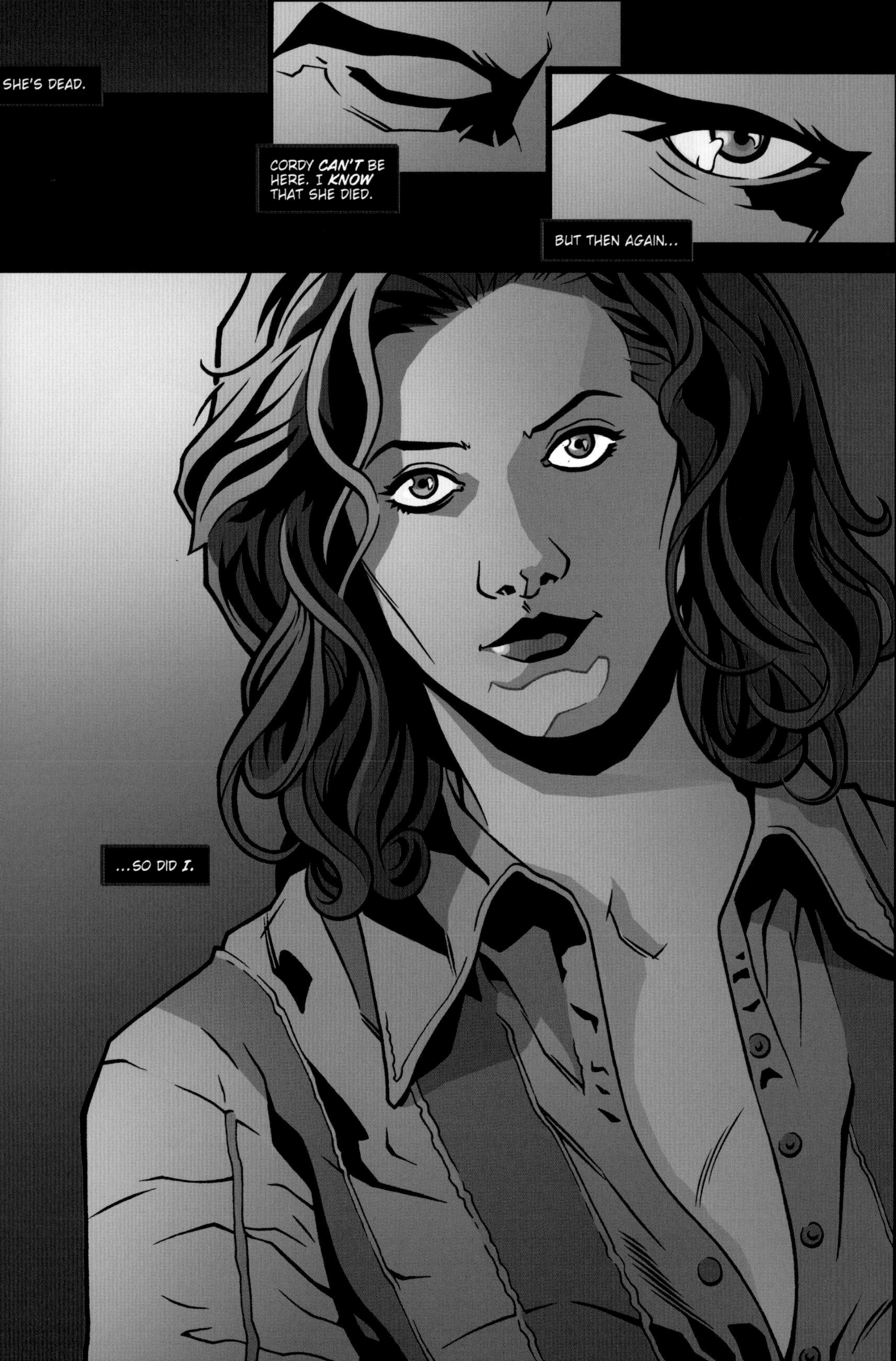
SHE'S DEAD.
CORDY *CAN'T* BE HERE. I *KNOW* THAT SHE DIED.
BUT THEN AGAIN...
...SO DID *I*.

ANGEL...

LET'S JUST DEAL WITH *THIS* LITTLE DISTRACTION FIRST.

YAAAGHH!

AAAIEE!

BOSS, THIS AIN'T—AAAARRH!

THAT'S *NOT* CORDELIA, Y'BIG SOT!

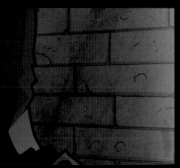

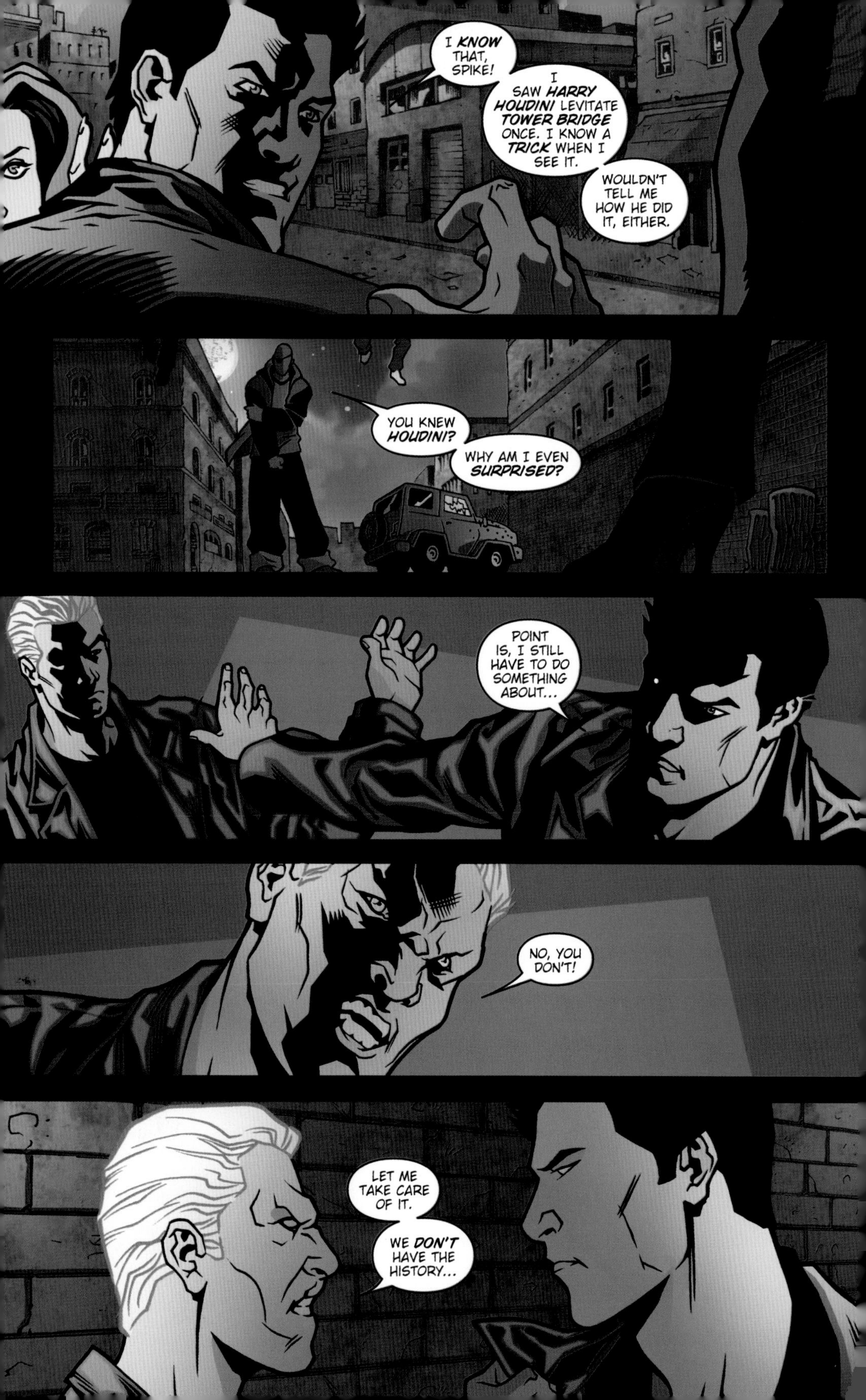
I KNOW THAT, SPIKE!
I SAW HARRY HOUDINI LEVITATE TOWER BRIDGE ONCE. I KNOW A TRICK WHEN I SEE IT.
WOULDN'T TELL ME HOW HE DID IT, EITHER.
YOU KNEW HOUDINI?
WHY AM I EVEN SURPRISED?
POINT IS, I STILL HAVE TO DO SOMETHING ABOUT...
NO, YOU DON'T!
LET ME TAKE CARE OF IT.
WE DON'T HAVE THE HISTORY...

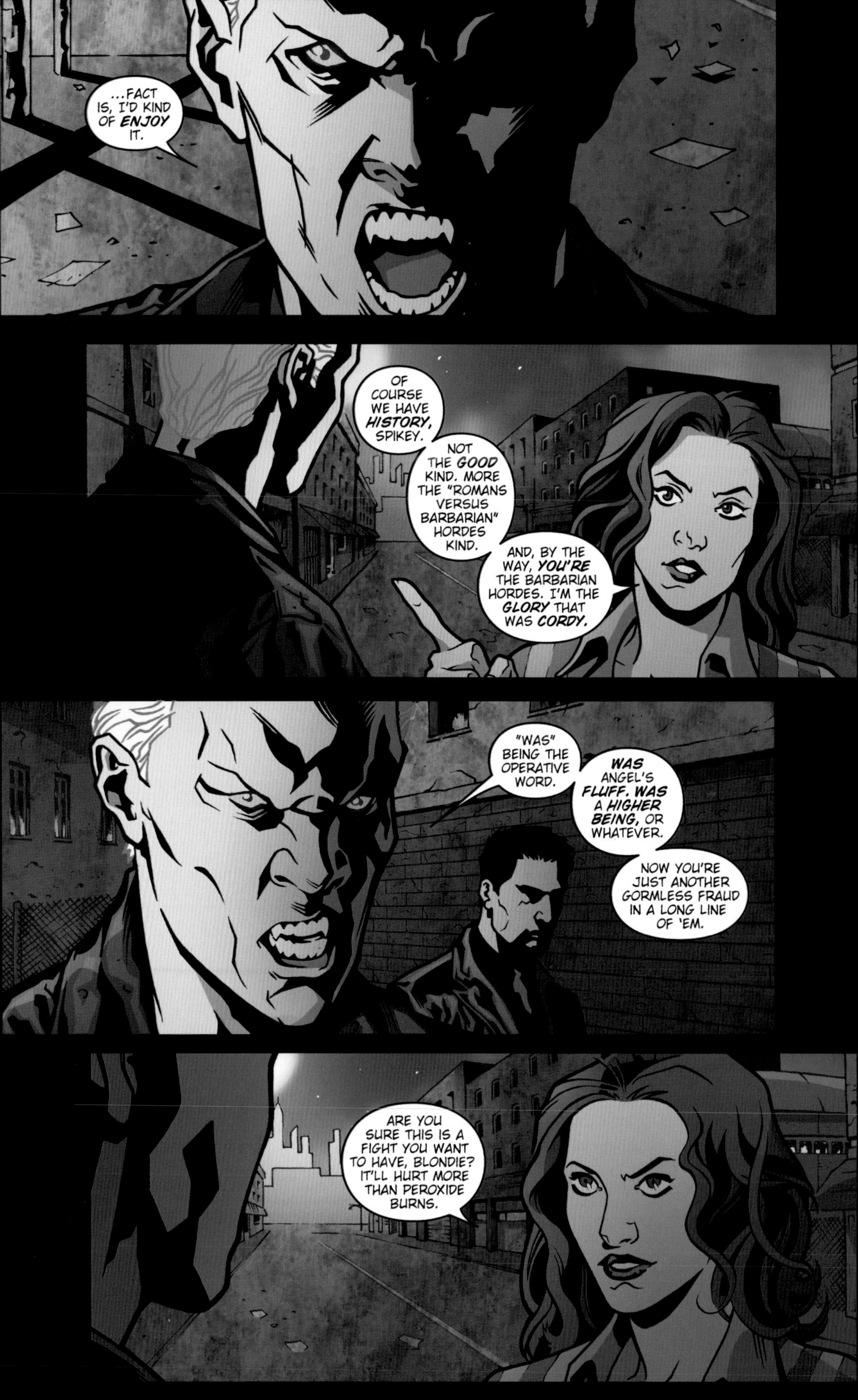
...FACT IS, I'D KIND OF ENJOY IT.
OF COURSE WE HAVE HISTORY, SPIKEY.
NOT THE GOOD KIND. MORE THE "ROMANS VERSUS BARBARIAN" HORDES KIND.
AND, BY THE WAY, YOU'RE THE BARBARIAN HORDES. I'M THE GLORY THAT WAS CORDY.
"WAS" BEING THE OPERATIVE WORD.
WAS ANGEL'S FLUFF. WAS A HIGHER BEING, OR WHATEVER.
NOW YOU'RE JUST ANOTHER GORMLESS FRAUD IN A LONG LINE OF 'EM.
ARE YOU SURE THIS IS A FIGHT YOU WANT TO HAVE, BLONDIE? IT'LL HURT MORE THAN PEROXIDE BURNS.

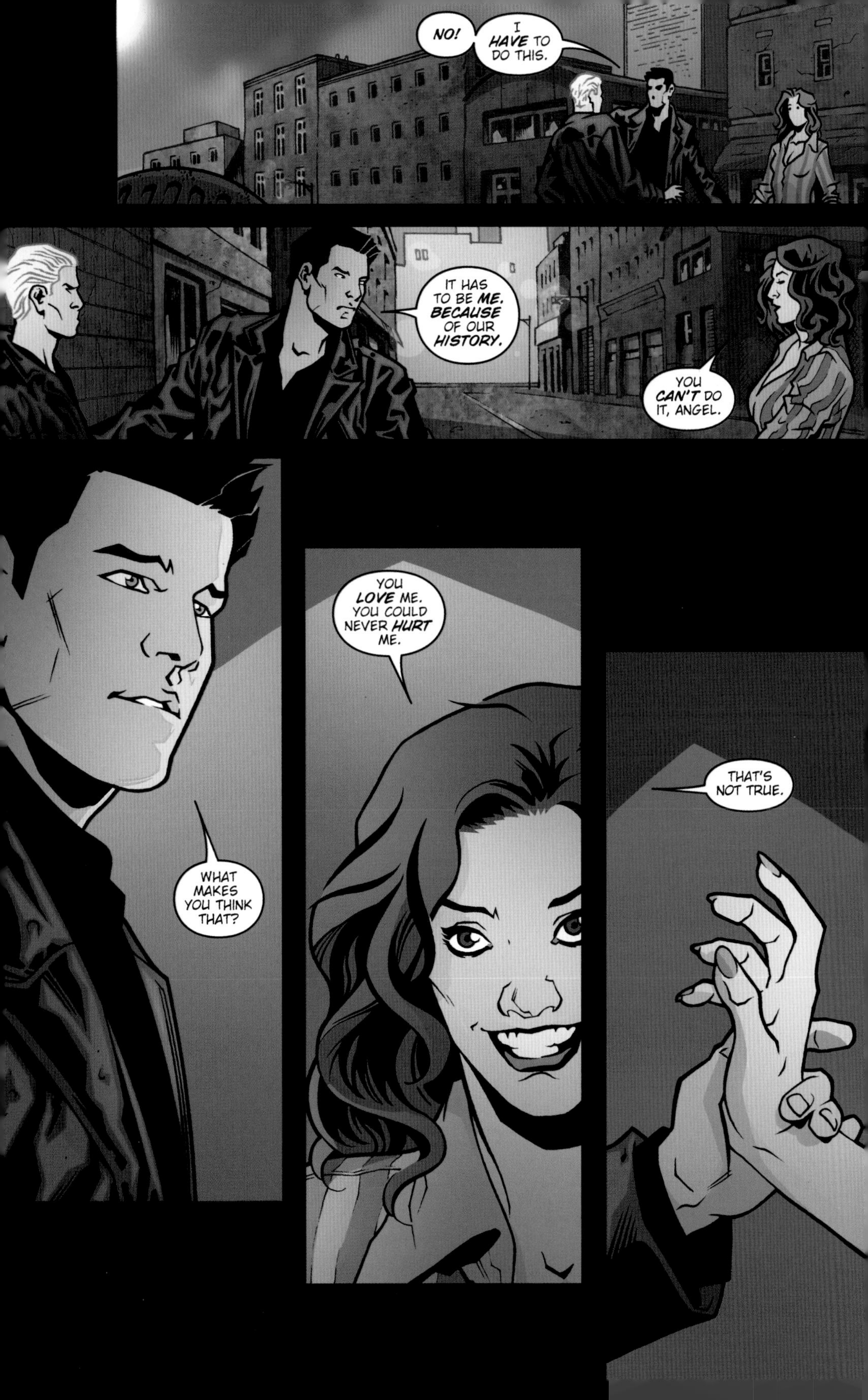
NO!
I HAVE TO DO THIS.
IT HAS TO BE ME. BECAUSE OF OUR HISTORY.
YOU CAN'T DO IT, ANGEL.
WHAT MAKES YOU THINK THAT?
YOU LOVE ME. YOU COULD NEVER HURT ME.
THAT'S NOT TRUE.

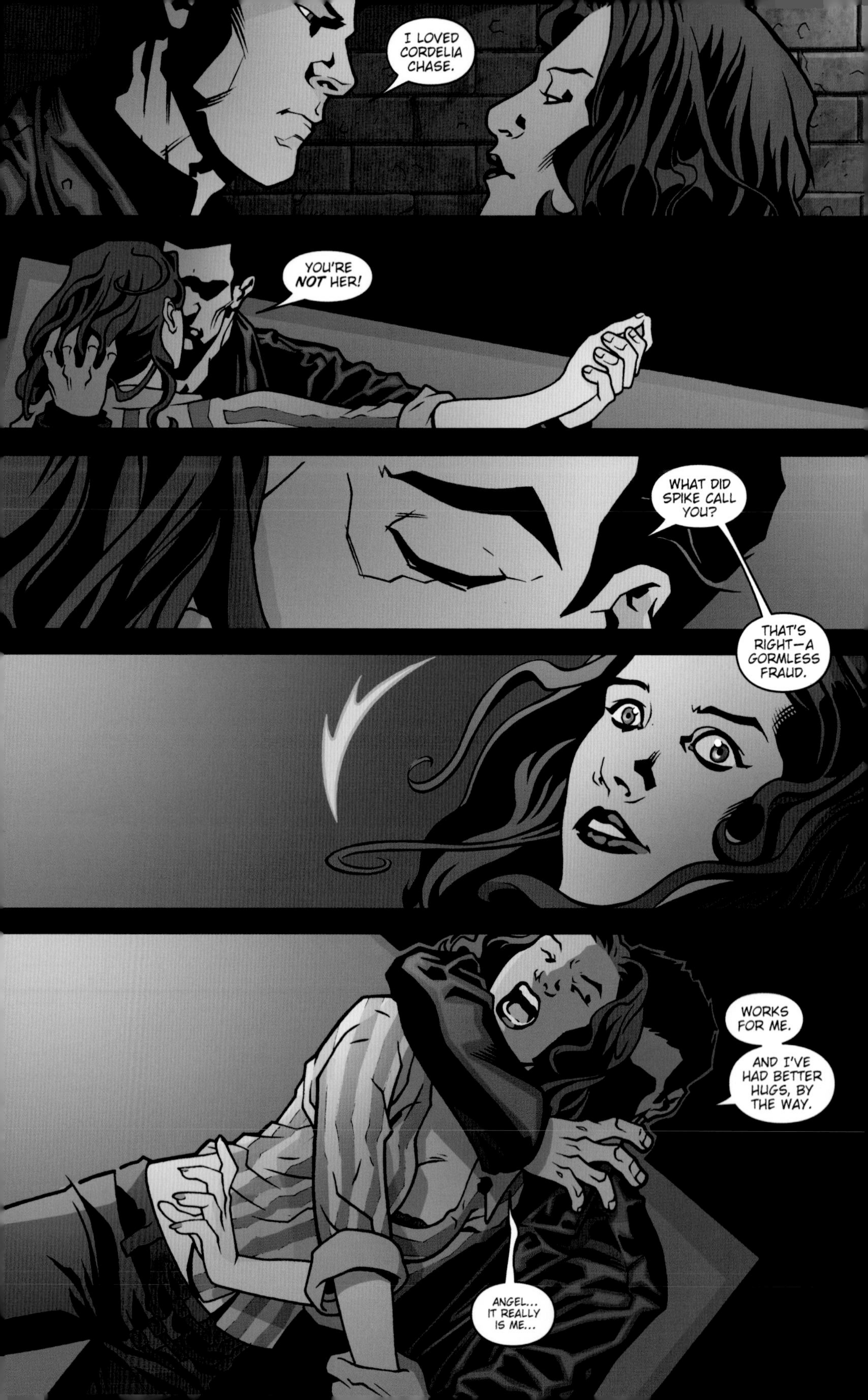
I LOVED CORDELIA CHASE.
YOU'RE **NOT** HER!
WHAT DID SPIKE CALL YOU?
THAT'S RIGHT—A GORMLESS FRAUD.
WORKS FOR ME.
AND I'VE HAD BETTER HUGS, BY THE WAY.
ANGEL... IT REALLY IS ME...

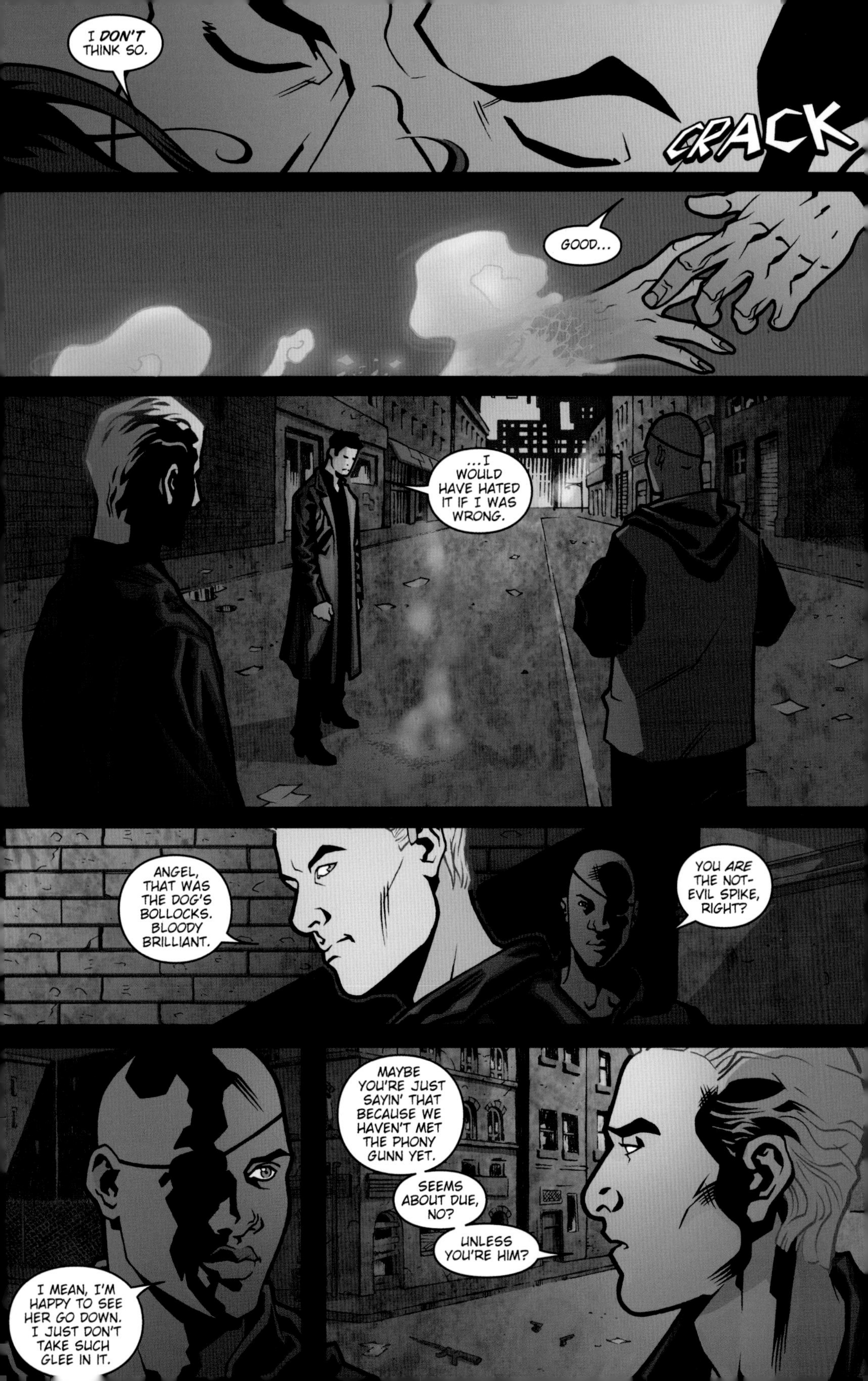
I DON'T THINK SO.
CRACK
GOOD...
...I WOULD HAVE HATED IT IF I WAS WRONG.
ANGEL, THAT WAS THE DOG'S BOLLOCKS. BLOODY BRILLIANT.
YOU ARE THE NOT-EVIL SPIKE, RIGHT?
MAYBE YOU'RE JUST SAYIN' THAT BECAUSE WE HAVEN'T MET THE PHONY GUNN YET.
SEEMS ABOUT DUE, NO?
UNLESS YOU'RE HIM?
I MEAN, I'M HAPPY TO SEE HER GO DOWN. I JUST DON'T TAKE SUCH GLEE IN IT.

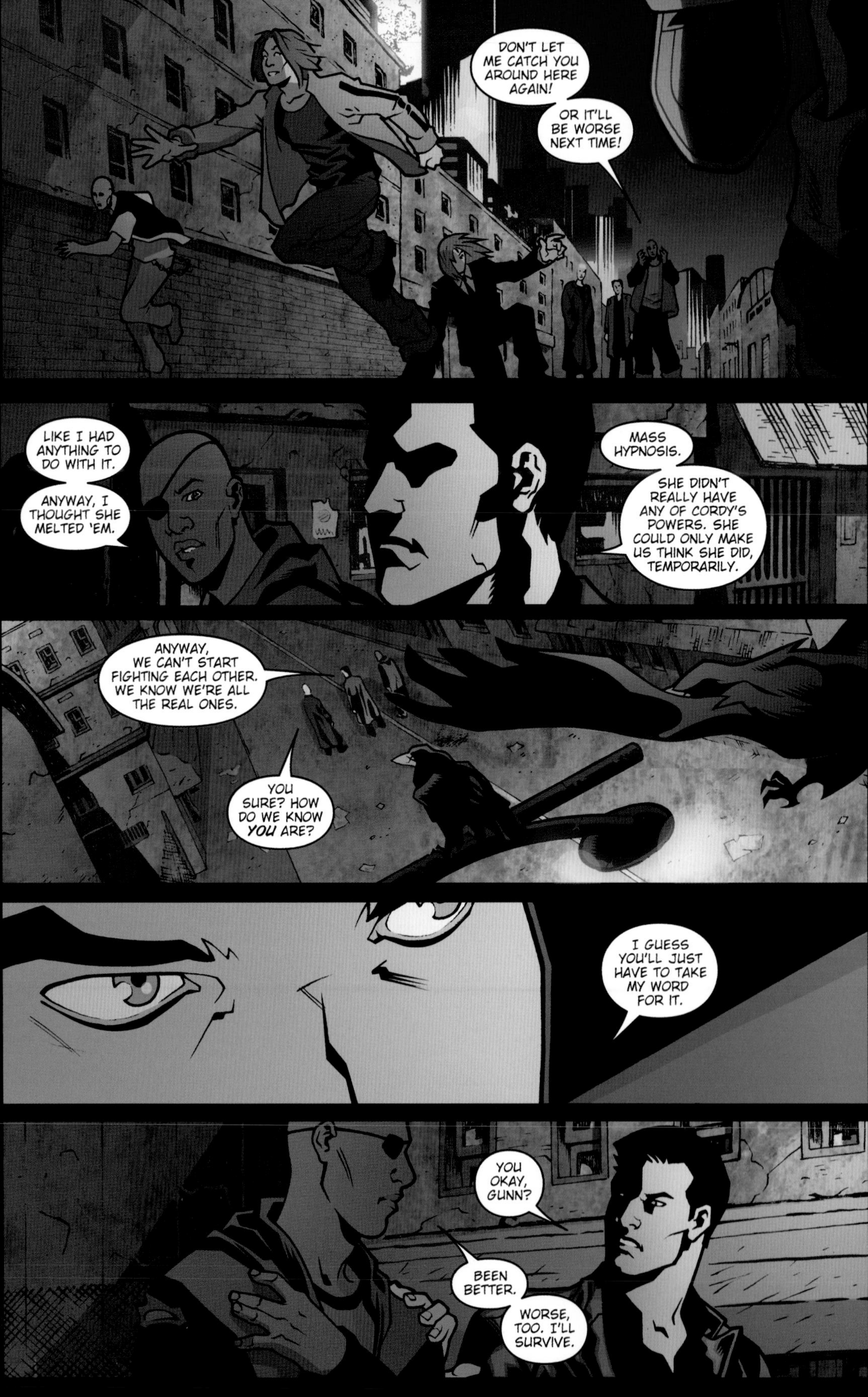
DON'T LET ME CATCH YOU AROUND HERE AGAIN!
OR IT'LL BE WORSE NEXT TIME!
LIKE I HAD ANYTHING TO DO WITH IT.
ANYWAY, I THOUGHT SHE MELTED 'EM.
MASS HYPNOSIS.
SHE DIDN'T REALLY HAVE ANY OF CORDY'S POWERS. SHE COULD ONLY MAKE US THINK SHE DID, TEMPORARILY.
ANYWAY, WE CAN'T START FIGHTING EACH OTHER. WE KNOW WE'RE ALL THE REAL ONES.
YOU SURE? HOW DO WE KNOW *YOU* ARE?
I GUESS YOU'LL JUST HAVE TO TAKE MY WORD FOR IT.
YOU OKAY, GUNN?
BEEN BETTER.
WORSE, TOO. I'LL SURVIVE.

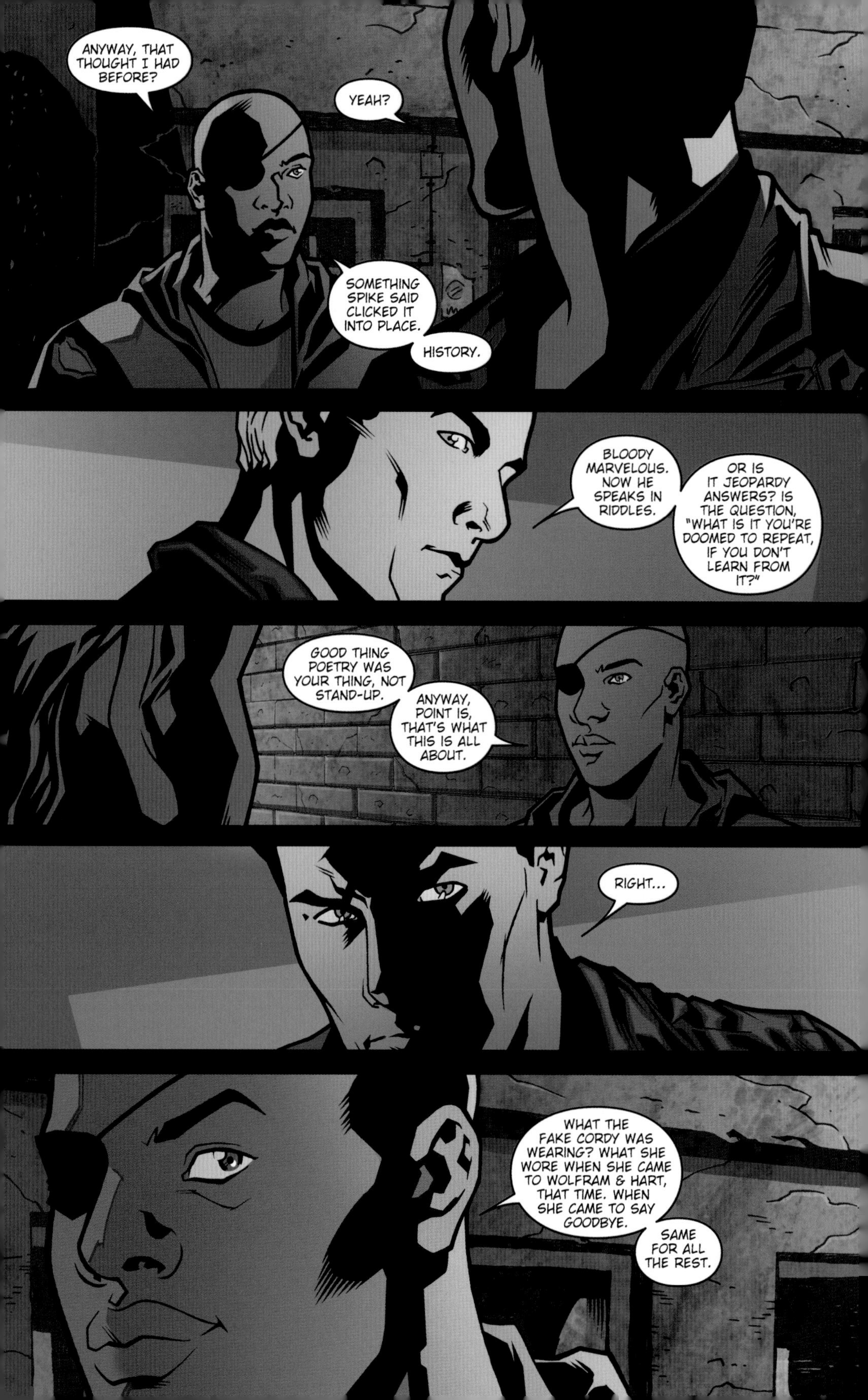
ANYWAY, THAT THOUGHT I HAD BEFORE?
YEAH?
SOMETHING SPIKE SAID CLICKED IT INTO PLACE.
HISTORY.
BLOODY MARVELOUS. NOW HE SPEAKS IN RIDDLES.
OR IS IT JEOPARDY ANSWERS? IS THE QUESTION, "WHAT IS IT YOU'RE DOOMED TO REPEAT, IF YOU DON'T LEARN FROM IT?"
GOOD THING POETRY WAS YOUR THING, NOT STAND-UP.
ANYWAY, POINT IS, THAT'S WHAT THIS IS ALL ABOUT.
RIGHT...
WHAT THE FAKE CORDY WAS WEARING? WHAT SHE WORE WHEN SHE CAME TO WOLFRAM & HART, THAT TIME. WHEN SHE CAME TO SAY GOODBYE.
SAME FOR ALL THE REST.

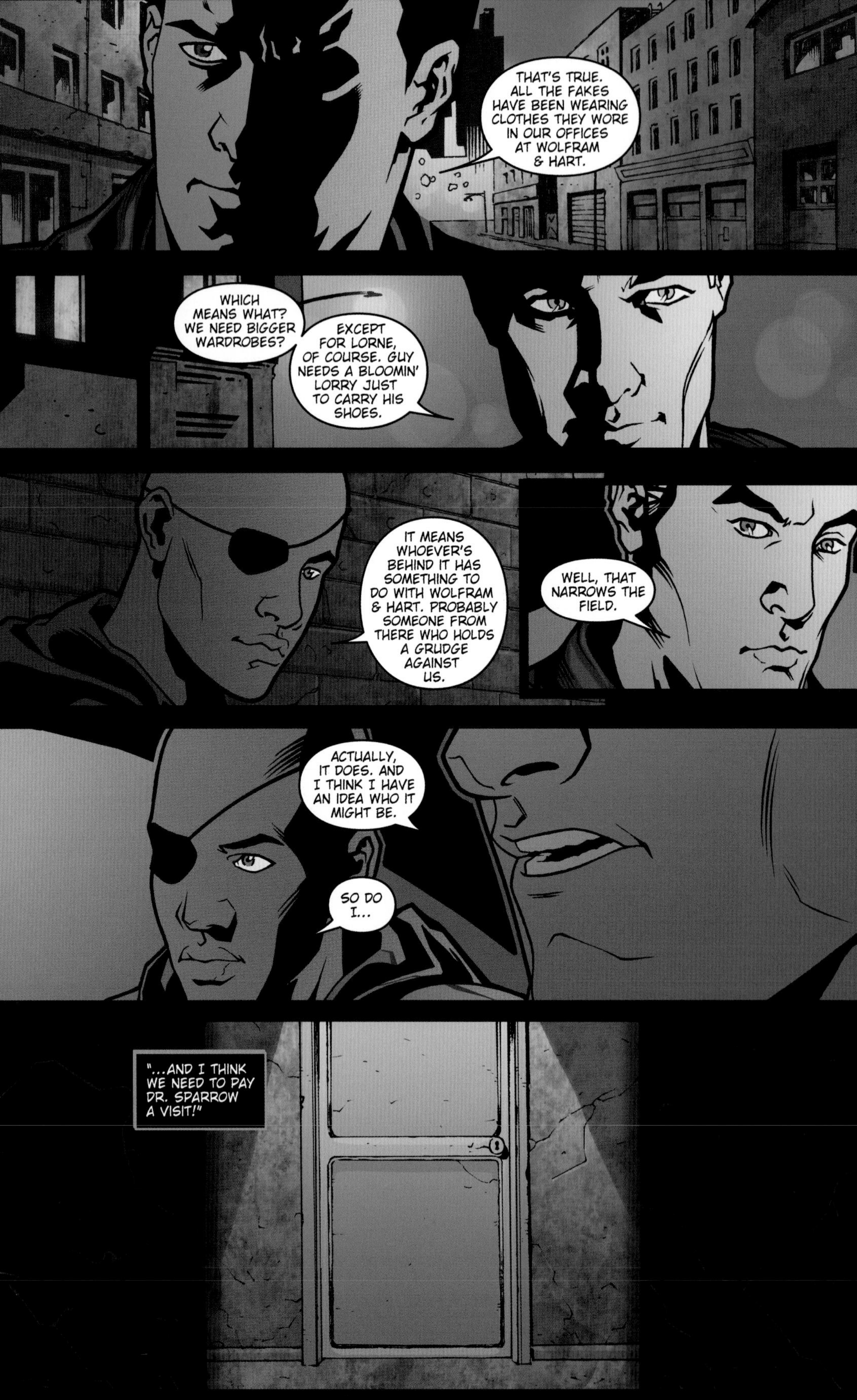
THAT'S TRUE. ALL THE FAKES HAVE BEEN WEARING CLOTHES THEY WORE IN OUR OFFICES AT WOLFRAM & HART.
WHICH MEANS WHAT? WE NEED BIGGER WARDROBES?
EXCEPT FOR LORNE, OF COURSE. GUY NEEDS A BLOOMIN' LORRY JUST TO CARRY HIS SHOES.
IT MEANS WHOEVER'S BEHIND IT HAS SOMETHING TO DO WITH WOLFRAM & HART. PROBABLY SOMEONE FROM THERE WHO HOLDS A GRUDGE AGAINST US.
WELL, THAT NARROWS THE FIELD.
ACTUALLY, IT DOES. AND I THINK I HAVE AN IDEA WHO IT MIGHT BE.
SO DO I...
"...AND I THINK WE NEED TO PAY DR. SPARROW A VISIT!"

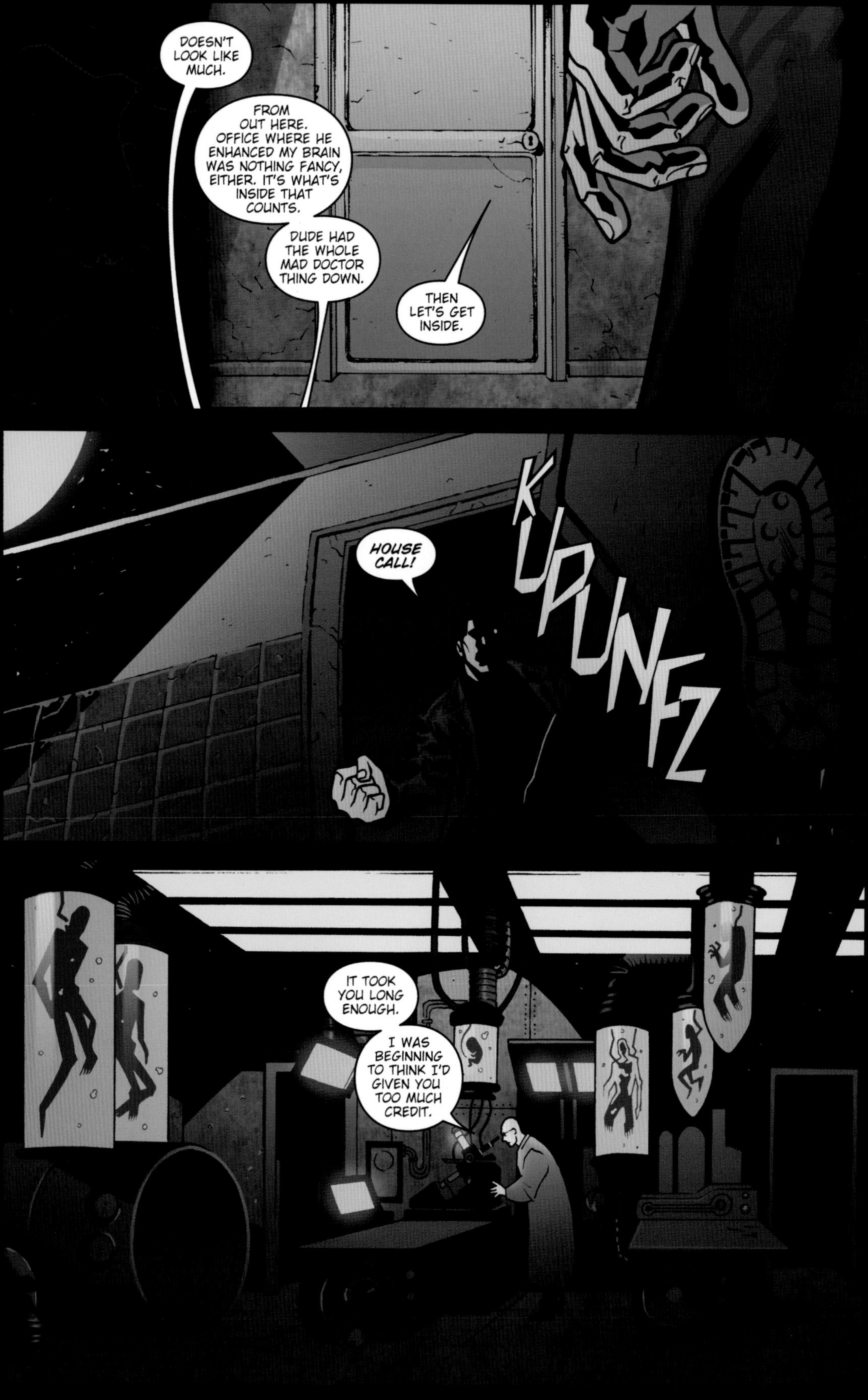
DOESN'T LOOK LIKE MUCH.
FROM OUT HERE. OFFICE WHERE HE ENHANCED MY BRAIN WAS NOTHING FANCY, EITHER. IT'S WHAT'S INSIDE THAT COUNTS.
DUDE HAD THE WHOLE MAD DOCTOR THING DOWN.
THEN LET'S GET INSIDE.
KUDUNFZ
HOUSE CALL!
IT TOOK YOU LONG ENOUGH.
I WAS BEGINNING TO THINK I'D GIVEN YOU TOO MUCH CREDIT.

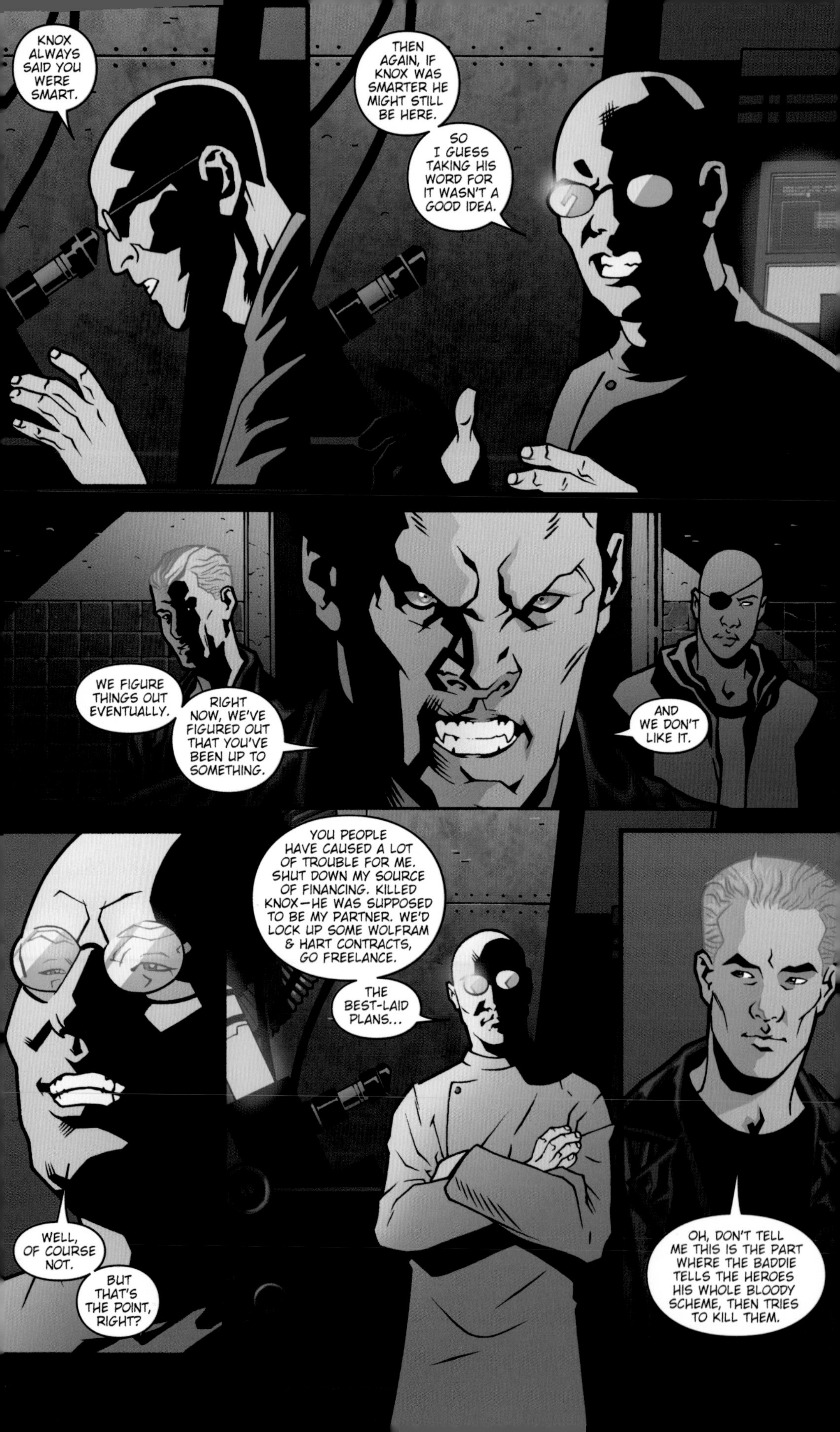
KNOX ALWAYS SAID YOU WERE SMART.
THEN AGAIN, IF KNOX WAS SMARTER HE MIGHT STILL BE HERE.
SO I GUESS TAKING HIS WORD FOR IT WASN'T A GOOD IDEA.
WE FIGURE THINGS OUT EVENTUALLY.
RIGHT NOW, WE'VE FIGURED OUT THAT YOU'VE BEEN UP TO SOMETHING.
AND WE DON'T LIKE IT.
WELL, OF COURSE NOT.
BUT THAT'S THE POINT, RIGHT?
YOU PEOPLE HAVE CAUSED A LOT OF TROUBLE FOR ME. SHUT DOWN MY SOURCE OF FINANCING. KILLED KNOX—HE WAS SUPPOSED TO BE MY PARTNER. WE'D LOCK UP SOME WOLFRAM & HART CONTRACTS, GO FREELANCE.
THE BEST-LAID PLANS...
OH, DON'T TELL ME THIS IS THE PART WHERE THE BADDIE TELLS THE HEROES HIS WHOLE BLOODY SCHEME, THEN TRIES TO KILL THEM.

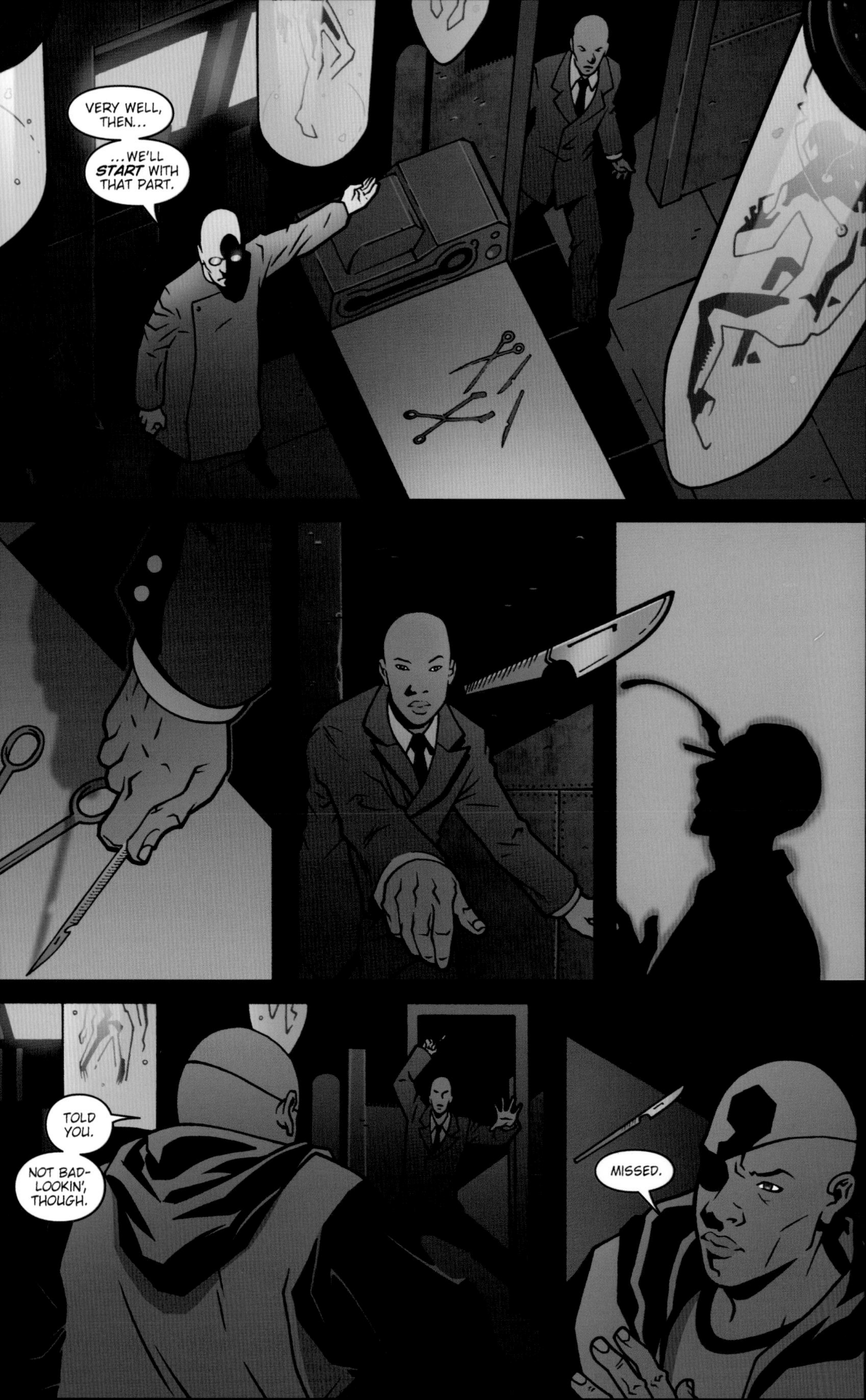
VERY WELL, THEN...
...WE'LL *START* WITH THAT PART.
TOLD YOU.
NOT BAD-LOOKIN', THOUGH.
MISSED.

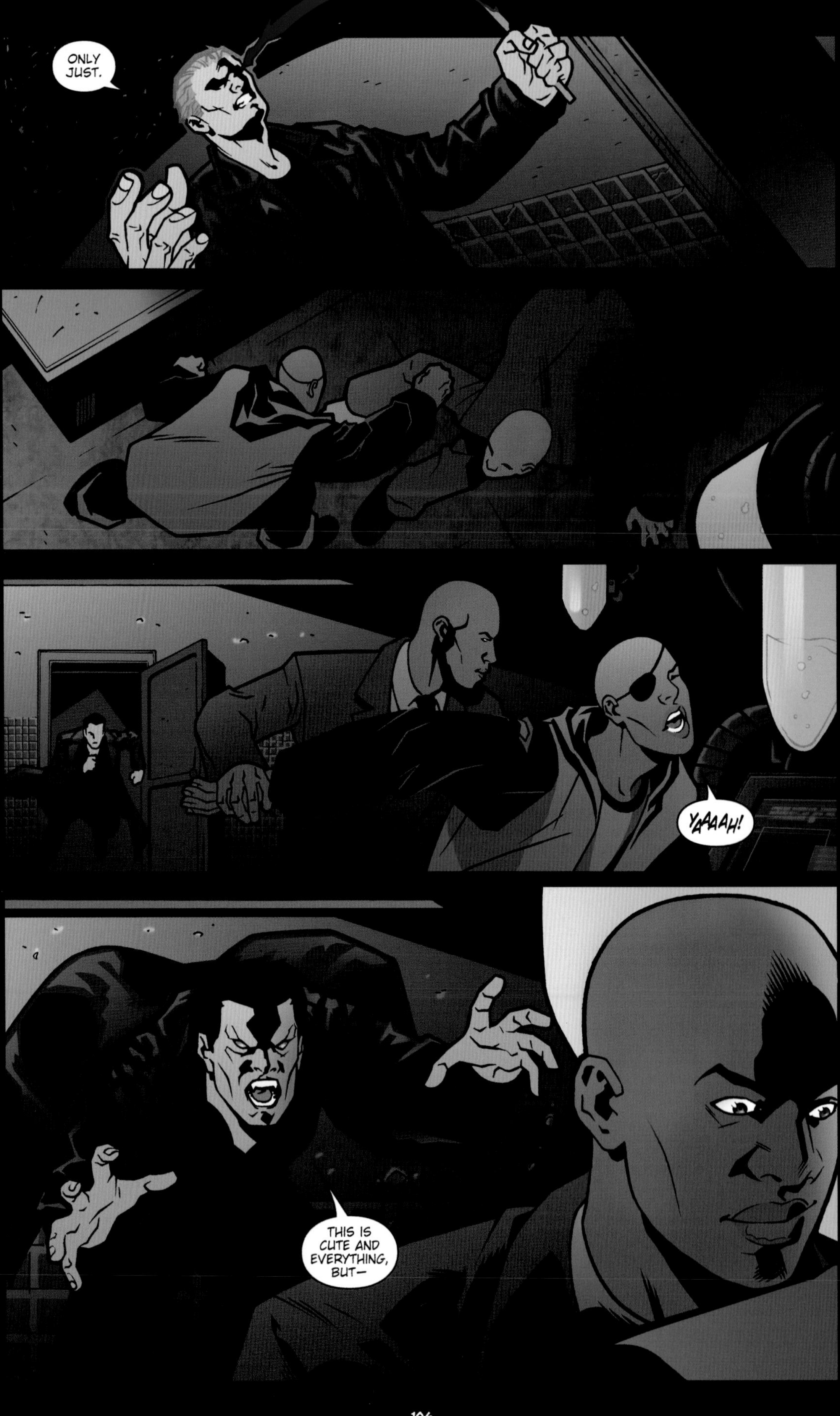
ONLY JUST.
YAAAAH!
THIS IS CUTE AND EVERYTHING, BUT—

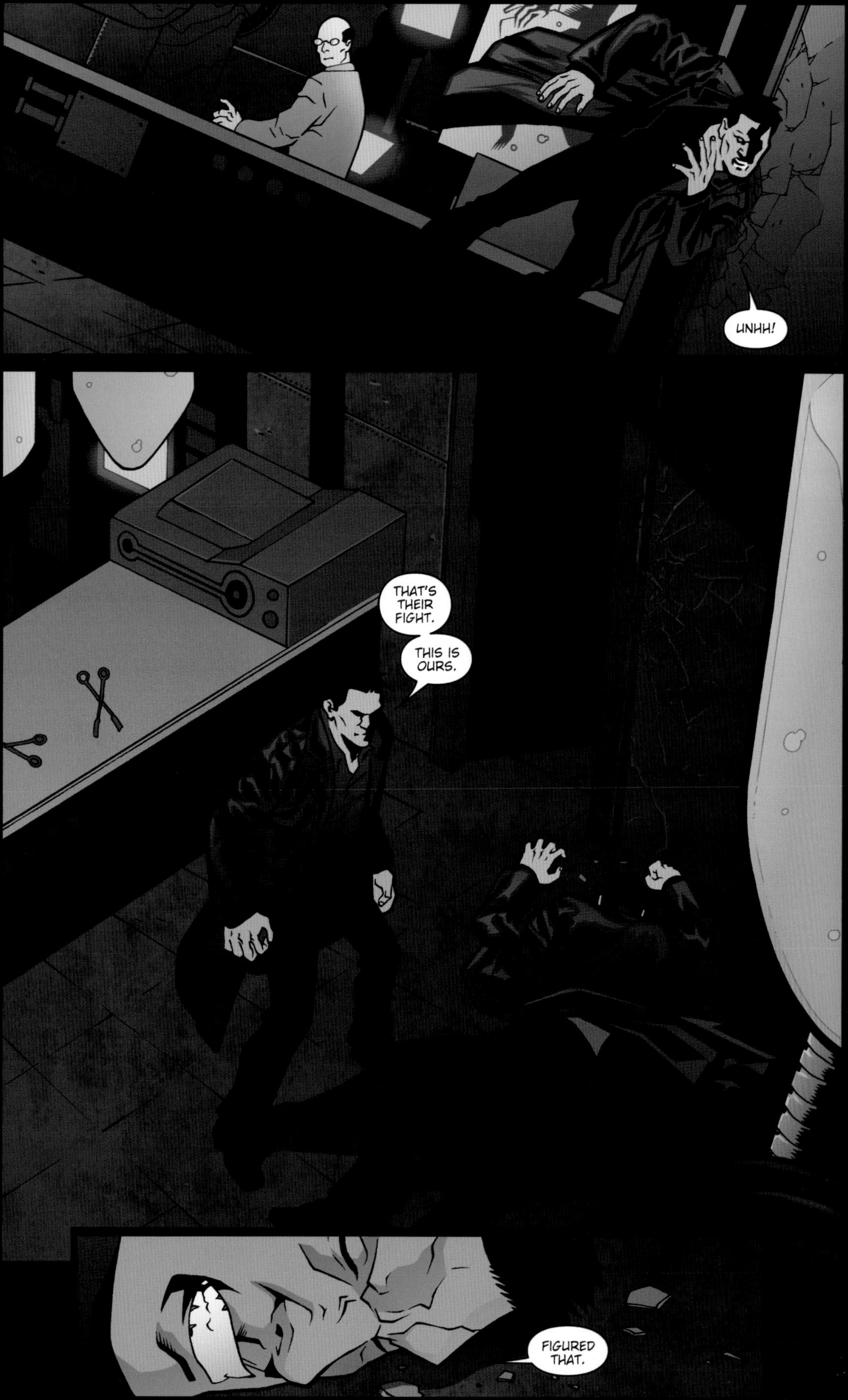
UNHH!
THAT'S THEIR FIGHT.
THIS IS OURS.
FIGURED THAT.

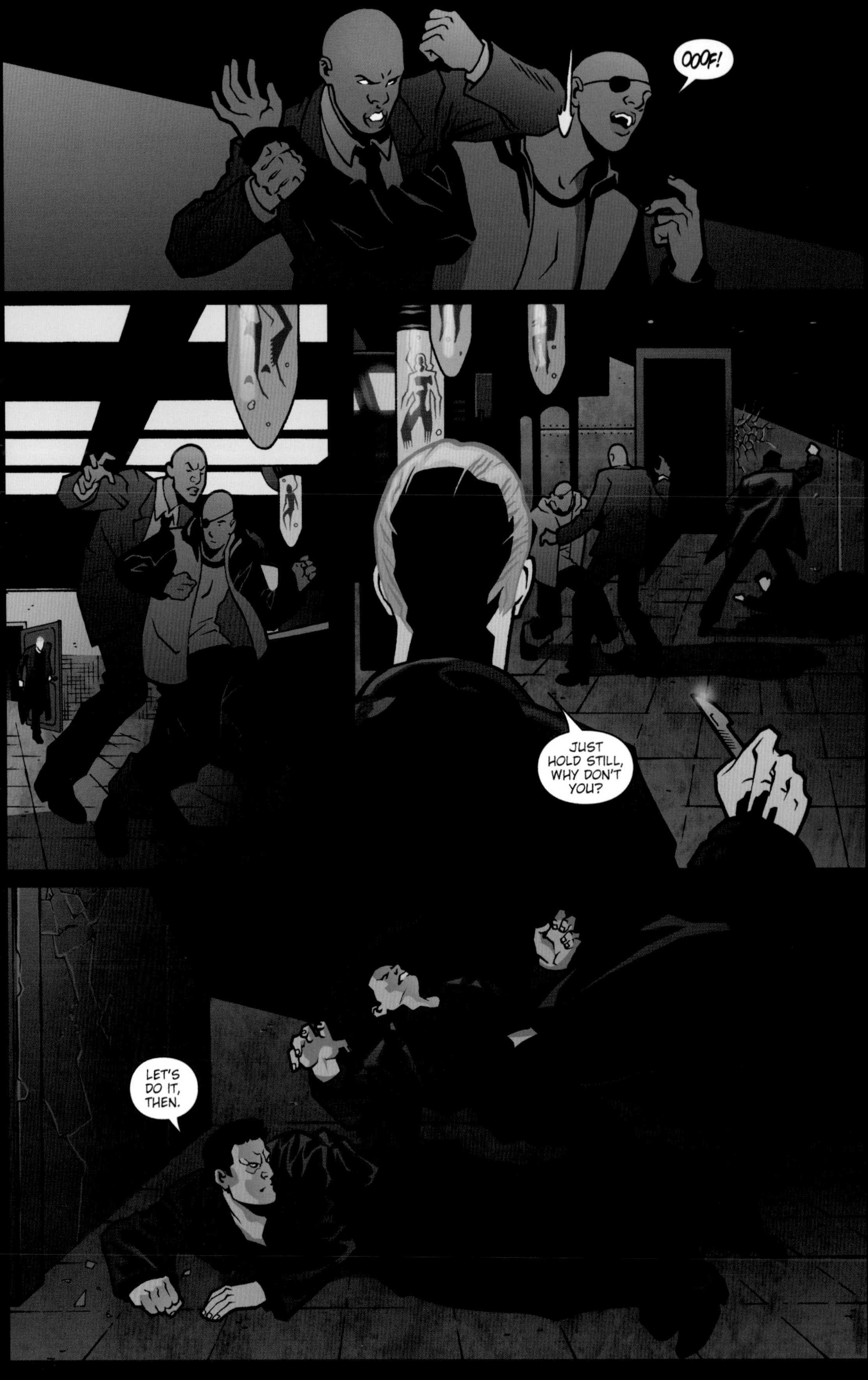
OOOF!
JUST HOLD STILL, WHY DON'T YOU?
LET'S DO IT, THEN.

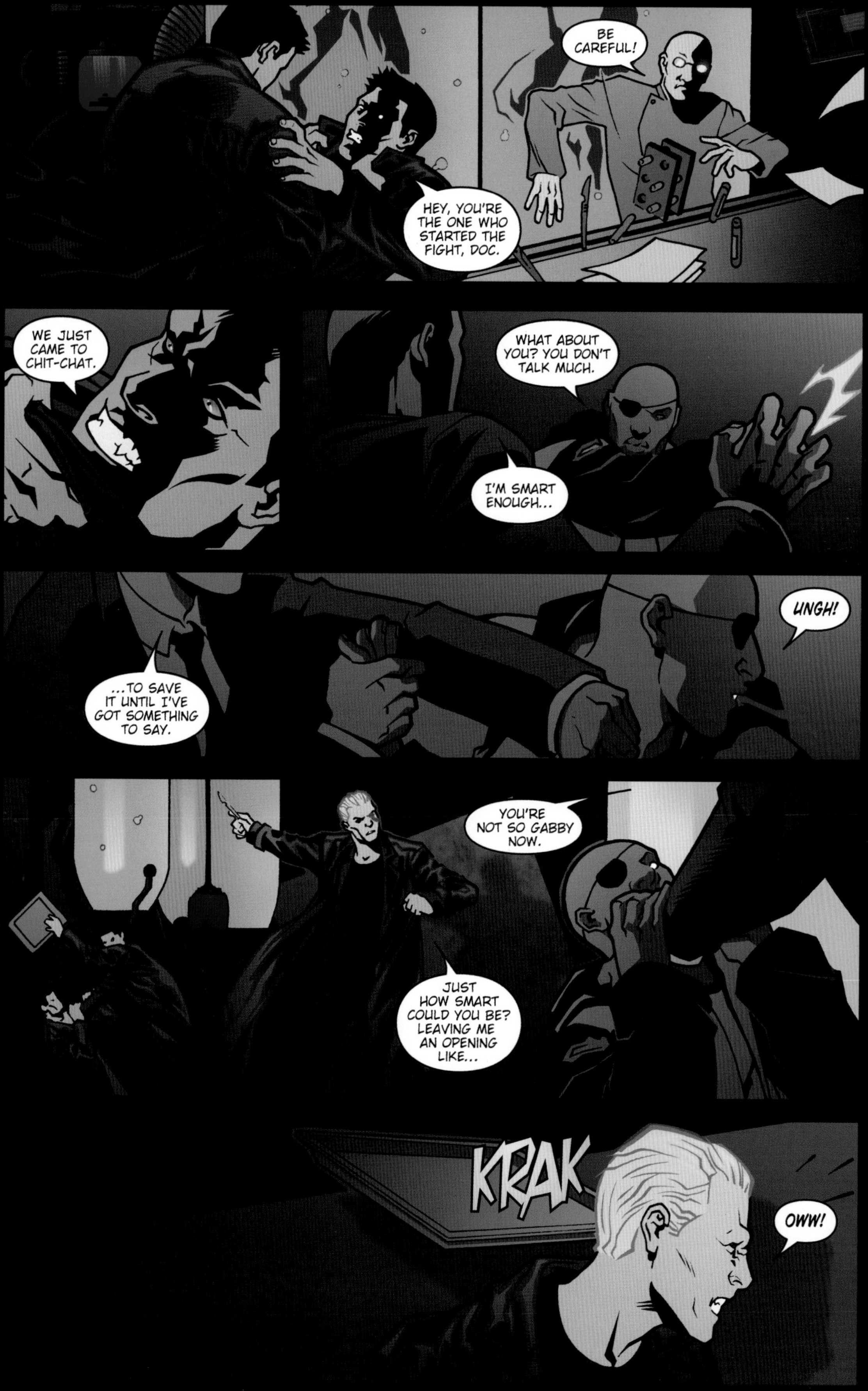
BE CAREFUL!
HEY, YOU'RE THE ONE WHO STARTED THE FIGHT, DOC.
WE JUST CAME TO CHIT-CHAT.
WHAT ABOUT YOU? YOU DON'T TALK MUCH.
I'M SMART ENOUGH...
...TO SAVE IT UNTIL I'VE GOT SOMETHING TO SAY.
UNGH!
YOU'RE NOT SO GABBY NOW.
JUST HOW SMART COULD YOU BE? LEAVING ME AN OPENING LIKE...
KRAK
OWW!

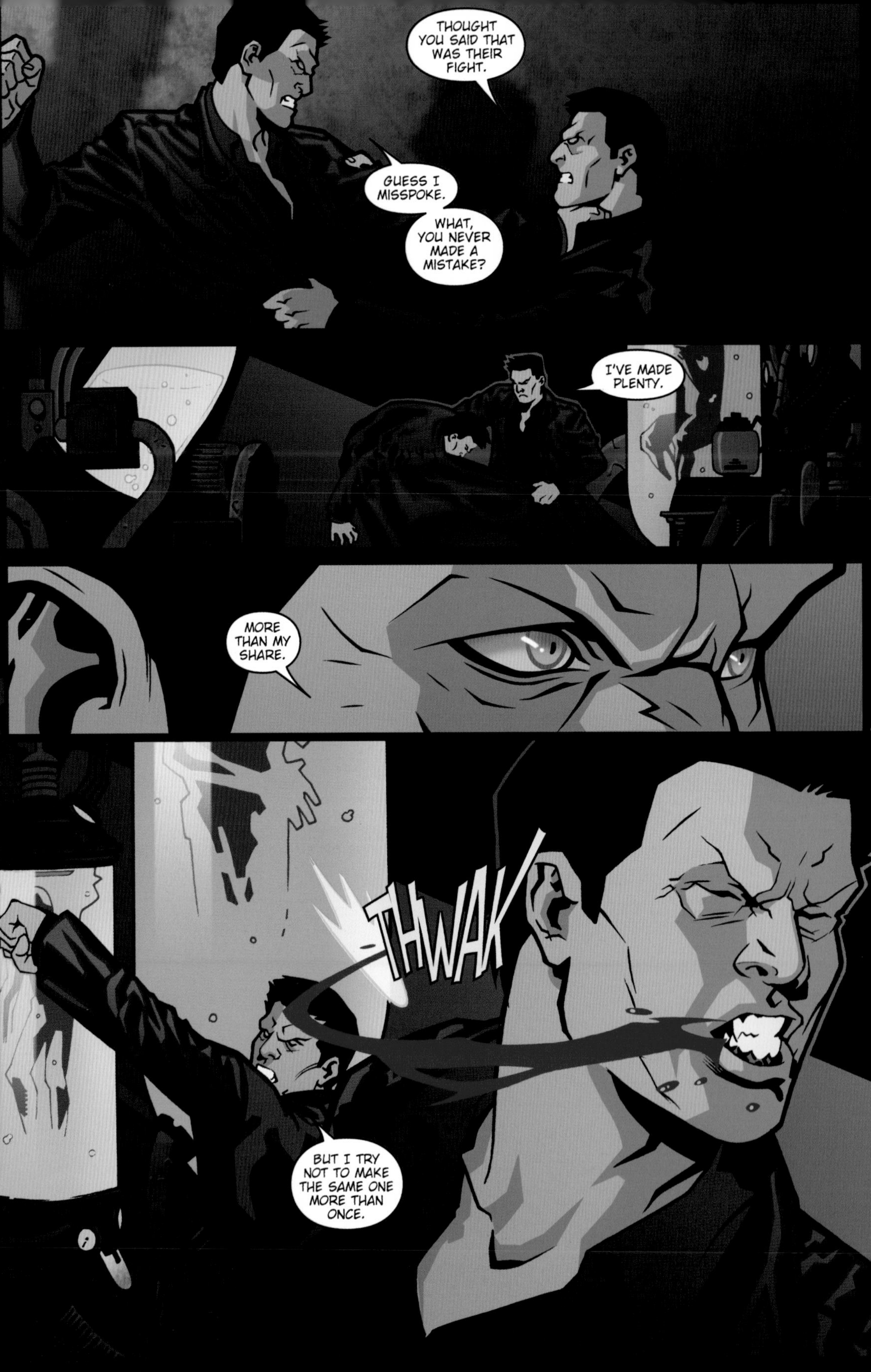
THOUGHT YOU SAID THAT WAS THEIR FIGHT.
GUESS I MISSPOKE.
WHAT, YOU NEVER MADE A MISTAKE?
I'VE MADE PLENTY.
MORE THAN MY SHARE.
THWAK
BUT I TRY NOT TO MAKE THE SAME ONE MORE THAN ONCE.

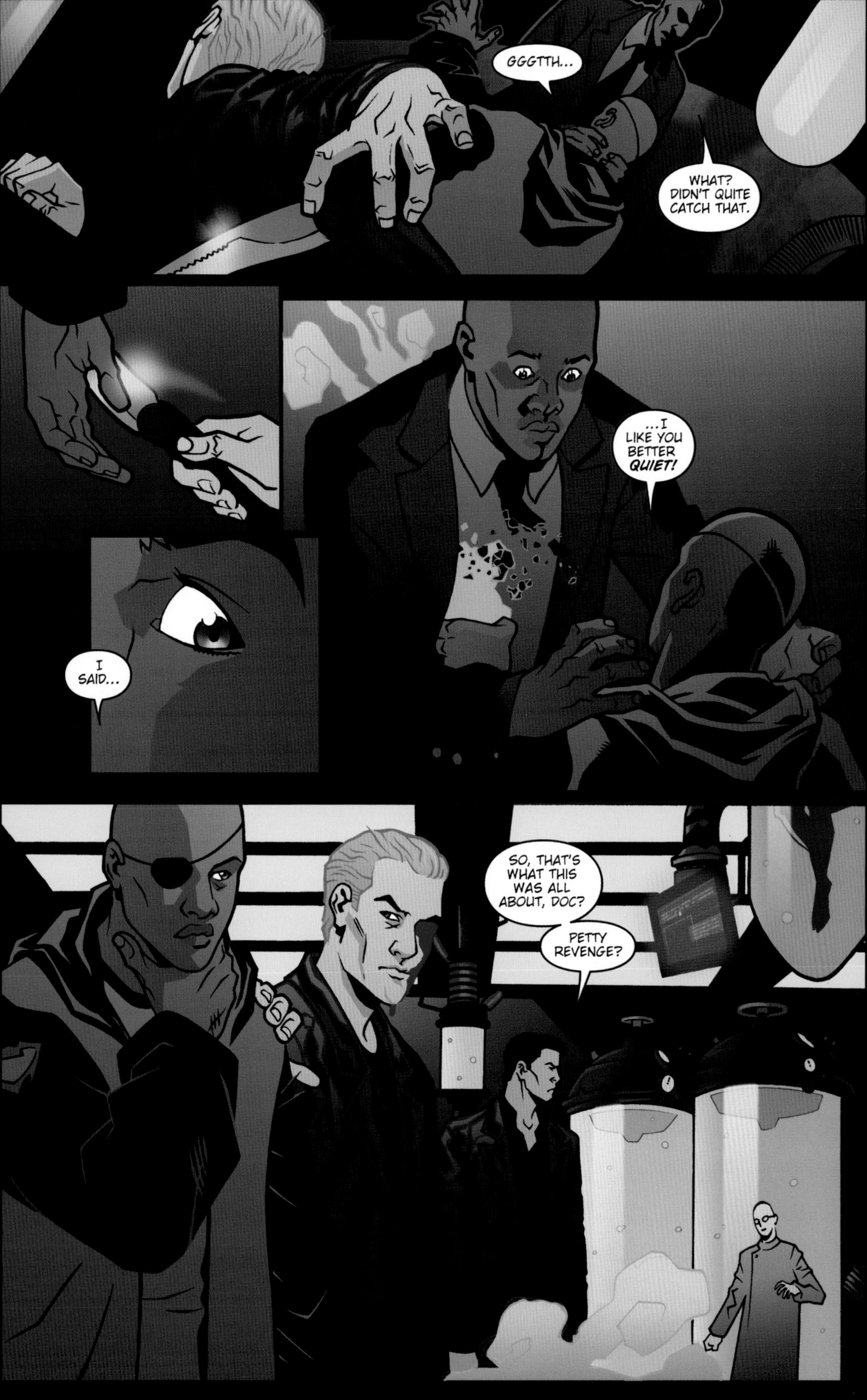
GGGTTH...
WHAT? DIDN'T QUITE CATCH THAT.
I SAID...
...I LIKE YOU BETTER *QUIET!*
SO, THAT'S WHAT THIS WAS ALL ABOUT, DOC?
PETTY REVENGE?

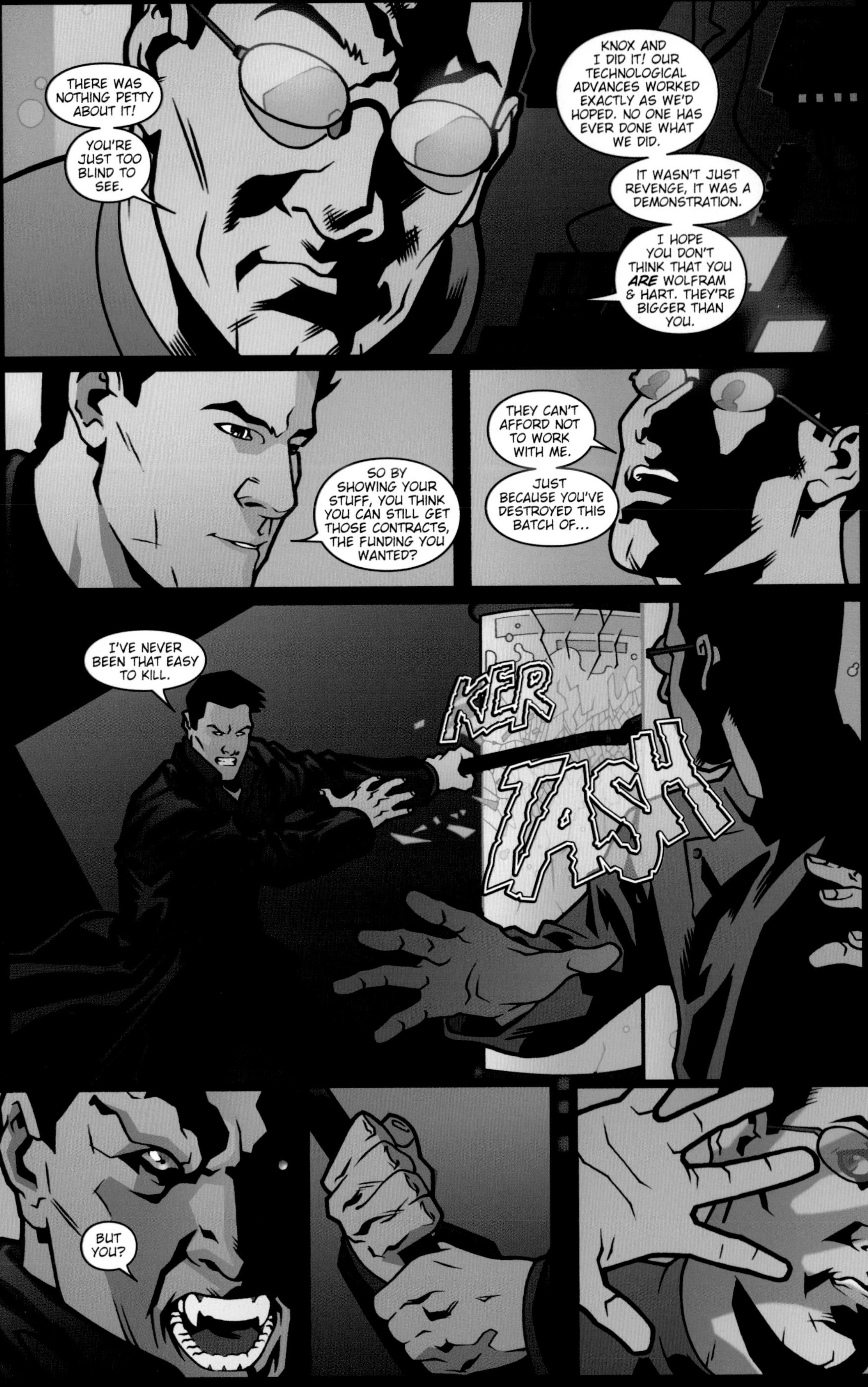
THERE WAS NOTHING PETTY ABOUT IT!
YOU'RE JUST TOO BLIND TO SEE.
KNOX AND I DID IT! OUR TECHNOLOGICAL ADVANCES WORKED EXACTLY AS WE'D HOPED. NO ONE HAS EVER DONE WHAT WE DID.
IT WASN'T JUST REVENGE, IT WAS A DEMONSTRATION.
I HOPE YOU DON'T THINK THAT YOU ***ARE*** WOLFRAM & HART. THEY'RE BIGGER THAN YOU.
SO BY SHOWING YOUR STUFF, YOU THINK YOU CAN STILL GET THOSE CONTRACTS, THE FUNDING YOU WANTED?
THEY CAN'T AFFORD NOT TO WORK WITH ME.
JUST BECAUSE YOU'VE DESTROYED THIS BATCH OF...
I'VE NEVER BEEN THAT EASY TO KILL.
KER TASH
BUT YOU?

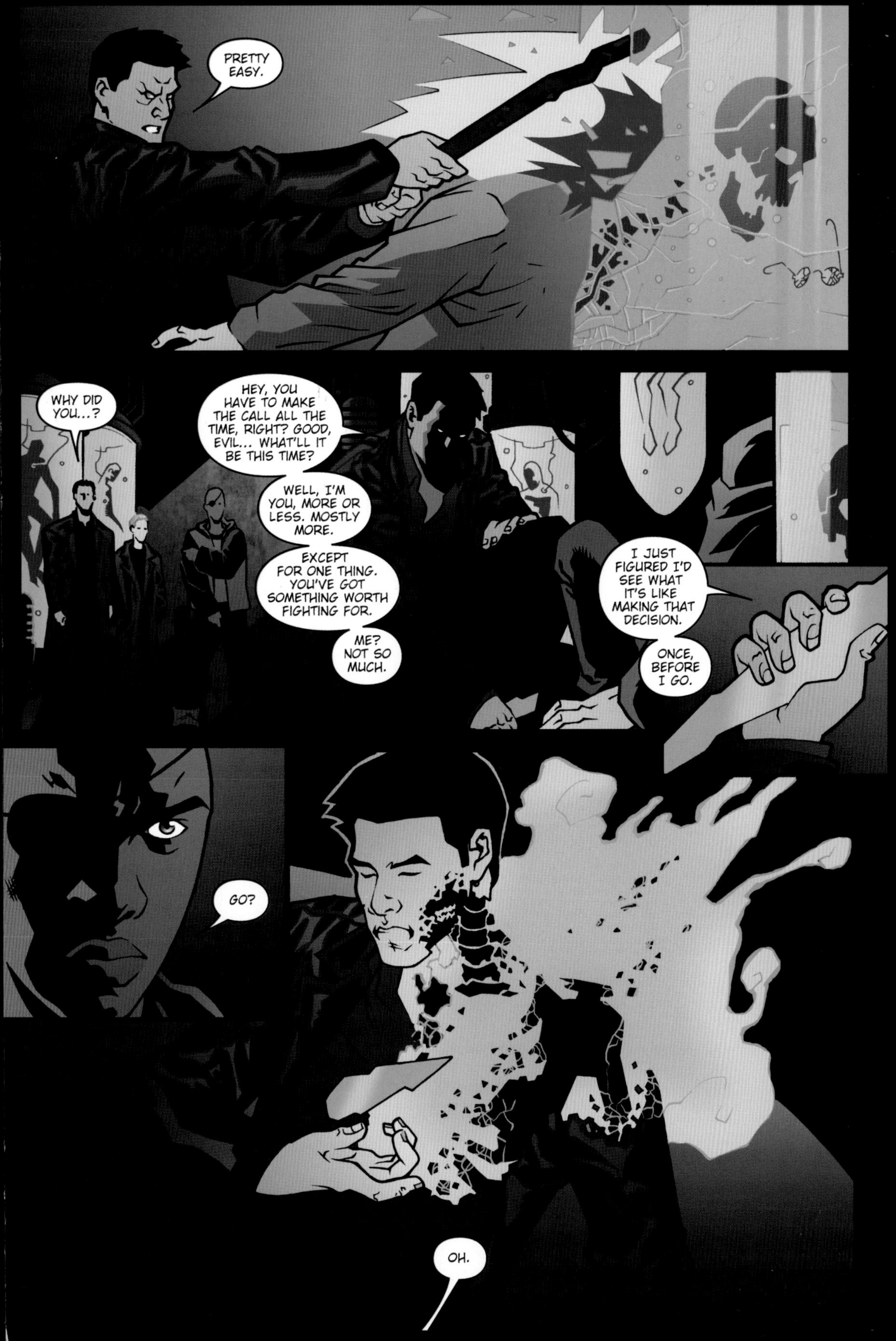
PRETTY EASY.
WHY DID YOU...?
HEY, YOU HAVE TO MAKE THE CALL ALL THE TIME, RIGHT? GOOD, EVIL... WHAT'LL IT BE THIS TIME?
WELL, I'M YOU, MORE OR LESS. MOSTLY MORE.
EXCEPT FOR ONE THING. YOU'VE GOT SOMETHING WORTH FIGHTING FOR.
ME? NOT SO MUCH.
I JUST FIGURED I'D SEE WHAT IT'S LIKE MAKING THAT DECISION.
ONCE, BEFORE I GO.
GO?
OH.

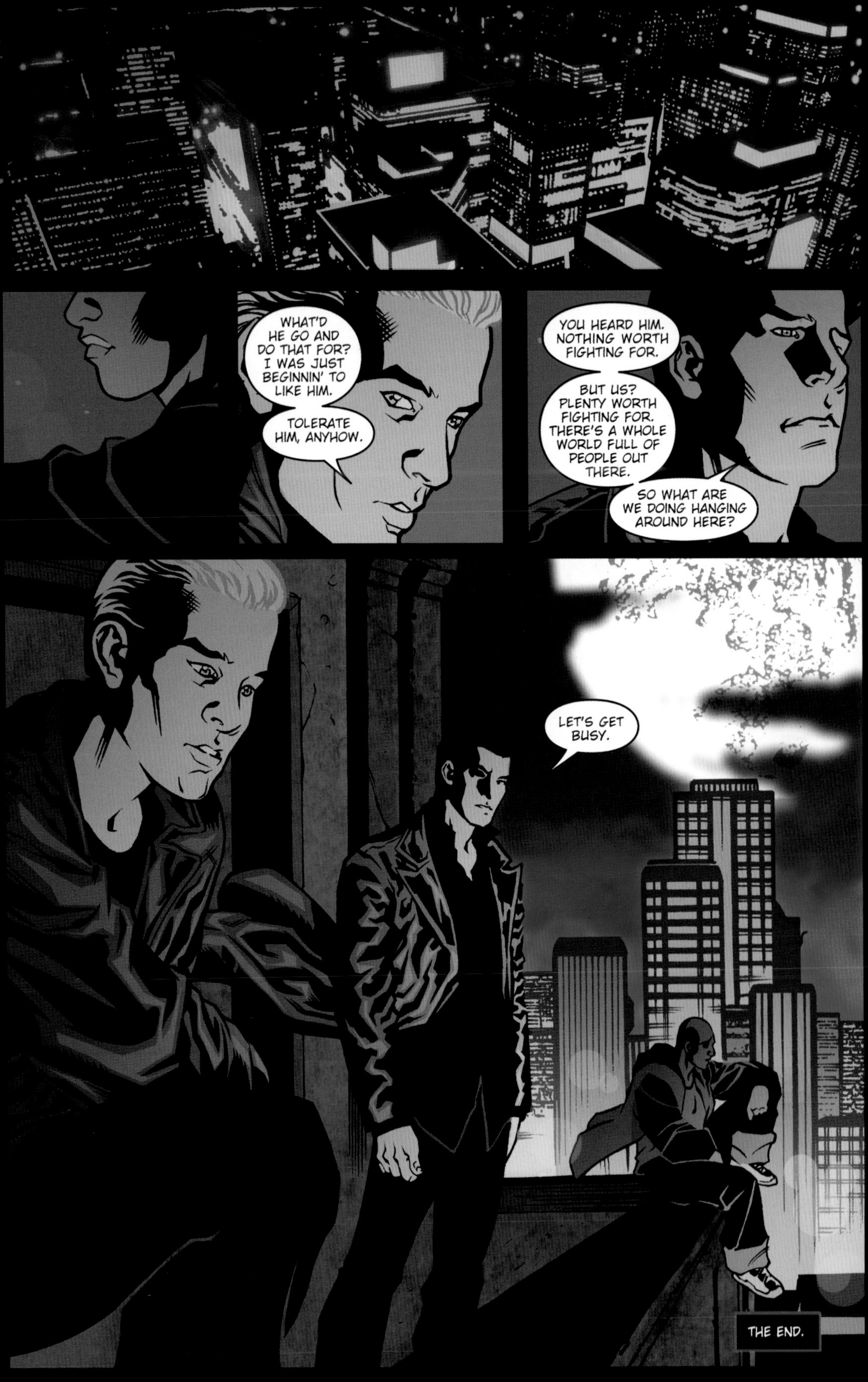
WHAT'D HE GO AND DO THAT FOR? I WAS JUST BEGINNIN' TO LIKE HIM.
TOLERATE HIM, ANYHOW.
YOU HEARD HIM. NOTHING WORTH FIGHTING FOR.
BUT US? PLENTY WORTH FIGHTING FOR. THERE'S A WHOLE WORLD FULL OF PEOPLE OUT THERE.
SO WHAT ARE WE DOING HANGING AROUND HERE?
LET'S GET BUSY.
THE END.

COVER GALLERY

art by David Messina

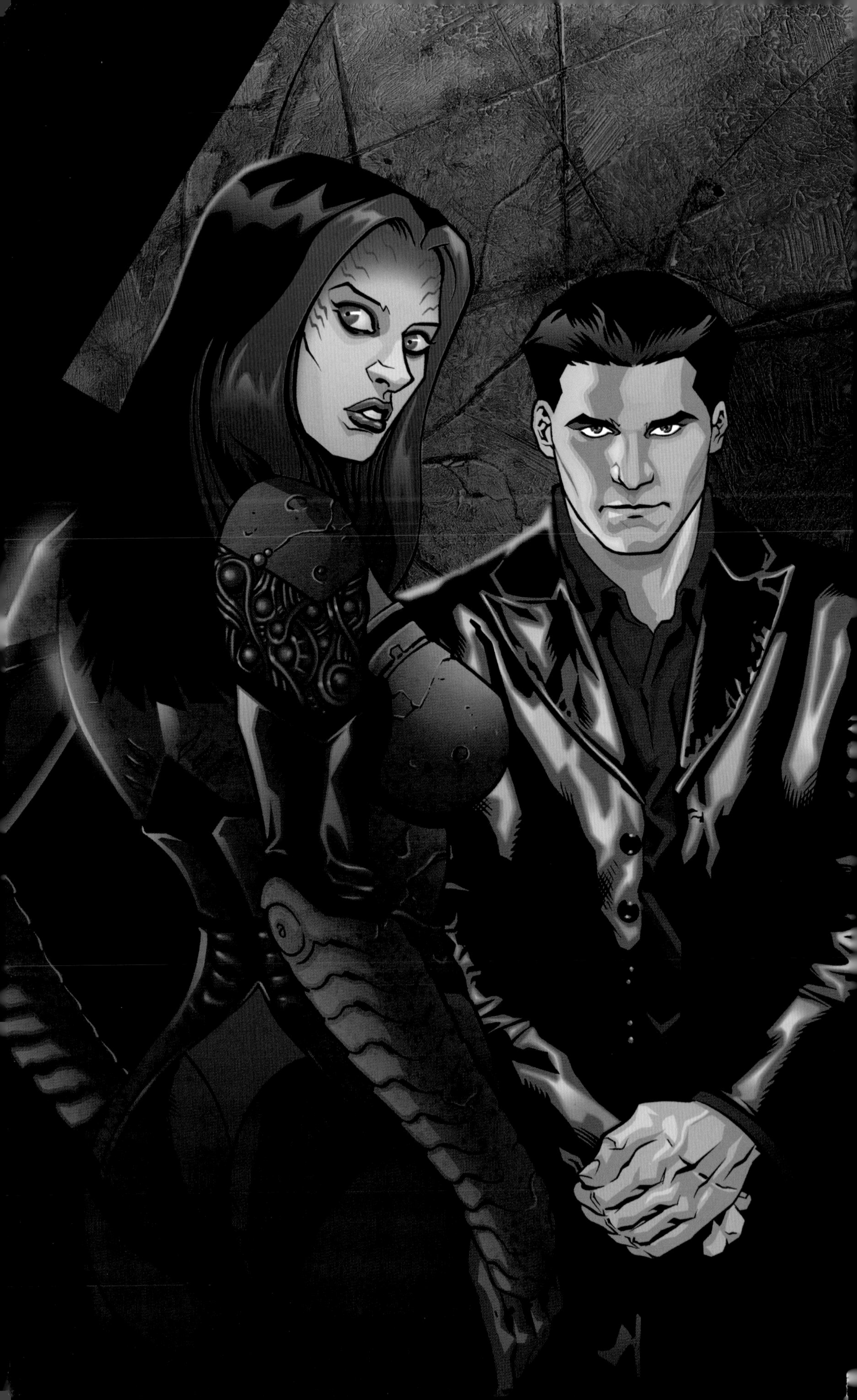

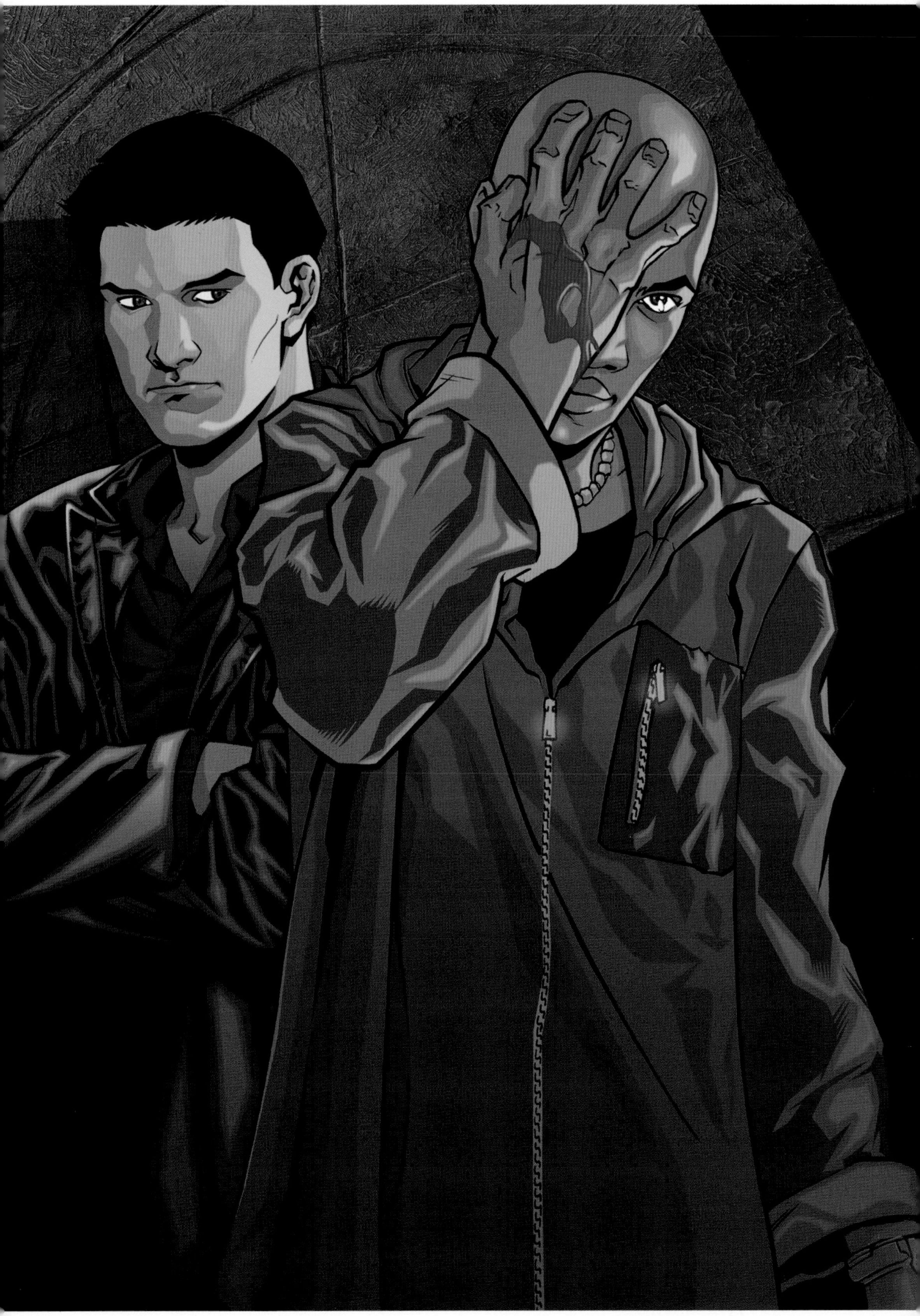

Facing page : Cover issue #1
This page : Cover issue #2

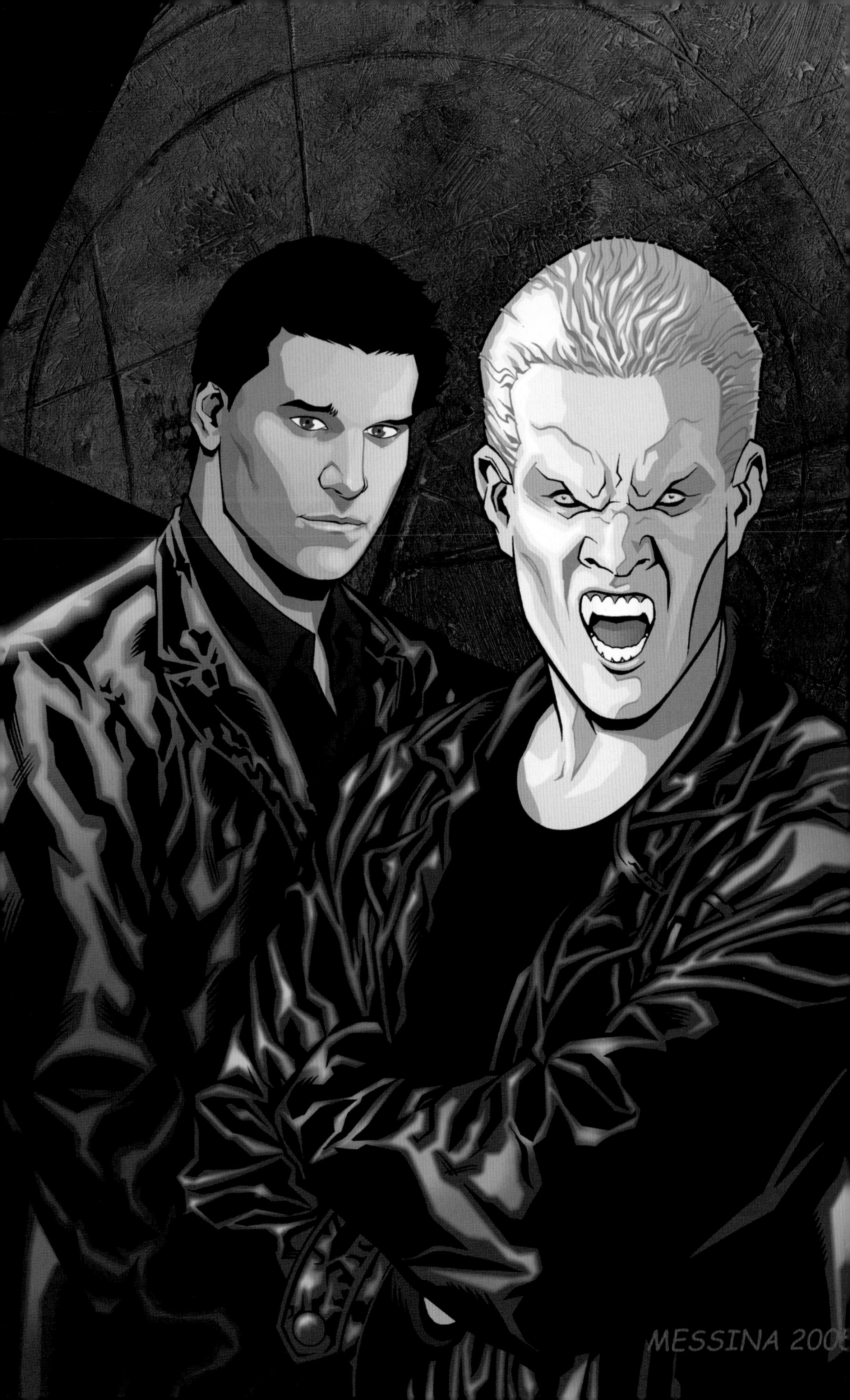
MESSINA 200

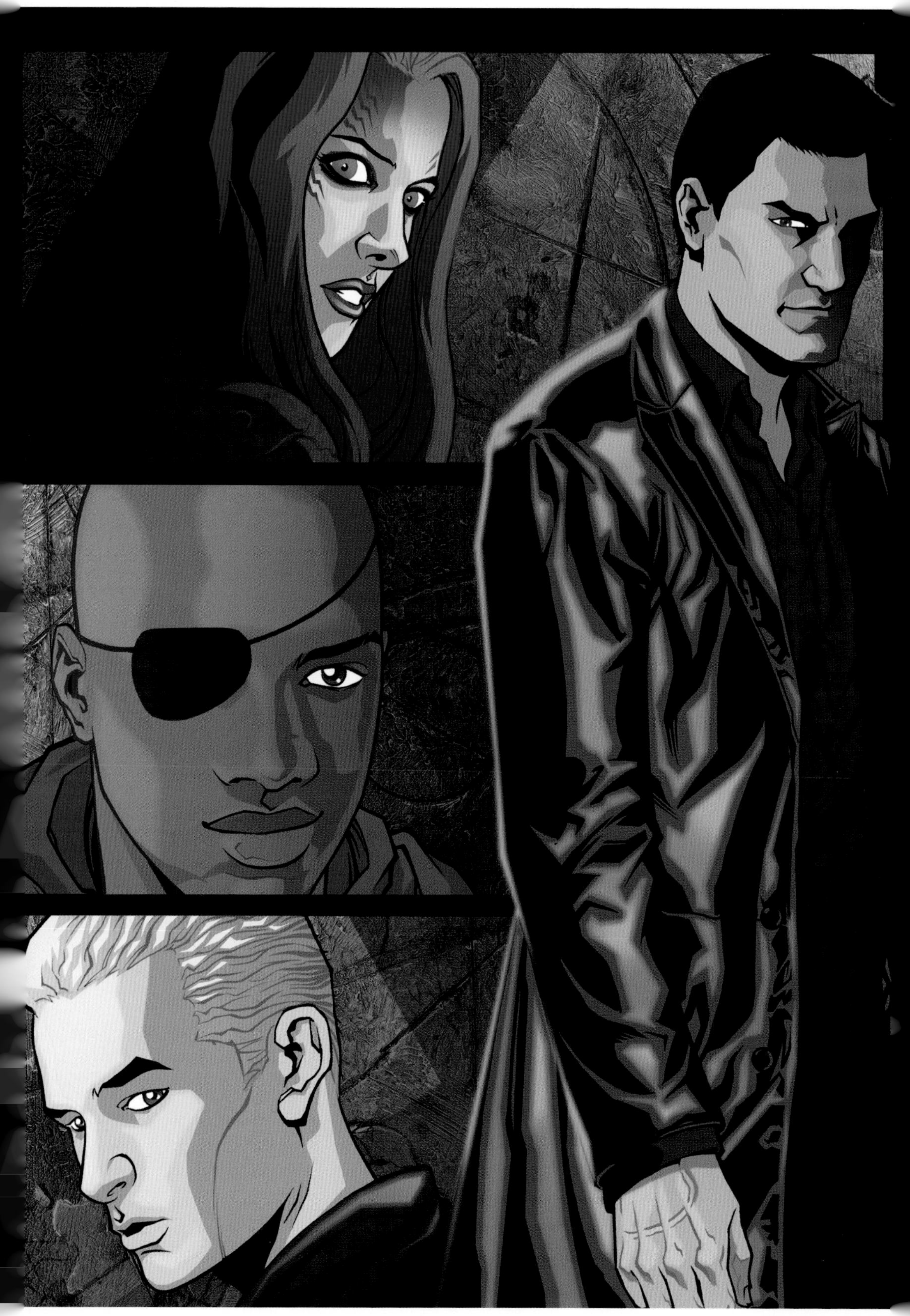

Facing page : Cover issue #3
This page : Cover issue #4
Next page : Cover issue #5

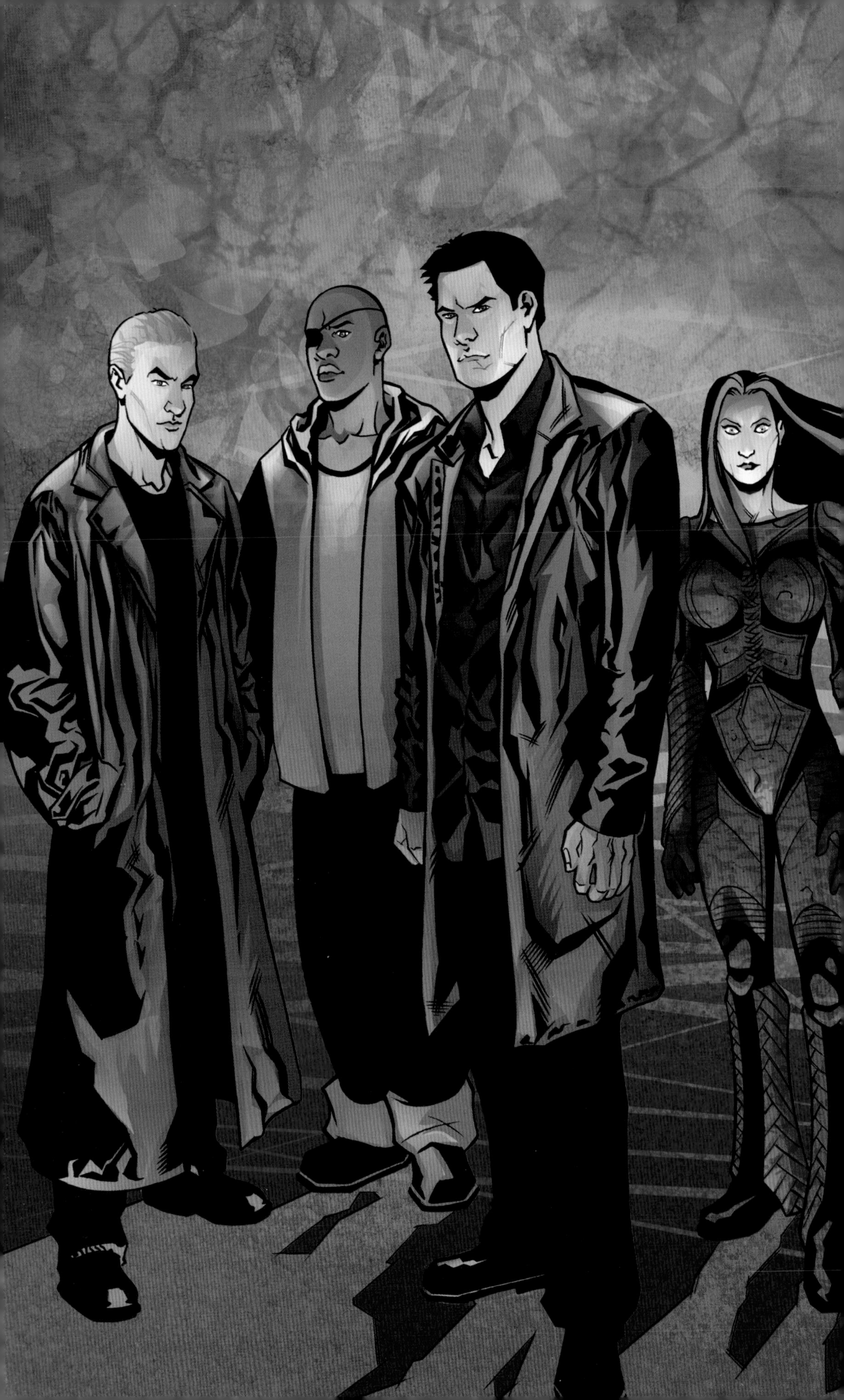